The Rediscovery of Meaning,
and Other Essays

Other Books by Owen Barfield

✳

Published by Wesleyan University Press
What Coleridge Thought
Speaker's Meaning
Romanticism Comes of Age
(new and augmented edition)
Unancestral Voice
Worlds Apart: A Dialogue of the 1960's
Poetic Diction: A Study in Meaning
(third edition, with afterword by the author)

Published Elsewhere
History in English Words
Saving the Appearances: A Study in Idolatry
This Ever Diverse Pair
(as by G. A. L. Burgeon)

The Rediscovery of Meaning,
and Other Essays

by

OWEN BARFIELD

WESLEYAN UNIVERSITY PRESS

Middletown, Connecticut

Library of Congress Cataloging in Publication Data

Barfield, Owen, 1898–
    The rediscovery of meaning, and other essays.

    1. Philosophy — Addresses, essays, lectures. 2. General semantics — Addresses, essays, lectures. 3. Philology — Addresses, essays, lectures. I. Title.
B1618.B281R4   121   76–41479
ISBN 0–8195–5006–X

Manufactured in the United States of America
First edition

Table of Contents

Part One

INTRODUCTION

Introduction

There are three possible justifications for the presumptuous gesture of collecting and publishing in one volume a number of lectures and essays on widely different topics elicited by widely different occasions. The first is that each essay (I will so refer to all of them), regardless of what it is about, is a little gem of mellifluous literature; the second that they all present the reader with separate facets of a single engaging and scintillating personality; and the third that there is an effective unity of content underlying the apparent fragmentation. This little miscellany rests its case exclusively on claim number three.

The validity of any such claim is, it must be admitted, rendered additionally improbable by the fact that a very long period of time is here involved. "Poetic Diction and Legal Fiction" for example was first printed in 1947 and had been delivered as a paper something like ten years earlier, while "The Coming Trauma of Materialism" was written as late as December 1974. As against that it was once observed by a fairly wise man, whose name for the moment escapes me, that all authors, however many books they write and however long they go on doing it, are always really saying the same thing over and over again. I do not know whether this was intended as an insult or a compliment, or merely as a neutral statement of fact, but as far as I am concerned, I should not wish to deny it. The contents of this book indeed, including therein this ostensibly quite *ad hoc* Introduction, rather go to confirm it, since in my case the "same thing" that is always being reaffirmed is the importance of penetrating to the antecedent unity underlying apparent or actual fragmentation.

That is after all one way of approaching the problem of meaning or, as it has become for us today, the problem of meaninglessness. Anyone who takes the trouble of reading all or most of the book will, I think, have little difficulty in feeling the presence of that problem and that approach, not only in the title essay, where it is most explicitly stated, but also in or close behind all the others. It is for instance often argued that the fragmentation of knowledge itself, which is characteristic of our age of specialization, has been brought about simply by an increase in the quantity of things known. Contrariwise "Science and Quality" argues that it has been brought about by the fact that human "knowledge" was formerly different in character from what it is today. But the same contention, differently stated, pervades most of the essays. If knowledge formerly connoted a certain awareness of an antecedent immaterial unity, then the perception or intuition of such unities is a historical as well as an ontological topic. The problems both of knowledge and of meaning involve in fact the evolution of consciousness, and it is as implicit in many of the essays as it is explicit in "Self and Reality" that the evolution of consciousness has been at the same time the evolution of phenomena, or "evolution" *tout simple.*

It is a fact—and if this book illustrates it, all the better—that anyone who has once contemplated the evolution of the earth and man as a progress from unity to fragmentation and from meaning to meaninglessness, and then, if all goes well, from meaninglessness through to meaning and from fragmentation through to unity, will see traces of that universal process wherever he looks. Is this because he will be seeing what he is determined to see, or because he will be seeing what is there? The reader must answer that question for himself. Meanwhile he will perhaps be persuaded that to see them in that way makes most things more interesting and many things more intelligible. The fragmentation of humanity itself, that "alienation" of unit from unit and group from group which is posing such a formidable threat to civilization, is one such thing and is accordingly the subject of "Participation and Isolation."

If evolution of consciousness is the thread you hold in your hand, it may lead you into discrete and scattered places, but it will still be the same thread. It will be the same thread, whether it leads straight into a fairly abrupt critique of the philosophy of science and the basis of scientific method, as in "Science and Quality," or whether it winds a long course through literature to language, through language to history, through history to prehistory and the antecedent unity of man and nature, and back again from there to such matters as psychology, philosophy, and religion. That this, as a matter of biography, was the author's case is perhaps re-

flected in "The Harp and the Camera," while it is both reflected and affirmed in "Philology and the Incarnation." At the same time he would not
admit that the continuing length of the thread, the wide perspectives
opened up in the course of a journey that only *began* with literary experience, have ever led him away from literature as such in the sense of losing
a discriminating relish for it. He would venture to adduce "The Rediscovery of Allegory" as evidence that such a journey may sharpen rather than
dull the faculty of poetic appreciation which focuses on the *how* rather
than the the *what* of literary utterance.

But mention of "Philology and the Incarnation" raises a different question on which perhaps something needs to be said; and that is the relation
of the evolution of consciousness, and therefore of these essays, to Christianity. When I first published my book *Saving the Appearances* in England
in 1957, a reviewer in a humanist journal observed: "The argument seems
to be that we would be mistaken in trying to return to the primitive's
'original participation' because we are now able to move towards 'final
participation' made possible by Christian revelation." And this was something which "no humanist could accept." He had not read the book very
attentively. *Saving the Appearances*, like pretty well everything else I have
written, is about the evolution of consciousness. The first twenty-two
chapters seek to establish on various grounds that this must be seen as the
progressive metamorphosis of a universal or generalized consciousness,
which embraced both man and nature, into the individualized and alienated
self-consciousness we have today; and further that there are indications
that this contraction seeks to be followed by an expansion from the separate new centers thus created. This, it is argued, involves realizing that the
centers—human beings—are still, in their subconscious depths, transper-
sonal. It can be understood "*if*, but only if, we admit that in the course of
the earth's history, something like a Divine Word has been gradually clothing itself with the humanity it first gradually created—so that what was
first spoken by God may eventually be respoken by man." Nowhere is it
suggested that this process, or even our ability to perceive it, was "made
possible by the Christian revelation." Only the last three chapters are
written from the standpoint that the undoubted change of direction from
inward to outward, from centripetal to centrifugal, which is the heart of
the process, was made possible, not by the Christian revelation, but by the
historical event of the Incarnation. In other words the logical framework
of the book is precisely that of the essay "Philology and the Incarnation"
to be found herein. It is perfectly possible to accept as true such an account of the evolution of consciousness as is deducible from these essays

without relating it specially to the events recorded in the Christian gospels. On the other hand once it *has* been accepted, one may come to feel that such a special relation is almost self-evident. One may have the startling experience: Here is the antecedent Unity of unities, here is the interior Transforming Agent of evolution, here is the positive meaning of life on earth, here is the Meaning of meaning itself staring me in the face! It may be worth adding that this was the biographical, as well as the dialectical, sequence in the case of the author, who was reared as an agnostic.

It was from this second standpoint that one or two of the essays at the end of the book were conceived and written. Once it has been adopted, a different, indeed an opposite, order of interpretation is clearly possible. If it was formerly rational to—let us say—infer the validity of "the Christian revelation" from a perceived evolution of consciousness, it is now possible to infer the evolution of consciousness from the Christian revelation, or to apply the former for the purpose of elucidating the latter. Such an undertaking is attempted in "The 'Son of God' and the 'Son of Man,'" where the movement of thought is not from the evolution of consciousness toward theology and religion, but the opposite one from theology to the evolution of consciousness. More specifically it is from orthodox, that is trinitarian, Christianity to the psychological, and indeed psychosomatic— intricately psychosomatic—triunity which constitutes the nature of man, and without which his evolution and that of the earth he inhabits will, in my view, never be satisfactorily apprehended.

This extended application—for so it may be seen—of that "universal law of polarity," which was detected by Coleridge and sedulously ignored by both his critics and his admirers, seems to me to be peremptorily demanded of an age still fuddled by its discovery of an unconscious mind. It is also the distinguishing mark, if one single distinguishing mark should be insisted on, of the spiritual science, or "anthroposophy," associated with the name of Rudolf Steiner. Since some of my readers (though less so in the last few years than when I first began writing books) find my references to him a stumbling-block, I will mention here that a considered statement of my debt to Steiner, together with my estimate of his significance, is to be found in the Introduction to *Romanticism Comes of Age* and elsewhere throughout that book.

There is however one point, not mentioned there, to which I am minded—with some hesitation—to draw attention because of its relation to what I have just been saying. With some hesitation, because anything in the nature of a "parallel" is out of place between incommensurables. The relation between the doctrine, or system, or what you will, of the evolution of consciousness which I am sometimes credited with having developed, and what is to be found in the legacy bequeathed by Steiner to posterity is somewhat similar to that between, say, a primer of Greek grammar on the one hand and the whole corpus of Greek language and literature on the other. It happens to be true nonetheless that in each case its integral relation to the Christian religion was only realized *after* the system itself had been realized. It would be inappropriate to go further into this, which is clear from Steiner's *Autobiography*, or to attempt to expound the sporadic allusions in the ensuing pages into anything like an exposition of anthroposophy. What does need to be said, for the benefit of any who are unaware of it, is that the legacy I have referred to consists not simply, or mainly, of an epistemological theory and method, but of specific findings on a wide variety of subjects arrived at by applying that method. There are a good many now, and I am one of them, for whom these findings are so illuminating and so much in accord with their own deepest experience, that they accept them as reliable even for areas going beyond that experience. These people have Steiner's anthroposophy in common somewhat as we all have the natural world in common; and one of the ensuing essays, "Where is Fancy Bred?," was delivered to an audience that contained no others. I have included it nonetheless, though here as in the case of "The 'Son of God' and the 'Son of Man,'" there is a sort of reversal of the normal order, a starting from conclusions instead of ending with them; because I have judged rightly or wrongly that there may be some among those others to whom it need not be unintelligible and may be suggestive.

What have I been trying to say? At this point I am reminded of the uppity draft horse in Chaucer's *Troilus and Criseyde:*

> Than thenketh he, Though I praunce al beforn
> First in the trais, ful fat and newe shorn,
> Yit am I but an hors, and horses lawe
> I mot endure and with my feres drawe.

The idea was to insist that, in spite of appearances to the contrary, there is an interior unity informing the *disjecta membra* of which this published whole consists. I am now wondering if I may not have been seduced by the zest for persuasion into positively presenting it as something like a block of monolithic exposition. If so, I have lost my way. What was intended as a shield had better not start trying to turn itself into a sword. However it may have originated, an archipelago is not a continent. The book remains of course a miscellany, or call it even a medley, a container for preserving in a more permanent form a few things I hope may be worth preserving; and it is so that it is offered.

Part Two

MEANING, LANGUAGE, AND IMAGINATION

The Rediscovery of Meaning

Amid all the menacing signs that surround us in the middle of this twen-tieth century, perhaps the one which fills thoughtful people with the great-est foreboding is the growing general sense of meaninglessness. It is this which underlies most of the other threats. How is it that the more able man becomes to manipulate the world to his advantage, the less he can perceive any meaning in it? This is a paradox which has often been noted and has sometimes been attributed to a fundamental perversity, a sort of "pure cussedness," in human nature. In fact, however, it arises from a clear-ly identifiable and comparatively recent bit of history.

Most people are well aware that, with the advent of the Scientific Revo-lution about three hundred years ago, the mind of man began to relate it-self to the world around it in an entirely new way. The habit then first arose of meticulously observing the facts of nature and systematically in-terpreting them in terms of physical cause and effect; and this habit has been growing ever since, with incalculable and largely beneficial results for the accumulation of practical knowledge, or knowledge enabling the manip-ulation of nature. What is less clearly realized is the precise nature and significance of a certain further step which was taken in the nineteenth century. It was then that this habitual practice in the pursuit of knowledge was formulated as a dogma under the name of the "positive" philosophy, or positivism.

Positivism is the philosophical name for the belief now more widely known as "materialism." It is the doctrine—propounded originally by Auguste Comte—that the above-mentioned method of interpreting the facts of nature is not merely a useful but the only possible one. Obviously a proposition that only one method of scientific investigation is possible cannot itself (except for devout believers) be based on scientific investigation by that method. The proposition is, therefore, in fact a dogmatic belief; although it has been so thoroughly absorbed into the thought stream of Western humanity that it has come to be regarded, not as a dogma, but as a scientifically established fact.

Now there is usually little connection between the physical causes of a thing and its meaning. An important physical cause of what I am just now writing is the muscular pressure of my finger and thumb, but knowing this does not help anyone to grasp its meaning. Thus, in investigating the phenomena of nature, exclusive emphasis on physical causes and effects involves a corresponding inattention to their meaning. And it was just this exclusive emphasis which came into fashion about three hundred years ago. What happened later, in the nineteenth century, was that a *habit* of inattention, which had become inveterate, was finally superseded by an *assumption* (sometimes explicit but more often implicit) that scientific attention to the meaning, as distinct from the causes, of phenomena, was impossible—even if (which was considered improbable) there was anything to attend to. The meaning of a process is the inner being which the process expresses. The denial of any such inner being to the processes of nature leads inevitably to the denial of it to man himself. For if physical objects and physical causes and effects are all that we can know, it follows that man himself can be known only to the extent that he is a physical object among physical objects. Thus, it is implicit in positivism that man can never really know anything about his specifically human self—his own inner being—any more than he can ever really know anything about the meaning of the world of nature by which he is surrounded.

Up to now even those who reject materialism as an ultimate philosophy have been content to accept the limitations which positivism seeks to impose on the sphere of knowledge. True, they say, the spiritual values which constitute the true meaning of life can be dimly felt and are, in fact, what lie behind the symbols of religion and the mysterious phenomena of art. But we can never hope to know anything about them. There are—and this is often suggested with a certain unction—two kinds of truth: the scientific kind which can be demonstrated experimentally and which is limited to the physical world and, on the other side, the "truths" of mystical intuition and revelation, which can be felt and suggested but never known or scientifically stated. And if these seem to be incompatible with the truths of science—well, perhaps that is all the better. "The heart has its reasons whereof reason knoweth not."

In this way for a number of years a precarious equilibrium may be said to have been established between a meaningless and mechanical world of physical events described by science and some kind of ulterior spiritual significance which that world might be supposed to conceal and with which it had little if anything to do. The idealist philosophies of the nineteenth century made it their business to maintain this equilibrium by rationalizing it as best they could.

It was a state of affairs that could not last, and its latent instability has been exposed by a certain further step which the doctrine of positivism has taken in our time. The older positivism proclaimed that man could never know anything except the physical world-mechanism accessible to his senses. The twentieth-century variety — variously known as "logical positivism," "linguistic analysis," "the philosophy of science," and so on — goes further and avers that nothing can even be *said* about anything else. Language is meaningful only insofar as it communicates, or at least purports to communicate, information about physical events, which observation and experiment can then confirm or disprove. The ground is cut away from beneath the feet of any idealist interpretation of the universe by a new dogma, not that such an interpretation is untrue but that it cannot even be advanced. The language in which it is couched is not really language at all (although it may obey the rules of grammar) because it has no meaning. Not only that, the ground is cut away from any sort of inner life at all. Moral judgments, for instance, have no factual reference. If we say, "Cruelty is wicked," all we really mean is that we don't like it. Words which purport to refer to anything beyond the reach of the senses do not in fact refer to anything at all. Our conviction that they do is merely a mistake we make about the possible ways of using language. When we combine such words into sentences, we imagine we are saying something, but in fact we are merely making noises, which express our feelings, as laughter and tears and grunts express our feelings. This, it is claimed, has always been the case, and all mythology and religion, together with practically all philosophy before the rise of positivism, are simply examples of these linguistic errors.

The upshot of all this was once well put by C. S. Lewis, when he pointed out that by and large, if the new positivism is right, the history of the human mind since the beginning of time has consisted in "almost nobody making linguistic mistakes about almost nothing." Even so, modern "analytical" philosophy is interesting and significant just because it forces the issue to its logical conclusion and brings into the open the mental predicament which acceptance of positivism has always really implied. Like a sort of scalpel, linguistic analysis lays bare that connection which we began by affirming between the rise of positivism and the general sense of meaninglessness in the West. At last the choice is plain. Either we must concede that 99 per cent of all we say and think (or imagine we think) is meaningless verbiage, or we must — however great the wrench — abandon positivism.

"Wrench" is not too strong a word; for positivism is subtly entangled with our thinking at all points on almost all subjects. A rather similar wrench was required of the Western mind at the close of the Middle Ages. Those who have not studied medieval thought will hardly believe how stubborn and inveterate the assumption had become that it was impossible to go outside Aristotle. Originality, new discoveries, experiments were all very welcome — provided they remained within the encompassing framework of Aristotelian conceptions: for instance, that the earth is fixed in the center of the universe, that the heavenly bodies are weightless, that heat, or fire, is one of the elements. These were taken absolutely for granted and anything which seemed to throw doubt on their validity produced — above all in the acknowledged leaders of contemporary thought — a violent reaction, which made them condemn it as nonsense or even blasphemy. The study of the transition from medieval to modern thought is the study of the great and painful wrench with which this dogma was at last abandoned. Now if we substitute positivism for Aristotelianism, we may get some idea of what is in store for us when we first begin to cast doubts on it. For it is a mistake to suppose that we are more open-minded today; we are merely open-minded about different things.

We will, nevertheless, try the experiment and we will begin at the furthest point which positivism itself has reached, as we have seen, in its nihilistic advance; that is to say, at the primary vehicle which we possess for the understanding and expression of meaning; in other words, with language.

How did it come about that a very high proportion of the words in any modern language do refer (or appear to refer) to matters and events which are not part of the world accessible to our senses? To the historical student, language appears at first sight to consist of what has been well called "a tissue of faded metaphors." From the time of the nineteenth-century philosopher, Max Müller, onward this has been the common topic of innumerable books on words. Thus, as Ernest Weekley explained many years ago:

> Every expression that we employ, apart from those that are connected with the most rudimentary objects and actions, is a metaphor, though the original meaning is dulled by constant use.

And he went on to illustrate his meaning from the words used in that very sentence:

> Thus, in the above sentence, *expression* means "what is squeezed out," to *employ* is to "twine in" like a basket-maker, to *connect* is to "weave together," *rudimentary* means "in the rough state," and an *object* is "something thrown in our way."

Above all, we find that all words used to describe the "inside" of ourselves, whether it be a thought or feeling, can be clearly seen to have come down to us from an earlier period when they also had reference to the outside world. The further back you go in time, the more metaphorical you find language becoming; and some of the pioneers of etymology even anticipated the later positivism we have just described by claiming that mythology and religion were simply the result of the "mistake" which was made when, later on, the "metaphors" came to be taken literally.

Since their time, however, a great deal more thought has been given to the whole problem of meaning and symbolism. In particular it has been realized that symbolic significance is not the exclusive attribute of religion and art, but is an intrinsic element in language itself. How did it come about that the shapes and objects of the outside world could be employed, and were employed, by man to express the inner world of his thought? It is because he was able to use them, not merely as *signs* for drawing attention to his feelings and impulses, but as *symbols* for his concepts. A thing functions as a symbol when it not only announces, but *represents* something other than itself. We owe the existence of language to the fact that the mental images, into which memory converts the forms of the outer world, can function not only as signs and reminders of themselves but as symbols for concepts. If this were not so, they could never have given rise to words—which make abstract thought possible. If we reflect on this fact unprejudiced by any positivist assumptions, we must conclude that this symbolic significance is inherent in the forms of the outer world themselves. The first metaphors were not artificial but natural.

In other words, the positivists are right in their conclusion that *if* (they would say "because") nature is meaningless to the human mind, most language is also meaningless. But the converse is equally true that, if language is "meaningful," then nature herself must also be meaningful. In fact, as Emerson pointed out long ago, "It is not only words that are emblematic; it is things which are emblematic." Man, he reminded his unheeding contemporaries, "is placed in the center of beings and a ray of relation passes from every other being to him. And neither can man be understood without these objects, nor these objects without man." It is precisely in this "ray of relation," which positivism cannot admit and which has therefore come to be overlooked, that the secret of meaning resides.

I have reached the conclusion that the natural world can only be understood in depth as a series of images symbolizing concepts; further, that it was out of man's rich awareness of this meaningful relation between himself and nature that language originally came to birth. How is it, then, that early man possessed this rich awareness while we have lost it? In answering this question we already begin to feel the great wrench; for we find that the abandonment of positivism involves a drastic revision of our whole conception of prehistory.

Consider the conventional picture of the history of the earth and man. It shows us, first of all, a purely physical earth without life or consciousness; then the arrival on that earth of animals and men as physical objects moving about on it; finally the development by man, out of nothing, of a faculty of imagination and thought enabling him to mirror or copy inwardly an outer world which had existed solidly for millions of years before him. We see the inner world evolving at a comparatively late stage from the outer. For this picture we shall surely have to substitute the more difficult and less crude one of inner and outer worlds coming into being alongside one another. For the reciprocal relation between the two, which language reveals, will not allow of one's ever having existed without the other. It points back instead to a *common origin*. The distinction between inner and outer, which seems so fundamental to us, will be seen to have been brought about by man himself in the very process of exercising the symbolizing faculty which gave him his language.

Ernst Cassirer, dealing with language in his *Philosophy of Symbolic Forms,* showed how the history of human consciousness was not a progress from an initial condition of blank darkness toward wider and wider awareness of a pre-existent outer world, but the gradual extrication of a small, but a growing and an increasingly clear and self-determined focus of inner human experience from a dreamlike state of virtual identity with the *life* of the body and of its environment. Self-consciousness emerged from mere consciousness. It was only in the course of this process that the world of "objective" nature, which we now observe around us, came into being. Man did not start on his career as a self-conscious being in the form of a mindless or thoughtless unit, confronting a separate, unintelligible objective world very like our own, about which he then proceeded to invent all manner of myths. He was not an onlooker, learning to make a less and less hopelessly inaccurate mental copy. He has had to wrestle his subjectivity out of the world of his experience by polarizing that world gradually into a duality. And this is the duality of objective-subjective, or outer-inner, which now seems so fundamental because we have inherited it along with language. He did not *start* as an onlooker; the development of language enabled him to *become* one.

Let us digress for a moment and examine the other, the received view, that the history of human thought *is* the history of an onlooker learning to make a better and better mental copy of an independent outer world. All positivist science is based on mathematics and physics; and modern physics originally set out to investigate nature as something existing independently of the human mind. But this was a postulate which it had more and more to abandon as time went on. At a quite early stage a distinction was made between "primary" qualities, such as extension and mass, which were as-sumed to inhere in matter independently of the observer, and "secondary" qualities like color, which depend on the observer. Roughly speaking, physics has ended by having to conclude that *all* qualities are "secondary" in this sense, so that the whole world of nature as we actually experience it depends for its configuration on the mind and senses of man. It is what it is because we are what we are. Thus our common assumption that the main effort of human thinking has been to make a mental replica of a pre-existent outer world is incompatible even with the scientific approach to things out of which it arose. This assumption is indeed determined by sci-ence; but by a science of the day before yesterday.

Early man did not observe nature in our detached way. He participated mentally and physically in her inner and outer process. The evolution of man has signified not alone the steady expansion of consciousness (man getting to know more and more about more and more); there has been a parallel process of contraction—which was also a process of awakening— a gradual focusing or pinpointing down from an earlier kind of knowledge, which could also be called participation. It was at once more universal and less clear. We still have something of this older relation to nature when we are asleep, and it throws up the suprarational wisdom which many psycho-analysts detect in dreams. Thus, it is rather true to say that we have come to know more and more about less and less.

"Man is the dwarf of himself," said Emerson. It is this fact which under-lies the world-wide tradition of a fall from paradise; and it is this which still reverberates on in the nature-linked collective consciousness that we find expressed in myths, in older forms of language, and in the totemic thinking and ritual participation of primitive tribes. It is from some such origins as these and not from an alert, blank stare of incomprehension that

we have evolved the individual, sharpened, spatially determined consciousness of today.

It is a process which continued even into our own era. We have only to
go back as far as the period immediately before the Scientific Revolution
in Europe, when the world picture still held sway of man as a microcosm
within the macrocosm, and we shall find the felt severance between man's
inner being and the world around him still noticeably less than it is today.
There is not space to do more than casually allude to one or two examples;
but anyone who studies medieval art and medieval thought a little will find
that, for instance, the four elements, earth, water, air, and fire (which were
not conceived as merely physical substances) were assumed as a matter of
course to be functioning not only in the outside world but also in the human temperament as its four "humors"—melancholic, phlegmatic, san-
guine, and choleric—while similar links between the planets and the metals
and the dispositions of man were equally taken for granted. Of course,
positivist thinking assumes that these were all erroneous speculations and
had nothing to do with fact; but it transpires from the whole course of
history that they were in truth vestigial remains of the "common origin"
of man's outer and his inner worlds.

It remains to be considered whether the future development of scientific man must inevitably continue in the same direction, so that he becomes more and more a mere onlooker, measuring with greater and greater
precision and manipulating more and more cleverly an earth to which he
grows spiritually more and more a stranger. His detachment has enabled
him to describe, weigh, and measure the processes of nature and to a large
extent to control them; but the price he has paid has been the loss of his
grasp of any meaning in either nature or himself. Penetration to the meaning of a thing or process, as distinct from the ability to describe it exactly,
involves a participation by the knower in the known. The meaning of what
I am writing is not the physical pressure of thumb and forefinger, or the
size of the ink lines with which I form the letters; it is the concepts expressed in the words I am writing. But the only way of penetrating to these
is to participate in them—to bring them to life in your own mind by thinking them. A Chinese looking at this page would indeed be limited to describing its outer appearance. We are mere onlookers at a language we do
not understand. But confronted with a language we have learned to understand, we not merely observe the shapes of the letters—in the very act of
observing these we "read" their meaning through them. In the same way,
if we want to know the meaning of nature, we must learn to read as well as
to observe and describe. Is there any possibility of scientific man's ever re-

covering the old power to "read," while still retaining his hard-won treasure of exact observation and manipulative control—for no one would advocate a mere relapse into the past? Signs are not altogether wanting that there is such a possibility, though they are at present rudimentary.

We have seen that man can only begin to "read" the meaning of nature, when instead of merely copying and describing what he senses, he begins to apprehend it as a series of images symbolizing concepts. Now the word "imagination" has come to mean, for most people, the faculty of inventing fictions, especially poetic fictions; but in its deeper sense it signifies that very faculty of apprehending the outward form as the image or symbol of an inner meaning, for which we are looking. It is therefore not surprising that the first stirrings of a movement of thought in this new direction should have occurred among those who interested themselves in the deeper significance of art, and especially of poetry. Thus, it was held by Coleridge that the human imagination, at its highest level, does indeed inherit and continue the divine creative activity of the Logos (the "Word" of the opening verses of St. John's Gospel), which was the common origin of human language and consciousness, as well as of the world which contains them. Out of the whole development of the Romantic Movement in Europe at the turn of the eighteenth century and in the nineteenth a conviction arose in these circles that man's creative imagination can be applied, not only in the creation and contemplation of works of art but also in the contemplation of nature herself. Through its exercise we begin once more to experience nature as image; and indeed an obscure recognition of images underlies that feeling for the beauty of nature which differentiates us so sharply from the eighteenth century. It may even lead, as in some of Wordsworth's childhood recollections or in our own time in the poetic vision of Kathleen Raine, to glimpses of the "common origin":

> *Do you remember, when you were first a child,*
> *Nothing in the world seemed strange to you?*
> *You perceived, for the first time, shapes already familiar,*
> *And seeing, you knew that you have always known*
> *The lichen on the rock, fern-leaves, the flowers of thyme,*
> *As if the elements newly met in your body,*
> *Caught up into the momentary vortex of your living*
> *Still kept the knowledge of a former state. . . .*

But all this does not amount to very much more than that vague "idealism"—a general intuition of some sort of meaning behind the totality of things—which, as we have seen, can peacefully coexist with the positivist dogma, at all events in the latter's earlier stages, before it begins to disintegrate language. It is much too subtle for the man in the street; but most contemporary enthusiasts for art and poetry accept some form of the doctrine of "two kinds of truth" to which we have already referred. They are content that the business of detailed investigation should be left to positivist science. In the book of nature the whole may mean something, but the details mean nothing; or if they do, we can never know it.

This however is not what we feel when we read an actual book. There the meaning of the whole is articulated from the meaning of each part— chapters from sentences and sentences from words—and stands before us in clear, sharp outlines. The vital question is whether science can ever discover how to read the book of nature in *this* way. It would not matter so much if its field were limited to mechanics and physics. But in fact man looks more and more to science for guidance on *all* subjects. As we rise in the scale of creation from the lifeless to the living and from the living to the psychic and human—from mechanics to sociology—the question of the *meaning* of what we are dealing with becomes ever more insistent. Must this always be ignored or can science ever learn to supplement its weighing, measuring, and statistics with the systematic use of imagination? Of course, scientists already use imagination at a particular juncture in research— namely, the devising of hypotheses to explain new facts. But this would be something quite different; it would be the use of imagination at each point and in the very act of observation. Is such a development even conceivable?

It has not yet been very widely realized that the genius who was possibly Europe's greatest poet, but who was certainly the greatest figure in the Romantic Movement, actually devoted more of his time to scientific investigation than to poetry and at the end of his life attached more importance to this part of himself then he did to his world-famous poetry. Goethe was convinced that the scientific method which came into vogue with the Scientific Revolution was not the only possible one. In particular he held that for dealing with the phenomena of life and growth it was an inadequate method. For the whole process of "becoming" is one which eludes the categories of cause and effect. The method which he applied in his work on *The Metamorphosis of Plants,* and elsewhere, was based on the perception that nature has an "inside" which cannot be weighed and measured—or even (without training) observed—namely, the creative thoughts which underlie phenomenal manifestation. Before the Scientific Revolution, when some attention was still paid to such problems, they would have called it "potential," as distinct from "actual" nature. And, Goethe claimed that this side of nature, too, was perceptible, not indeed to the untrained senses, but to a perceptive faculty trained by systematic practice to participate in those creative thoughts.

By ordinary inductive science the unifying idea, or law, behind groups of related phenomena is treated as a generalization from particulars; it is an abstract notion, which can be inferred only from observations of their results; and it must be expressible in terms of measurable quantities. For Goethean science, on the other hand, this unifying idea is an objective reality, accessible to direct observation. In addition to measuring quantities, the scientist must train himself to perceive qualities. This he can do—as Goethe did when he saw the various parts of the plant as "metamorphoses" of the leaf—only by so sinking himself in contemplation of the outward form that his imagination penetrates to the activity which is producing it.

Goethe's morphological observations on plant and animal played a significant part in the development of the (then quite new) concept of evolution and are referred to by Darwin in the introduction to his *Origin of Species*. But, because their whole epistemological basis was undermined by, and submerged in, the rising flood of positivist assumptions, little attention has been paid to them. They have been looked at from time to time but almost always through the spectacles of positivism.

By detaching himself more and more from the world of nature—as he has been doing ever since the Scientific Revolution—man has gradually developed the exact quantitative approach which has given him, over such a wide area, his marvelous powers of manipulative control.

But in doing so he has necessarily lost for the time being that felt union with the inner origin of outward forms which constitutes perception of their meaning. He can begin to recover this only if he develops his science beyond its present positivist limitations; and it is just such a development to which the way has already been pointed by one of the greatest minds Europe has ever known. What is needed now is for someone to try the experiment of taking off his positivist spectacles and examining Goethe with the naked eye.

Further reading:

Barfield, Owen. SAVING THE APPEARANCES. New York: Hillary House, 1957.

Cassirer, Ernst. THE PHILOSOPHY OF SYMBOLIC FORMS. Vol. I, *Language.* New Haven: Yale University Press, 1953.

Langer, Susanne K. PHILOSOPHY IN A NEW KEY. New York: The New American Library of World Literature, Inc., 1948.

Lehrs, Ernest. MAN OR MATTER. New York: Harper & Brothers, 1958.

Dream, Myth, and
Philosophical Double Vision

My method will be argumentative rather than aphoristic, but because my time is limited, I shall occasionally claim the privilege of the aphorist, inasmuch as I shall be proffering unsupported assertions. I shall, however, at least on some occasions, draw attention to the fact that I am doing so.

When we reflect today on the nature of human consciousness, most of us find ourselves obliged to divide it into two distinguishable components, the first of which I shall (for simplicity) call "ordinary consciousness" and the second "extraordinary consciousness." Of course there are borderline cases, but they do not obviate the necessity of the distinction. There are borderline cases between light and darkness, but we should not get very far if we refused to distinguish the one from the other.

It has become customary to refer to extraordinary consciousness as the "unconscious" mind; but, when we thus distinguish between conscious and unconscious mind, we are using the word "unconscious" in a special way. Verbally and logically "conscious" and "unconscious" are contradictories, but we do not use them in that way. When we say "the unconscious," we do not mean simply "the non-conscious." We do not imply for instance that this unconscious we are talking about is related to consciousness as we suppose a rock is related to a sentient organism. It might be argued that, for that reason alone, the terms "ordinary" and "extraordinary" are more satisfactory; but that is not my main reason for employing them. I do so because, if I had used the word "unconscious," I should have been importing a whole battery of presuppositions, some of which it is my principal purpose to call in question. First and foremost in this battery of presuppositions is the one that is implicit in the illustration with which I myself incautiously clothed the distinction I have just made. When we speak of an "unconscious," we assume (or most of us do) that what we are speaking of is a certain condition of a sentient physical organism endowed with life — and consequently that it is contingent on the presence of such an organism. No organism: no consciousness, whether it be ordinary or extraordinary consciousness that we have in mind.

Further than this, it is assumed that, because consciousness is contingent on a physical organism, it must be the product of such an organism. I am not now concerned with the logic of this deduction (usually a tacit one), or with the fallacy of confusing conditions with causes. I merely say that it is in fact very widely assumed — explicitly so by the behavioral and allied schools of psychology and philosophy (and of course by a vast population that believes it to have been established by what they believe to be what they call "science"): implicitly so (as a long course of observation and reflection has convinced me) by nearly everyone in the West — including those who would hotly resent being called behaviorists, including those who would label themselves philosophical idealists, including those whose interests and convictions lead them to attend the kind of lectures that are being given here. I think for instance (in spite of occasional suggestions to the contrary) that it is firmly fixed in the mental picture out of which the speculations of C. G. Jung have reached us. I think the word "collective" in his term the "Collective Unconscious" points to its supposed origin in a numerable aggregate of such physical organisms.

Consequently the contrary assumption I am now going to make, and on which I shall base the rest of what I have to say, is either heterodox or preposterous. At least it is so for most of the Western world. It is however quite otherwise in the East. In the East it has remained for millennia the orthodox assumption — one could say the axiom — on which nearly all philosophy is based. There it is not only philosophical doctrine, but also the common sense of the common man, the background structure that determines his total experience of life and of the world around him.

I am wondering how much longer this contrast is going to endure. When the ultrapositivist Herbert Spencer said: "Mysterious as seems the consciousness of something which is yet *out* of consciousness, we are obliged to think it," it seems to me he was letting into the ring fence of nineteenth-century Western thought a good deal more than he realized. He was not only letting in the excluded middle between the terminological contradictories, *conscious* and *unconscious;* he was also letting in (it is really only another way of saying the same thing) a postulate that has been outlawed from the imagination of the West since the time of Descartes: namely the postulate of intermediate stages between consciousness, or mind, and the material world. In letting in, as a practical necessity, that rigorously excluded middle between conscious and unconscious we have also let in, alike for practical and for philosophical purposes, the postulate concerning the nature of consciousness that underlies the *Upanishads*. It is this assumption on which I am going to proceed without attempting to justify it further. I said I should warn you, and I have done so; but I should like to add to this warning (or confession) a respectful request that you should consider at your leisure whether it is not one that is loudly called for by the facts of psychology and of history (perhaps also of physics), as they are now being disclosed with accelerating rapidity in the West itself. We cannot, as even Freud discovered, investigate what we now quite happily refer to as the "unconscious mind" without investigating something that transcends the *individual* organism and its lifespan; and this discovery seems to have made things very complicated for us. The scheme of consciousness I am now going to outline seems to me to bear the like relation to the contortions of Western speculative psychology, with their biologically dubious foundation in the concept of "inherited memory," as did the astronomy of Kepler and Galileo to the more complex gyrations and epicycles of the Ptolemaic system . . . and even of the Copernican system on its *first* appearance; for the Copernican system, as Copernicus presented it, actually required a larger number of supposititious orbits than the Ptolemaic. Everyone at all acquainted with the history of science knows that the dawn of a new and simpler theory is often an unbearable increase in the complexities entailed by the old one.

The *Mandukya Upanishad,* in particular, does not simply distinguish between ordinary and extraordinary consciousness. It distinguishes four stages, or degrees, in a continuum of consciousness. Omitting the Sanskrit terminology, they are: (1) ordinary waking consciousness, (2) dream consciousness, (3) the consciousness of dreamless sleep, and (4) an even less conscious degree of consciousness than (3)—a degree that may be predicated even of inanimate objects such as rocks. For the reasons I have given, it would be confusing to call this last degree "unconscious." I will therefore call it "a-conscious" (as we can speak, not only of "immoral," but of "a-moral," not only of "illogical," but of "a-logical"). All except the first stage must of course be included under what I began by calling "extraordinary" consciousness. Only the first of the four stages is what I have called "ordinary" consciousness.

Clearly, it is the second of these four degrees with which we are more particularly concerned here; but, because it is a continuum we are now assuming, or a spectrum extending on either side of this dream consciousness on which we are focusing our attention, we are led to conceive of it in a rather different way from the one we are accustomed to. We can now see it as a *transition* from the third stage (dreamless sleep) to the first, or waking, stage of consciousness. (To some extent this is no more than a matter of experience. We appear to dream, for the most part, when we have already begun the process of awaking.) Another way of putting it would be to say that we can see the dream as the "coming-into-being" of waking consciousness, as the metamorphosis of sleeping into waking. Moreover we now see ordinary consciousness as an emergence from, or metamorphosis of, not only sleep consciousness but also the a-consciousness, which lies beyond it in the continuum.

Psychoanalysis distinguishes in the dream: (1) its source in the unconscious, that is in some somatic, or psychosomatic, tension; and (2) the manifestation of that tension in symbol and imagery. Whereas the alternative presupposition involves distinguishing more in this way: (1) the source of the dream in all that stretch of the entire spectrum of consciousness that is antecedent to it; (2) the psychosomatic tension that immediately occasioned the dream; and (3) the imagery or sumbolism that is—or that expresses—the content of the dream.

One important difference between these two ways of looking at it is this. The a-conscious end of the spectrum, beyond the point of dream, is not conditioned by any single organism. This is another of those assumptions, of which I gave due notice, but I believe a little reflection will show that there is no ground, unless it be habit, for imagining it otherwise. Since then, both sleep consciousness and a-consciousness are superindividual, the ultimate source of a dream may be traceable to tensions, or conditions, or events, antecedent not only to the dream itself but also to the physical organism that occasioned the dream and was its medium—primordial tensions and events which were not produced by, but which produced, the physical organism itself as well as producing the consciousness that is correlative to a physical organism.

Here let me point out that there is nothing in this point of view which need invalidate the results of empirical investigation, for clinical purposes, into the immediate psychosomatic causes of a dream; though it is otherwise with the philosophical, cosmological, and historical assumptions, which are sometimes based a priori on the premise that these are sole or ultimate causes.

Now occidental thought, as it has hitherto developed, has diverged from the oriental outlook, not only in the very different scheme it has proposed—or in its very different presuppositions concerning the nature and provenance of ordinary consciousness, but also in another very striking respect. The Western outlook emphasizes the importance of *history* and pays an ever increasing attention to it. It is interested in history, whereas the Eastern outlook, by and large, is not. There are those who maintain that the two attitudes go together, and that if (as these few also maintain) we are now called on to switch over, or switch back, from an occidental to an oriental view of the nature of consciousness, we should also abandon our concern with history and concentrate exclusively on the relation between the present moment and eternity—or between ordinary consciousness and a-consciousness.

I am of a different opinion. I believe it lies in the destiny of the West, not to abandon but rather to intensify its concern with history; not to abandon its interest in the past of mankind, and of the world, but to deepen its understanding of both. And I suspect that most people here feel the same. After all, it is because we are interested, not only in today but also in yesterday and the day before yesterday that we are also interested not only in the psychology of dream but also in the psychology of myth, which belongs to the day before yesterday. Here too, however, I am persuaded that occidental thought is disastrously hampered by the presupposition concerning the nature of all consciousness to which I have referred. There is, for instance, the primary issue, on which all else hangs: whether the myths are to be regarded as inventions of human fancy or whether they are something more. I see on many sides valiant efforts being made to maintain the latter, and I follow some of these with deep interest, but through it all I retain an uncomfortable scruple which whispers to me that, if not only ordinary consciousness but all consciousness has been occasioned by a sentient organism, then the origin of myth would have to be sought in something like arbitrary invention: whether in the animism of Tylor and the early anthropologists, or in Herbert Spencer's and Max Müller's theory of a "disease of language," or in the collective neuroses with which Freudian anthropology makes so free.

On the other hand, if the single organism, if the physical body is not the ultimate source of consciousness, if it conditions ordinary consciousness but is itself the product of an antecedent extraordinary one, then it follows, as a matter of course, that myth is not merely analogous to dream, but is a parallel manifestation; that it is the historical equivalent of what in the dream is present and personal. One could put it perhaps that the myth betrays the "phylogenetic" emergence, as the dream betrays the "ontogenetic" emergence, of ordinary from extraordinary consciousness.

Only one would have to be well aware that, in saying so, he is making bold to use these words in a new way, not sanctioned by their traditional use in biological theory.

I have said that we are hampered by occidental presuppositions in our approach to both dream and myth. Let me give an instance of what I mean. There is, I suppose, no commoner link between ideas about myth and ideas about dream than the name Oedipus. But the name Oedipus, when it is used in psychology, alludes to one selected part of the actual myth of Oedipus. For every ten thousand allusions to the patricide and incest of the Theban monarch I doubt if you will find one to his earlier encounter with the Sphinx. Yet the question asked by the Sphinx: What is man? — or rather the riddle posed by the Sphinx, to which the answer is "man" — what is it, if it is not the story, in image, of man's first awakening experience of emerging from extraordinary into ordinary consciousness? With that thought in mind, is it not some guide also to an individual man's experience of awakening from sleep in the twentieth century? Though he may not often attend to the moment as it passes, the first thing he has to do on waking in the morning is to answer the question: Who, or what, am I? And what if the vanishing dream, at whose skirts we sometimes clutch, sometimes prove to have as much to do with this question, and the answer to it, as with our more immediate personal anxieties and tensions? I suspect that, if only half as much attention and fancy and imagination had been concentrated on the whole Oedipus myth as has in fact been concentrated on the spicier part, we should have learned by now to pay more regard to this marvelous experience — which only does not seem marvelous because it occurs, like the sunrise, every morning.

Once again, we must not forget that, if the spectrum of consciousness is in fact one and all-embracing, then it will not be only the transition from extraordinary to ordinary consciousness that a receptive imagination will detect in the myths, but also the emergence from extraordinary consciousness of the inseparable condition and occasion of ordinary consciousness, that is, of the physical body itself. This is, I believe, the most unsavory gnat which the West is now called on to swallow in lieu of the numerous beasts of burden it has been happily devouring since psychoanalysis was first invented.

Gnat and camel! Am I exaggerating? Perhaps. It is a first principle of Western science that, of two hypotheses, either of which furnishes an adequate explanation, the simpler should always be preferred. That no doubt is why, in order to explain a dream, we reject the complex notion that the physical organism emerged from a condition anterior to the physical and adopt the simpler and more elegant hypothesis that the psyche desires (but without knowing that it desires) to return to a physical womb, regarding that (but without knowing that it regards it) as a convenient base from which to commence the further operation of becoming its own father.

The philosopher Schelling maintained that mythology represents the repetition in the human spirit and consciousness of the processes of nature . . . that the myths also disclose the ties uniting man with the primary processes of world-creation and formation . . . that deep natural processes were at work even before the consolidation of matter; and man's destiny was still rooted in them, although his divorce from higher spiritual sources had already taken place.

I must remark here, since I have referred to Schelling, who (I suppose) is not much read today, and is probably regarded by most philosophy students as having been "written off" in some way, that it depresses me when I hear it said, or implied, that we have passed on from Descartes to Kant, from Kant to the post-Kantians and neo-Kantians, and from the neo-Kantians to phenomenology or something else—rather as if philosophy were a kind of railroad train—and of course it depresses me especially when the writing off is done by people who perhaps have not themselves read a line of the discarded material. If we insist on thinking of the history of philosophy as a train, we must conceive of a train, some of whose coaches (perhaps even the most important ones) have got uncoupled and left behind on the rails until a donkey engine comes along and picks them up. The coach may be a whole philosopher, such as Vico, or Coleridge, or Schelling, or Thomas Reid; or it may be a particular part of a philosopher's whole thought, such as Kant's *Critique of Teleological Judgment,* or Goethe's *Metamorphosenlehre.*

I have mentioned the Oedipus myth as evincing the emergence of ordinary from extraordinary consciousness. I could also have mentioned the myth of Medusa—and of course many another. If we hold (with or without the help of Schelling) that the myths "disclose the ties uniting man the primary processes of world-creation and formation," we are likely to see in that unforgettable picture of the Gorgon's head, with serpents writhing about it instead of hair, that turns to stone all who look on it, not only an image of ordinary consciousness cut off from extraordinary consciousness, but also (and here I am indebted, as I so often have been, to Rudolf Steiner) an image of the writhing convolutions of the physical brain in process of formation, before the consolidation of matter.

It is in my mind that those of us in the West who feel a special interest in myth and dream are mostly impelled thereto by a feeling that the world in which we reside with our ordinary consciousness, and which is correlative to that ordinary consciousness, is precisely that world that has already been blasted by Medusa. From such a world they feel the need of liberation. That is a point of view to which the East also is, to say the least of it, no stranger. And "liberation" in this context means, for both East and West, somehow receiving the freedom of extraordinary consciousness. Yet there is a difference between the oriental and the occidental point of view, and a very important one. The Eastern teacher of "Moksha" or liberation has eyes for little but the ultimate goal, which is the attainment of what I have called "a-consciousness." He is not much interested in any intermediate stages, though (as we have seen) he may carefully enumerate them. He is not much interested in any intermediate stages, whether of the descent from extraordinary into ordinary consciousness by way of myth (which is history) or of dream (which is personal) or in a gradual reascent from ordinary to extraordinary consciousness. It seems to be otherwise in the West.

But there is a deeper difference than this between the Eastern concept of "liberation" and the Western one—a deeper difference, but one that is not unconnected, I would say, with that other difference between a lack of interest in intermediate stages and a burning interest in them. For the Eastern sage liberation from ordinary consciousness and the attainment of a-consciousness entails, in effect, the absorption of ordinary consciousness. Whereas the true Western impulse is rather to add extraordinary consciousness to ordinary consciousness—though the word "add" is lame one, as any other word must be in such a context. Another way of putting it would be to say that the impulse of the West is toward liberation by "vision" rather than liberation by absorption. But of course it is a special sort of vision — one not incompatible with an experienced identity between the seer and what he sees.

There is a certain kind of nocturnal dream, in which we dream with one part of ourselves, and yet at the same time we know with another part that we are dreaming. The dream continues, and is a real dream (that is, it is not just a waking reverie). And yet we know that we are dreaming; we are there outside the dream, as well as being there within it. I think we may let ourselves be instructed by such dreams in the nature of true vision.

Poets have sometimes been called "visionaries" and sometimes "dreamers"; but they are likely to be poor poets, unless it is *this* kind of dream that we are connoting when we use the word. Poetic imagination is very close to the dreaming of such dreams, and has little to do with reverie. In

reverie we lose ourselves (we speak of being "lost in reverie"), we are absorbed; but in imagination we find ourselves in finding vision. The vision is
objective (as if it were part of ordinary consciousness); but its very objectivity is as much our own as what we call subjectivity—for it is the content of extraordinary consciousness; and that is what we now mean by
"objectivity"; it is what we mean (in terms of the spectrum of consciousness) even by rocks and stones and trees. Imagination is a Western concept, and imagination is potentially extraordinary consciousness—not just
the dream stage, but the whole gamut of it—*present with* ordinary consciousness.

I believe moreover that this potential lies at the root of the "tension"
that is often spoken of in connection with the use of metaphor. Metaphor
involves a tension between two ostensibly incompatible meanings; but it
also involves a tension between that part of ourselves which experiences
the incompatibles as a mysterious unity and that part which remains well
able to appreciate their duality and their incompatibility. Without the
former metaphor is nonsense language, but without the latter it is not even
language.

That, I take it, is why, on the part of those who reject metaphor, and
the whole organic and organizing concept of art and poetry which it presupposes, as effete and superseded, we are at the moment witnessing a
number of attempts to produce a poetry, or a literature, which is not even
language. Metaphor is objectionable to these pioneers of aphasia for the
same reason that it is acceptable to me: because it can be objectively meaningful. It can be objectively meaningful because language itself (though it
is inextricably involved with ordinary consciousness) is the product, not
only of ordinary consciousness but also of the extraordinary consciousness
from which ordinary consciousness has emerged. That is also the case with
myth. All the richness and variety of myth, and all the richness and variety
of language, arise from intermediate stages between the one consciousness
and the other. Accordingly a good, a wise, a true metaphor is not just a
device for lobbing us abruptly out of ordinary consciousness into a-consciousness, out of time into eternity, out of the communicable into the
ineffable, but one for affording us vision of some particular intermediate
stage between the two extremes of the continuum. It trains us in the ten-
sive and laborious problem of adding extraordinary consciousness to our
ordinary consciousness. It is likely, then, to become more rather than less
unpopular with those who are primarily interested in short cuts to bliss.
Intermediate stages are not their portion.

My time has run out just as I approach what many regard as the major problem, that of communication; and I mean by that communication of particular noetic vision, or vision of noetic particulars, as distinct from communicating the general flavor of extraordinary consciousness. As I see it, it is this problem with which the poets, from Dante to the Romantics, have been experimenting; and the question arises for me whether it can any longer be safely left in their hands alone, especially as there is an increasing tendency on their part to disclaim all responsibility for it. Whether that is so or not, I am persuaded that the problem cannot even be fruitfully debated except on the basis of the three positions I have been seeking to establish: (1) that there is such a thing as noetic vision—as distinct from liberation, which is its condition but not its content; (2) that this is a philosophical as well as an aesthetic problem; (3) that the act of vision, though not the objective content of the vision, requires the maintenance, and not the sacrifice, of ordinary consciousness.

It was for this reason that, when the phrase "philosophical double vision" was suggested to me as part of my title, I accepted it. But any attempt to develop it further would have to be left for another occasion.

The Meaning of "Literal"

We call a sentence "literal" when it means what it affirms on the face of it, and nothing else. If some sentences are not literal, that is because it is possible, by recognized linguistic usage, to affirm or express one thing and to mean another thing, either instead of or as well as the first. An extreme case of meaning another thing instead (which I will call "substituted meaning") is the prearranged code. In P. G. Wodehouse's *Leave it to Psmith,* a young man outside an Underground Station goes up to a number of complete strangers in turn and tells them to their surprise (and sometimes annoyance) that "There will be rain in Northumberland tomorrow." But what he really means is: "Are you the person who advertised in the Personal Column and later wrote asking me to meet you here?" Perhaps the code is hardly a *linguistic* device; but it will serve as a kind of marker for the terminal point of "substitution"; and we may profitably compare with it the *cliché,* or completely *fossilized metaphor.* If, for example, I tell anyone to "leave no stone unturned," there is hardly more of "stone" in my meaning than there was of "rain" in Psmith's. All that is left is the substituted meaning: "Try every way you can think of!"

When we turn from "instead of" to "as well as," that is, to sentences which convey a secondary meaning, while still in some measure retaining the primary, or literal, one (I will call this "concomitant meaning"), we have already crossed the frontier between prose and poetry. At least I think our examples would practically all have to be taken from among sentences which are characteristically—though not necessarily successfully—poetic. They would range from allegory at one end of the scale, where the two meanings continue alongside, on more or less parallel lines, to

32

what I suppose is best called "symbolism" at the other — loaded sentences like:

E il naufragar m'è dolce in questo mare,

or:

The cat looked long and softly at the king.

I have distinguished concomitant meaning from substituted meaning, but no doubt in all cases, where it makes any sense at all to distinguish the literal meaning from some other or others, a possibility is implied of transference or substitution. For if there are at least two concomitant meanings, and these are distinguishable from one another, we must be able to attend to either one to the exclusion of the other; and if we attend only to the nonliteral meaning, we are substituting it for the literal. Thus, the ordinary word for the converse of "literal" is "metaphorical," from μεταφέρειν — meaning "to carry across" or "transfer"; and the problems of the relation between the literal meaning and any other confront us nowhere more strikingly than in the metaphors of poets.

As an example of such problems, you might expect that the element of concomitance (retention of the literal meaning alongside the substituted one) would bear some relation to the verisimilitude of the literal meaning. But that is not in practice the case. The literal meaning of

The moon is my eye,
Smiling only at night . . .

or

There is a garden in her face . . .

is a pretty tall story; whereas Psmith's remark about the rain was all too likely to be true. Yet it is in the first two cases that the literal meaning continues to command our attention, while in the last it drops out altogether. I only mention this in passing and am not proposing to pursue it.

So far, I should imagine, everyone is with me. But at this point opinions begin to differ. It was Dr. I. A. Richards in *The Philosophy of Rhetoric* (1936) who introduced two terms which are very useful to people who try to deal with this kind of subject, when he referred to the literal or surface meaning of an expression as the *vehicle* and any other meaning which it also properly conveys as the *tenor*. These two terms I propose, with grateful acknowledgments, to adopt.

Now there is a school of thought which holds that the tenor of a meaningful metaphor could always, if it were thought fit, be expressed literally. The passenger in the vehicle could, if he chose, get out and walk. If it were not so, these thinkers hold, the tenor would not deserve the name of "meaning" at all; it would amount to no more than an emotional overtone. A meaningful expression, as distinct from an emotive one, imparts information; and there is no information (they insist) which is not communicable by discursive and literal statement. It is not, by the way, only those who are insensitive to the working of imagination who take this view. Apart from Dr. Richards, Susanne Langer, in her book *Problems of Art* (1957), in the course of making an acute and valuable distinction between art as symbol and the use of symbols *in* art, commits herself to the general statement that "there is a literal meaning (sometimes more than one) connoted by the symbol that occurs in art." And again, genuine symbols "have meanings, *and the meanings may be stated.*"

The other school of thought holds that the tenor of a meaningful metaphor or symbol *cannot* always be expressed literally. However it may be with codes and allegories, there are also "creative," or "seminal," or anyway some sort of metaphors and symbols, whose tenor cannot be communicated in any other way than through the symbol, and yet whose tenor is not purely emotive. Whether what is so communicated is information will depend on how we choose to limit the word "information"; but it is certainly meaning. The adherents of this school might well object to my use of the word "concomitant" and prefer some such term as "manifold" or "multiple," but I will continue to use the word "concomitant" without implying any particular relation between vehicle and tenor, or that the one is always clearly distinguishable from the other.

The meaning we attach to the word "literal" in many of the contexts in which it is commonly used (and these are of course not limited to the realms of poetry and art) will be found, I believe, to depend a good deal on the issue between these two contrasted views. At the moment, however, I shall content myself with having stated them, while I move on into another field and try approaching the subject from a different direction.

Hitherto we have been considering only sentences, but it is not only sentences that possess this quality of being a vehicle with a tenor. That is also very frequently the case with individual words. Since I shall be saying a good deal about "meaning," I had better mention that I am aware that there is a sense of the word "meaning" in which an individual word outside a sentence has no meaning. But this limiting sense of the term "meaning" is really based on the premise that all meaningful language is discursive and therefore that the only meaningful symbols are the discursive symbols of logic. In other words it presupposes that the first of the two schools of thought which I have mentioned is right and the second is wrong. I shall be suggesting later that there are difficulties in the way of such a supposition. Meanwhile it is enough that, when I talk about the meanings of individual words, I shall be talking about whatever it is that lexicographers and etymologists do talk about. For reasons which I hope will appear, I do not think it is possible to form any reliable ideas on this subject without taking full account of the historical approach, and it is so that I approach it.

Consider the four words, *outsider, noble, gentle,* and *scruple.* If we approach them etymologically, we find a sort of graduated scale in the relation between vehicle and tenor which they exemplify. When we meet the word *outsider,* we are normally still aware, even without reflection, of its vehicular connotation of spatial externality, even though our main concern is with its tenorial significance—which will be caddishness, or original genius, according to the context. *Noble* is still used occasionally to signify social rank, irrespective of high character (which is of course its tenor). *Gentle,* a word with a similar history, has already ceased to be used with a class or social import except in the obsolescent compounds *gentleman* and *gentlewoman.* In the case of *scruple,* it takes a little erudition to be aware that once upon a time it, too, was a vehicle with a distinguishable tenor; for we have to go to another language (Latin), from which it is derived, in order to ascertain that *scrupulus* originally meant a small, sharp stone—the kind that gets into your shoe and worries you.

In all these four cases the vehicle is a reference to something in the outside world, while the tenor conveys a moral quality or a feeling not accessible to sense-observation. (I am going to call it something in the "inside" world. There will not be much danger, during this paper, of anyone forgetting that we talk in metaphors.) And of course, as soon as we start exploring the history of language in this way, the deluge of available examples makes us feel like the sorcerer's apprentice. The shortest way I can think of to get our minds straight into the middle of all that line of country is to quote a few sentences from the section on language in Emerson's longer essay on Nature:

> Every word which is used to express a moral or intellectual fact, if
> traced to its root, is found to be borrowed from material appearance.
> *Right* means *straight; wrong* means *twisted. Spirit* primarily means

wind; transgression, the *crossing of a line; supercilious,* the *raising of the eyebrows.* We say the *heart* to express emotion, the *head* to denote thought, and *thought* and *emotion* are words borrowed from sensible things, and now appropriated to spiritual nature. Most of the process by which this transformation is made is hidden from us in the remote time when language was formed . . . .

I have chosen Emerson, but the observation is one with which, it seems, everyone agrees. For instance, it was summed up as follows by Jeremy Bentham:

> Throughout the whole field of language, parallel to the line of what may be termed the material language, and expressed by the same words, runs a line of what may be termed the immaterial language. Not that to every word that has a material import there belongs also an immaterial one; but that to every word that has an immaterial import, there belongs, or at least did belong, a material one.
>
> Essay on Language, Section IV

It is fairly obvious that, if we are to consider the meaning of the word "literal" in any general sense—that is, not simply as a technical term in the art of rhetoric—all this is very relevant indeed and requires further examination. For instance, it is clear that the words of this "immaterial" language, of which Bentham speaks, are, or were at one time, what we have been calling *vehicles,* with an immediately physical reference, but having as their *tenor* the "immaterial" language. Or, avoiding the technical terms, it is clear that they were used *figuratively.* Are we equally justified in saying that they are, or were, used *metaphorically*? Was the figurative import always created by a definite mental act of substitution? In some cases it certainly was. The word *scrupulus* is a good example of these cases—I am not even sure that there isn't a passage in Cicero somewhere, where he introduces the metaphor with a rhetorical flourish. But the facility with which, from a few such cases, the general inference has been drawn that *all* immaterial language came about in this way is remarkable. Bentham, Herbert Spencer, Max Müller all take this long jump in their stride and, though other voices have been raised in this century—for instance, Ernst Cassirer, Bruno Snell, and R. B. Onians—it is still the general view. Dr. A. S. Diamond, in his book *The History and Origin of Language* (1959), simply takes it for granted.

If this inference were correct, it would follow that all nouns which today have an immaterial import and no other (*transgression, supercilious, emotion,* and so forth), have behind them a history in which we can distinguish the following four stages: a first stage, in which they had an exclusively literal meaning and referred to a material object; a second stage, in which they had concomitant meanings; a third stage, in which they had a substituted meaning, though the original one had not quite vanished; and a fourth and final stage, in which their meaning has again become (though much altered) exclusively *literal.* The Greek word πνεῦμα and Latin *spiritus* and *anima* are commonly given as the typical examples of stage 2. We think of the third chapter of St. John's Gospel where the same Greek word πνεῦμα has to be translated *spirit* in one sentence and *wind* in the next sentence of the same verse. I have already given *outsider* as an example of stage 3 (for the *quality* it denotes is immaterial) and the modern English word *spirit* will do very well once more for our example of stage 4.

Under examination, however, this presumed historical progress gives rise to a number of questions, two of which were briefly considered many years ago by Professor C. S. Lewis in a paper entitled "Bluspels and Flalansferes," which was printed in his *Rehabilitations* (1939). He distinguished between the *magistral* and the *pupillary* metaphor: "The first is freely chosen; it does not at all hinder, and only very slightly helps, the thought of its maker. The second is not chosen at all; it is the unique expression of a meaning that we cannot have on any other terms" (pp. 140–41). The two questions he raised are: *When?* and *What?* When exactly, at what point in its history, did the stage 3 meaning of the word *spiritus* (during which it still connoted something to do with *wind* or *breath*) turn into stage 4 — the present-day meaning of our word *spirit*? And (much more difficult semantically) *what* happened, when it ceased to be a vehicle with a tenor, and became a mere literal word? Now the fact that we cannot say exactly *when* a change has taken place does not of course mean that it did not take place; and we perhaps need not worry unduly about the first question — though in point of fact it is a good deal easier to presume a gradual transition in such a case than actually to imagine the process in detail. Just as it is easy to talk of an emendation "creeping" into a text, but very difficult to form a concrete picture of any halfway point in that mysterious journey.

The problem of *what* happened is a much more prickly one; for it raises the whole question of what a literal word of immaterial import *does* mean. What does it refer to? Anatole France had a very simple answer for this question. He said these words really still have only their original, material import — and for that reason we need not worry too much about philósophy. The metaphysician constructs his system by putting together noises which are no more than the perfected cries of dogs and monkeys, cries to which we have gradually attached a significance which we believe to be abstract, when they are in fact only loose or vague. Obviously this will not do. Nobody except an *esprit fort* seriously thinks that the word *spirit* means "wind" today; but what *does* it mean? Nor is it only words like *spirit, soul, mind* which are puzzling. To what, precisely, does each one of them refer—the tens of thousands of abstract nouns which daily fill the columns of our newspapers, the debating chambers of our legislatures, the consulting rooms of our psychiatrists? *Progress, tendency, culture, democracy, liberality, inhibition, motivation, responsibility*—there was a time when each one of them, either itself or its progenitor in another tongue, was a vehicle referring to the concrete world of sensuous experience with a tenor of some sort peeping, or breathing, or bursting through. But now they are just "literal" words—the sort of words we have to use, when we are admonished *not* to speak in metaphors. What do we mean when we say that?

It is here that the blessed word "entity" generally rears its head. An abstract noun, used literally, means—or is thought to mean—an entity of some sort, a real entity, if you are a Hegelian idealist; a fictitious entity, if you are a positivist. Bentham tells us that:

> With every name employed an entity stands associated in the minds of the hearers, as well as speakers; and that entity, though in one half of the whole number of instances, no other than a fictitious one, is, in all of them, apt to be taken for a real one.

And he goes on to emphasize the misconceptions, errors, and ambiguities that have arisen as the result. I do not know that the logical positivists have added much to this way of putting it. What I want to question is the validity of this whole approach to the problem, this whole way of thinking about it.

Why have people fallen into the habit of talking and thinking on the footing that nouns refer, or at all events are expected to refer, to entities? You will remember that the presumed history of these literal words of immaterial import has gone through four stages, in the first and last of which their meanings were exclusively literal, while in the two intermediate stages they functioned as vehicles having a tenor. We may call the first stage—at which they are presumed to have referred solely to material objects—the "born" literal, and the last stage—at which they are presumed

to refer to immaterial entities, real or fictitious – the "achieved" literal.
Now I believe it will be found that our whole way of thinking about the
achieved literal is based on a tacitly assumed analogy with the born literal.
We assume that it is not the natural, simple nature of a noun to be a vehicle
with a tenor, because nouns did not begin that way. They began life as
plain labels for plain objects and that is their true nature. It was only later,
as a result of the operation of human fancy in metaphor-making, that they
came to be used for a time as vehicles with a tenor; and when that stage is
over and they have once more achieved literalness, we feel that they have
reverted to their pristine innocence and become once more labels for objects, even if we are firmly convinced that the new objects do not exist.
Better a fictitious entity than none at all – for a noun to be the name of!

If I am right about this, and there is a confusion between our notion of
achieved literalness and our notion of born literalness, it is clearly important to be sure that at least our notion of born literalness is roughly correct. And that is what I now propose to examine.

At the beginning of this paper we found that there were two schools of
thought about the relation between vehicle and tenor; one holding that
they are always detachable, and that the tenor could also be expressed literally; the other holding that that is not always the case. Let us therefore
consider the concept of born literalness from each of these contrasted
points of view in turn.

The concept of born literalness assumes that all words of immaterial
import began with an exclusively material reference and subsequently acquired an immaterial tenor as a result of the metaphor-making activity of
human minds. Now adherents of the first, or detachable, school of
thought – which I will call the *explicationist* theory of metaphor – are
bound to assume that the immaterial tenor, upon its first appearance
among our primitive ancestors, could in the alternative have been expressed literally. But in order to achieve this, those ancestors must already
have possessed other words with an immaterial reference. But how did
those words acquire their immaterial reference? Not by metaphorical activity – unless there had already been still other words available; and so on
ad infinitum. It follows that, *if* you believe that whatever can be expressed
metaphorically can also be expressed literally, you cannot at the same time
believe that man's first words had a purely material reference and that an
immaterial tenor was subsequently added by way of metaphor.

The second – or *implicationist* – theory of metaphor, which holds that
the tenor cannot necessarily be taken apart from its vehicle and expressed
literally, escapes this difficulty. But it still has to assume that the immater-

ial content, which afterwards became the tenor, was *conceived* separately and without the help of any verbal vehicle. Somehow or other our ancestors had acquired a bit of self-knowledge (knowledge of the "inner" world) without the help of the instrument of speech and then they chose a word with which to clothe that bit of knowledge metaphorically. I am a primitive man, who has just become aware of a sort of immaterial something within me, but I have no word for it. In my experience up to now, it is not even the sort of thing for which there *are* words. What I *have* got available is a bunch of strictly literal labels for things like *sun, moon, cloud, rock, river, wind,* etc. None of these words has any immaterial overtone at all. That is an essential condition; for otherwise they would not be literal (as born literals are assumed to be literal); they would already be vehicles with a tenor. The word for *wind,* for example, means to me simply what we today call *air* or *oxygen,* the physical stuff that keeps on coming into and going out of me. I now take the step of substituting my word for, and with it my thought of, *wind* for my wordless thought of the sort of something. That is the picture.

And of course it is an impossible one. It is not impossible that new meanings should make their first appearance as metaphor. On the contrary in our time it is the common way. Discovery, consciousness itself, and symbolization go hand-in-hand. But we must remember that metaphors and symbols today are created by minds already acquainted with figurative language as a normal mode of expression. What we are trying to imagine now is the first metaphor in a wholly literal world. And that does imply precisely this primitive and verbally unsupported notion of the "sort of something" which I have tried to depict. But it is impossible to believe that things happened in this way.

It is impossible to believe, because consciousness and symbolization are simultaneous and correlative. We can believe that a growing awareness of the sort of something which we today mean by *spirit* was inextricably linked with a new use of the word for *wind.* What it is impossible to believe is, that up to that moment the word for *wind* had been as semantically aloof from the sort of something as Psmith's remark about rain in Northumberland was semantically aloof from the information he intended to convey to Freddie Threepwood.

If there was no prior, no "given" affinity between the concept "wind" and the other immaterial concept of "spirit," the latter concept must have been originally framed without the aid of any symbol. It must moreover, as tenor, have been separable from its vehicle when it acquired one. The first of these two consequences is, in my view, epistemologically untenable on several grounds; but it is enough that the second is pointedly inconsistent with just that "implicational" type of metaphor which is the only one we are any longer concerned with, since the explicational type has already been shown to be incompatible with born literalness. If, on the other hand, there *was* any prior affinity between the concept of *wind* and the other (immaterial) concept, then the word must already, from the moment of its birth, have been a vehicle with a tenor.

I think we are bound to conclude that this was in fact the case. We have escorted the concept of "born literalness" to the frontier and there is really nothing left to do but to hand it over to the consular representatives of the land of Not-being, or perhaps better say the land of dream. It occupies a clear and conspicuous place in so many minds that I hardly know what to call it. "Chimera" suggests fancifulness and vagueness, but the historical fallacy of born literalness is neither vague nor fanciful. Perhaps *specter* is the best word. Literalness is a quality which some words have achieved in the course of their history; it is not a quality with which the first words were born. And let us be clear about the consequences. The born literalness which we have rejected is a literalness of the material, not of the immaterial language. We mean by a "literal" word or meaning one which is not a vehicle with a tenor or one which is a vehicle without a tenor. But the vast majority of the words by which we today denote the objects of the outer world have at some stage in their history been vehicles with a tenor, and, if that is so, it follows (except in places where a tenor was added by late and deliberate metaphorical construction) that they *began* life as vehicles with a tenor. They too can only have *achieved* a literalness with which they were not born. Just as our immaterial language has acquired its literal meanings by dropping the vehicular reference, so our material language has acquired its literalness by dropping the tenorial reference. That which the physiologist takes to be the literal meaning of the word *heart,* for example, is no less "achieved" than that which the theologian takes to be the literal meaning of the word *spirit.* Whatever else the word "literal" means, then, it normally means something which is the end-product of a long historical process.

Abandoning the specter of born literalness, we shall also abandon the whole dream of fixed entities with which literal meanings must somehow correspond. What then are we left with? What solid ground have we to stand on? The linguistic analysts have already suggested that there is none. According to them, the meaning of a word is the way it is used in sentences, and it may be that there is not much to quarrel with in this doctrine, if it stops there. They do not however appear to stop there, for they seem to infer from this a sort of lowest common measure and to equate the meaning of any word with (to quote Mr. Gellner) "the way it is used by an unimaginative man about the middle of the morning." On the other hand, when it is a question, not of inference or assumption, but of any further development of the doctrine, they *do* stop there. For they do not appear to be interested in any sort of historical enquiry. Whereas, if the meaning of a word in the twentieth century is the way it is used in the twentieth century, I would have thought that that makes it all the more interesting and important to enquire into the way it was used from time to time in previous centuries.

Although I have been dealing with words, it cannot be said that my conclusions affect words only. If the word on its very first appearance was already a vehicle with a tenor, then the given affinity which I suggested between the concept of *wind* and the concept of *spirit* must have been "given" in the nature of things and not by some kind of friction in the machinery of language. I think it will be found that to assume otherwise is merely to smuggle back into our thinking the specter of born literalness, or at all events of the sort of world, the sort of relation between nature and the mind of man which must have given rise to born literalness and could not therefore (as we saw when we laid the specter) have given rise to an immaterial import. Bruno Snell put it neatly in his book *The Discovery of Mind* (1946, translated 1953), when, in dealing with one of Homer's metaphors, he maintained that man could never have come to experience a rock anthropomorphically if he had not also experienced himself "petromorphically."

It follows that neither nature nor man will ever be understood, though certainly physical nature—and perhaps physical man, too—may in the meantime be very skillfully *manipulated,* until we accept that nature is the reflected image of man's conscious and unconscious self. We must remember that the human body is itself a part of nature. As long as the historical fallacy of born literalness holds sway, Freud's half-truth that many images have a bodily significance will be swallowed, without leading, as it should, to the reflection that this is only possible because the body itself has an imaginal significance. I think it also follows that the mind of man is not, as Coleridge put it, "a lazy onlooker" on an external world but itself a structural component of the world it comtemplates.

I conclude that the second of the two schools of thought mentioned at the start—the implicationist school—has hold of the truth. The other, the explicationist, view is founded on the assumption that all meaningful langauge is discursive; this assumption is itself based on the premise that literalness of meaning is some kind of unclouded correspondence with a mindless external reality which was given from the start; and this premise in its turn requires the specter of born literalness to keep it in countenance.

As to the meaning of the word "literal," there is no difficulty about it, and everyone knows what it means as a technical term in the art of rhetoric. In any wider sense, bearing on the general relation between material and immaterial language, what we call literalness is a late stage in a long-drawn-out historical process.

There is of course a sense in which words must be said to mean what they are believed, and therefore intended, to mean; but nouns of the so-called material language do not in fact correspond with real and wholly material entities. The belief that they do so is responsible for the fuss about entities, real or fictitious, upon which to found the meanings of nouns of the so-called immaterial language. In this factual sense there is indeed no such thing as literalness. The most we can safely say, therefore, is that the literal and discursive use of language is the way in which it is used by a speaker, who is either unaware of, or is deliberately ignoring, that real and figurative relation between man and his environment, out of which the words he is using were born and without which they could never have been born.

Poetic Diction and Legal Fiction

The house of poetry contains many mansions. These mansions are so diverse in their qualities and in their effect on the indweller and some of them are so distant from others that the inhabitants of one mansion have sometimes been heard to deny that another is part of the same building at all. For instance, Edgar Allen Poe said that there is no such thing as a long poem, and the difference between a long narrative poem and a short lyric is admittedly rather baffling, seeming almost to be one of kind. What I have to say here touches mainly lyric poetry, and will interest those who love to dwell with recurring delight on special felicities of expression more than those to whom poetry means taking their *Iliad* or their *Faerie Queene* a thousand lines at a time and enjoying the story. It is highly specialized. Think for a moment of poems as of pieces of fabric, large tapestries, or minute embroideries as the case may be. What I have to say does not concern the whole form of even one of the embroideries, but only the texture itself, the nature of the process at any given point, as the fabric comes into being, the movements which the shuttle or the needle must have made. It is still more specialized than this; for in examining the texture of poetry one of the most important elements (a mansion to itself) is rhythm, sound, music; and all this is of necessity excluded. I am fully aware that this involves the corollary that the kind of poetry I am talking about may also be written in prose; but that is a difficulty which is chronic to the subject. I wish, however, to treat of that element in poetry which is best called "meaning" pure and simple. Not the meaning of poetry, nor the meaning of any poem as a whole, but just meaning. If this sounds like an essay in microscopy, or if it be objected that what I am talking about is not poetic

44

diction, but etymology or philosophy or even genetic psychology, I can only reply that whatever it ought to be called, it is, to some people, extraordinarily interesting, and that if, in all good faith, I have given it a wrong address, it is still to me the roomiest, the most commodious, and the most exciting of all the mansions which I rightly or wrongly include in the plan and elevation of the great house.

The language of poetry has always been in a high degree *figurative;* it is always illustrating or expressing what it wishes to put before us by comparing that with something else. Sometimes the comparison is open and avowed, as when Shelley compares the skylark to a poet, to a high-born maiden, and to a rose embowered in its own green leaves; when Keats tells us that a summer's day is:

> like the passage of an angel's tear
> That falls through the clear ether silently.

Or when Burns writes simply: "My love is like a red red rose." And then we call it a "simile." Sometimes it is concealed in the form of a bare statement, as when Shelley says of the west wind, not that it is *like*, but that it *is* "the breath of Autumn's being," calls upon it to "make him its lyre," and says of himself that *his* leaves are falling. This is known as "metaphor." Sometimes the element of comparison drops still farther out of sight. Instead of saying that A is like B or that A is B, the poet simply talks about B, without making any overt reference to A at all. You know, however, that he intends A all the time, or, better say that you know he intends *an* A; for you may not have a very clear idea of what A is and even if you have got an idea, somebody else may have a different one. This is generally called "symbolism."

I do not say that these particular methods of expression are an absolute *sine qua non* of poetic diction. They are not. Poetry may also take the form of simple and literal statement. But figurative expression is found everywhere; its roots descend very deep, as we shall see, into the nature, not only of poetry, but of language itself. If you took away from the stream of European poetry every passage of a metaphorical nature, you would reduce it to a very thin trickle indeed, pure though the remainder beverage might be to the taste. Perhaps our English poetry would suffer the heaviest damage of all. Aristotle, when treating of diction in his *Poetics,* provides the right expression by calling the element of metaphor πολὺ μέγιστον —far the most important.

It may be noticed that I am now using the word "metaphor" in a slightly different and wider sense than when I placed it in the midst between simile on the one hand and symbol on the other. I am now using it, and shall use it frequently throughout this article, to cover the whole gamut of figurative language including simile and symbol. I do not think this need confuse us. Strict metaphor occurs about the middle of the gamut and expresses the essential nature of such language more perfectly perhaps than either of the extremes. In something the same way Goethe found that the leaf of a plant expressed its essential nature as plant, while the blossom and the root could be considered as metamorphoses of the leaf. Here I want to try and consider a little more closely what the essential nature of figurative language is and how that nature is most clearly apparent in the figure called metaphor.

But first of all let us return to the "gamut" and take some examples. This time let us move along it in the reverse direction, beginning from symbolism.

> Does the road wind uphill all the way?
> > Yes, to the very end.
> Will the day's journey take the whole long day?
> > From morn to night, my friend.
>
> But is there for the night a resting-place?
> > A roof for when the slow, dark hours begin.
> May not the darkness hide it from my face?
> > You cannot miss that inn.
>
> Shall I meet other wayfarers at night?
> > Those who have gone before.
> Then must I knock or call when just in sight?
> > They will not keep you waiting at that door.
>
> Shall I find comfort, travel-sore and weak?
> > Of labour you shall find the sum.
> Will there be beds for me and all who seek?
> > Yea, beds for all who come.

As I have already suggested, the ordinary way of characterizing this kind of language would be to say that the poet says one thing and means another. Is this true? Is it fair to say that Christina Rossetti says B but that she *really means* A? I do not think this is a question which can be an-

swered with a simple "yes" or "no." In fact the difficult and elusive relation between A and B is the heart of my matter. For the time being let me
hazard, as a rather hedging sort of answer, that the truer it is to say "yes,"
the worse is the poem, the truer it is to say "no," the better is the poem.
We feel that B, which is actually said, ought to be necessary, even inevitable in some way. It ought to be in some sense the best, if not the only, way
of expressing A satisfactorily. The mind should dwell on it as well as on A
and thus the two should be somehow inevitably fused together into one
simple meaning. But if A is too obvious and could be equally or almost as
well expressed by other and more direct means, then the mind jumps
straight to A, remains focused on it, and loses interest in B, which shrinks
to a kind of dry and hollow husk. I think this is a fault of Christina Rossetti's poem. We know just what A is. A = "The good life is an effort" plus
"All men are mortal." Consequently it detaches itself from B, like a soul
leaving a body, and the road and the inn and the beds are not a real road
and inn and beds, they look faintly heraldic — or as if portrayed in lacquer.
They are not even poetically real. We never get a fair chance to accord to
their existence that willing suspension of disbelief which we are told constitutes "poetic faith." Let us try another:

> 'Is there anybody there?' said the Traveller,
>   Knocking on the moonlit door;
> And his horse in the silence champed the grasses
>   Of the forest's ferny floor:
> And a bird flew up out of the turret,
>   Above the Traveller's head:
> And he smote upon the door again a second time:
>   'Is there anybody there?' he said.
> But no one descended to the Traveller;
>   No head from the leaf-fringed sill
> Leaned over and looked into his grey eyes,
>   Where he stood perplexed and still.
> But only a host of phantom listeners
>   That dwelt in the lone house then
> Stood listening in the quiet of the moonlight
>   To that voice from the world of men:
> Stood thronging the faint moonbeams on the dark stair,
>   That goes down to the empty hall,
> Hearkening in an air stirred and shaken
>   By the lonely Traveller's call.

And he felt in his heart their strangeness,
  Their stillness answering his cry,
While his horse moved, cropping the dark turf,
  'Neath the starred and leafy sky;
For he suddenly smote on the door, even
  Louder, and lifted his head: —
'Tell them I came, and no one answered,
  That I kept my word', he said.
Never the least stir made the listeners,
  Though every word he spake
Fell echoing through the shadowiness of the still house
  From the one man left awake:
Ay, they heard his foot upon the stirrup
  And the sound of iron on stone,
And how the silence surged softly backward,
  When the plunging hoofs were gone.

This poem seems to me to possess as symbolism most of the virtues which I miss in Christina Rossetti's. First it obviously *is* a symbol. There *is* an A and a good solid one, though we do not know what it is, because we cannot put it into a separate container of words. But that is just the point. A has not got (perhaps I should say, it has not *yet* got) a separate existence in our apprehension; so it makes itself felt by modifying and enriching the meaning of B—it hides itself in B, hides itself in language which still *could* on the face of it be heard and interpreted as though no A came into the question at all.

I must here remark that merely making A obscure is not in itself a recipe for writing good symbolical poetry. William Blake at his worst, and, I fancy, many modern poets who write or intend to write symbolically, go astray here. They are so anxious to avoid the error of intending too obvious an A, so anxious to avoid a mere old-fashioned simile, that we end by being mystified or disgusted by the impossibility of getting any sort of feeling at all of what they are talking about, or why. Why are they talking about B at all? we ask ourselves. If they are doing it simply for the sake of B, it is pure drivel. On the other hand, if they intend an A, what evidence is there of it? We do not mind A being intangible, because it is still only half born from the poet's unconscious, but you cannot make poetry by cunningly removing all the clues which, if left, would discover the staleness of your meaning. In other words, if you set out to say one thing and mean another, you must really mean another, and that other must be worth meaning.

It will be observed that when we started from the simile and moved towards the symbol, the criterion or yard-stick by which we measured our progress was the element of *comparison* — paramount in the simile and very nearly vanished out of sight in the symbol. When, on the other hand, we move backwards, starting from the symbol, we find ourselves with another yard-stick, viz., the fact of saying one thing and meaning another. The poet says B but he means A. He hides A in B. B is the normal everyday meaning which the words so to speak "ought" to have on the face of them, and A is what the poet *really* has to say to us, and which he can only say through or alongside of, or by modifying, these normal everyday meanings. A is his own new, original, or poetic meaning. If I were writing this article in Greek or German, my public would no doubt be severely restricted, but there would be this advantage to me — that I could run the six words "say-one-thing-and-mean-another" together and use the resulting conglomerate as a noun throughout the rest of it. I cannot do this, but I will make bold to borrow another German word instead. The word *Tarnung* was, I believe, extensively used under the heel of the Nazi tyranny in Germany for the precautionary practice of hiding one meaning in another, the allusion being to the *Tarnhelm* of the Nibelungs. I shall give it an English form and call it "tarning." When I say "tarning," therefore, the reader is asked to substitute mentally the concept of saying one thing and meaning another, in the sense in which I have just been trying to expound it. We have already seen that the more A lives as a modification or enrichment of B, the better is the tarning.

Now let us proceed to the next step in our backward progress from symbol to simile. We come to the metaphor. And here we find both the best and the most numerous examples of tarning. Almost any poem, almost any passage of really vivid prose which you pick up is sure to contain them in abundance. I will choose an example (the source of which he does not disclose) given by Dr. Hugh Blair, the eighteenth-century writer on style.

"Those persons who gain the hearts of most people, who are chosen as the companions of their softer hours, and their reliefs from anxiety and care, are seldom persons of shining qualities or strong virtues: it is rather *the soft green* of the soul on which we rest our eyes, that are fatigued with beholding more glaring objects."

Consider how the ordinary literal meaning of the word "green" blends with the ineffable psychic quality which it is the writer's object to convey! How much weaker it would be, had he written: "It is rather persons whose

souls we find restful, as the eye finds green fields restful, etc." Put it that
way and nearly all the tarning, and with it half the poetry, is lost. The passage reminds me of this from Andrew Marvell's *Garden:*

> The Mind, that Ocean where each kind
> Does straight its own resemblance find;
> Yet it creates, transcending these,
> Far other Worlds, and other Seas;
> Annihilating all that's made
> To a green Thought in a green Shade.

What a lot of tarning can be done with the word "green"!

We see that any striking and original use of even a single word tends to
be metaphorical and shows us the process of tarning at work. On the
whole, I think it is true to say that the fewer the words containing the
metaphor, the more the expression is in the strict sense a "trope" rather
than a metaphor — the morn tarning we shall feel. For the long and elaborate metaphor is already almost a simile — a simile with the word "like"
missed out. We must, however, remember that the tarning may not have
actually occurred in the particular place where we find it. People copy one
another and the metaphor may be a cliché or, if not a cliché, part of our
common heritage of speech. Thus, when Tennyson writes:

> When the happy Yes
>   Falters from her lips,
> Pass and blush the news
>   Over glowing ships.

we feel that the peculiarly effective use of the word "blush" throughout
this lyric is a tarning of his own. It actually goes on in us as we read. When,
on the other hand, Arnold writes in the *Scholar Gypsy:*

> O Life unlike to ours!
>   Who fluctuate idly without term or scope

or:

> Vague half-believers of our casual creeds,
>   Who never deeply felt, nor clearly willed,
> Whose insight never has borne fruit in deeds

though none of this writing can be described as cliché, yet we feel that the
metaphorical element in "fluctuate" and in "borne fruit" is the product of

a tarning that happened before Arnold was born. So, too, in the passage I first quoted the "*shining* qualities" and the "*softer* hours" are metaphors of the kind we are all using every day, almost without thinking of them as metaphors. We all speak of *clear* heads, of *brilliant* wit, of *seeing* somebody's meaning, of so-and-so being the *pick of the bunch,* and so on: and most of us must use at least, say, a hundred of these dead or half-dead metaphors every day of our lives. In fact, in dealing with metaphor, we soon find ourselves talking, not of poetry, but of language itself. Everywhere in language we seem to find that the process of tarning, or something very like it, either is or has been at work.

We seem to owe all these tropes and metaphors embedded in language to the fact that somebody at some time had the wit to say one thing and mean another, and that somebody else had the wit to tumble to the new meaning, to detect the bouquet of a new wine emanating from the old bottle. We owe them all to tarning, a process which we find prolifically at work wherever there is poetry—from the symbol, where it shouts at us and is all too easily mishandled, to the simile, where we already hear the first faint stirrings of its presence, inasmuch as the B image even here is modified, enriched, or colored by the A image with which it is this time overtly compared.

> Then fly our greetings, fly our speech and smiles!
> — As some grave Tyrian trader, from the sea,
> Descried at sunrise an emerging prow
> Lifting the cool-hair'd creepers stealthily,
> The fringes of a southward-facing brow
> Among the Aegean isles;
> And saw the merry Grecian coaster come,
> Freighted with amber grapes, and Chian wine,
> Green bursting figs, and tunnies steep'd in brine;
> And knew the intruders on his ancient home,
> The young light-hearted masters of the waves.

The grave Tyrian trader and the merry Grecian coaster are not the same figures that we should meet in a history book. They have their own life, they take in the imagination a special color from the things with which they are compared—that is, the *Scholar Gypsy* on the one hand and our too modern selves on the other. They are pregnant with the whole of the poem that has gone before.

I said at the beginning that I might be accused of indulging in a kind of aesthetic microscopy. The drawback of the microscope is this, that even if the grain of sand which we see through it does indeed contain a world, mere magnification is not enough to enable us to see that world. Unfortunately the processes which are said to give to the infinitesimal a cosmic character are not merely minute; they are also very rapid. This is certainly true of the process of tarning as it takes place in the mind of the poet and his reader. It is both rapid and delicate and, as the reader may have felt already, it is difficult to take it out and examine it without rushing in where angels fear to tread. But there is another modern invention which may be brought to the aid of the microscope in order to meet this drawback; and that is the slow-motion film. Can we find in any sphere of human life something analogous to a slow-motion picture of the tarning process? I think we can. I have said that tarning can be detected not only in accredited poetry or literature but also in the history of language as a whole. Is there any other human institution in which tarning also happens, and in which it happens on a broader scale and at a more leisurely pace? I think there is. I think we shall find such an illustration as we want in the law, notably in the development of law by means of fictions.

We are accustomed to find something crabbed and something comic in legal fictions. When we read in an old pleading an averment that the plaintiff resides in the Island of Minorca, "to wit in the parish of St. Mary le Bow in the Ward of Cheap"—or, in a Note in the *Annual Practice* for 1945, that every man-of-war is deemed to be situated permanently in the parish of Stepney—it sounds funny. But it must be admitted that it is not any funnier *per se* than Shelley's telling us that his leaves are falling or Campion informing us as to his mistress that "there is a garden in her face." It is funny when we take it literally, not particularly funny when we understand what is meant and why it is expressed in that particular way.

There is one kind of metaphor which occurs both in law and in poetry and which is on the whole commoner and less odd-sounding in modern law than it is in modern poetry. This is personification of abstractions:

> Let not Ambition mock their useful toil,
>   Their homely joys, and destiny obscure;
> Nor Grandeur hear with a disdainful smile
>   The short and simple annals of the poor.

We find this particular usage almost vanished from English poetry by the beginning of the twentieth century. The personification of abstractions and attributes which we find in the more high-flown sort of eighteenth-century poetry or in the occasional allegorical papers which Johnson inserted in the *Rambler* sound stiff and unnatural to us, and a modern poet would hardly bring himself to try and introduce the device at all. On the other hand, the personification of limited companies by which they are enabled to sue and be sued at law, to commit trespasses, and generally to be spoken of as carrying on all sorts of activities which can only *really* be carried on by sentient beings, is as common as dirt and no one ever dreams of laughing at it. But these examples will hardly do for our slow-motion picture. On the contrary, in them the gap between the B meaning and the A meaning is as wide and the prima facie absurdity of the B or surface-meaning is hardly less than in, let us say, Ossian's description of the Hero: "In peace, thou art the Gale of Spring, in war, the Mountain Storm."

The important thing is to see how and why the legal fiction comes into being and what is its positive function in the life of human beings. If you have suffered a wrong at the hands of another human being, the practical question for you, the point at which law really touches your life as a member of society, is, Can you do anything about it? Can you bring the transgressor to book and obtain restitution? In other words, can you bring an action against him, obtain judgment, and get that judgment executed? Now the answer to that question must always depend to some extent, and in the earlier stages of a society governed by law it depends to a very large extent indeed, on the answer to another question. It is not enough simply to show that the transgressor has, in common parlance, broken the law. What you or your advisers have to make up your mind about is something rather different and often much more complicated. You have to ask yourselves, Is there a form of procedure under which I can move against him? If so, is it sufficiently cheap and expeditious for me to be able to adopt it with some hope of success? Where, as in the case of English Common Law down to the middle of the nineteenth century, these forms of procedure, or forms of action as they are more often called, are severely restricted in number, these questions are very serious ones indeed.

While the so-called historical fictions (which are the only ones I am concerned with) have no doubt played a broadly similar part in every known system of law, I think it will be best if I confine myself to England and take a particular example. The forms of action were not the arbitrary inventions of an ingenious legislator. They grew up out of the whole history of English social life, and one of the results of this was a wide difference between those forms of action which had their roots in the feudal system and those which sprang from later and different sources. I think it is true to say that they were different because they were really based on two different ways of looking at human beings in society. You may look at a hu-

man being in what I will call the genealogical way, in which case you will
conceive of his legal rights and position as being determined by what he *is*
rather than by what he may choose to *do*. They will then seem to be determined by the kind of father he had, by the piece of land to which he and
his ancestors were attached or which was attached to them, and by its relations to adjoining land attached to other people and their ancestors and
descendants. Or alternatively you may look at him in what I will call the
personal way, in which case his position will seem to be determined more
by the things which he himself has chosen to *do* of his own free will. Maine
in his *Ancient Law* calls the first way "Status" and the second way "Contract," and he depicts society as evolving from the first towards the second.
Broadly speaking, forms of action having to do with the ownership of land
had grown up out of the first way, forms of action having to do with the
ownership of personal property out of the second way, of looking at human beings.

Now suppose you had a good claim to the ownership of a piece of land,
perhaps with a pleasant house on it, which was in the possession of somebody else who also, but wrongfully, claimed to be the owner. Your proper
normal form of action, say, five hundred years ago, was by Writ of Right, a
form of action which was very much of the first type and hedged about
accordingly with all sorts of ceremonies, difficulties, and delays.

At trahere atque moras tantis licet addere rebus!

One of the drawbacks of this type of action was that it was subject to
things called *essoins*. Essoins seem to have corresponded roughly to what
we should call "adjournments"; they no doubt grew up procedurally with
a view to preventing an unscrupulous plaintiff from taking unfair advantage of the defendant's ill health, absence, or other accidental disability.
But they must have been corn in Egypt for a usurping defendant. I am
tempted to let Glanville,[1] in his own sedate language and at his own pace,
give the reader some idea of their nature and complexity:

If the Tenant, being summoned, appear not on the first day, but Essoin
himself, such Essoin shall, if reasonable, be received; and he may, in this
manner, essoin himself three times successively; and since the causes on
account of which a person may justly essoin himself are various, let us
consider the different kinds of Essoins.

1. Beame's *Translation of Glanville* (London, 1812).

Of Essoins, some arise on account of ill health, others from other sources.

(I will here interpose that, among the essoins arising from other sources were the *de ultra mare* and the *de esse in peregrinatione* and that, if a person cast the essoin *de esse in peregrinatione,* "it must be distinguished whether he went to Jerusalem or to another place. If to the former place, then a year and a day at least is generally allowed him." And with that I will let Glanville proceed again in his own order:)

Of those Essoins which arise from ill health, one kind is that *ex infirmitate veniendi,* another *ex infirmitate de reseantisa.*

If the Tenant, being summoned, should on the first day cast the Essoin *de infirmitate veniendi,* it is in the election of his Adversary, being present, either to require from the Essoiner a lawful proof of the truth of the Essoin in question on that very day, or that he should find pledges or bind himself solemnly that at the day appointed he will have his Warrantor of the Essoin . . . and he may thus Essoin himself three times successively. If on the third day, he neither appear nor essoin himself, then let it be ordered that he be forthcoming in person on another day; or that he send a fit Attorney in his place, to gain or lose for him. . . . It may be asked, what will be the consequence if the Tenant appear at the fourth day, after having cast three Essoins, and warrant all the Essoins? In that case, he shall prove the truth of each Essoin by his own oath and that of another; and, on the same day, he shall answer to the suit. . . .

If anyone desire to cast the Essoin *de infirmitate de reseantisa,* he may thrice do it. Yet should the Essoiner, on the third day preceding that appointed, at a proper place and before a proper person, present his Essoin. If, on the third Summons the Tenant appear not, the Court should direct that it may be seen whether his indisposition amount to a languor, or not. For this purpose let the following Writ issue, directed to the Sheriff of the County . . .:

"The King to the Sheriff, Health. I command you that, without delay, you send 4 lawful men of your County to see if the infirmity of which B. hath essoined himself in my Court, against R., be a languor or not. And, if they perceive that it is a languor, then, that they should put to him a day of one year and one day, from that day of the view, to appear before me or my justices. . . ."

Nor was it forgotten that essoiners themselves may be subject to infirmities and languors:

The principal Essoiner is also at liberty, if so disposed, to essoin himself by another Essoiner. In this case the second Essoiner must state to the Court that the Tenant, having a just cause of Essoin, had been detained, so that he could not appear at the day appointed, neither to lose nor gain, and that therefore he had appointed a certain other person to essoin him; and that the Essoiner himself had met with such an impediment, which had prevented his appearance on that day: and this he is prepared to prove according to the practice of the Court. . . .

Having at last succeeded in getting your opponent out of bed and fixing the day for the trial, you still could not be certain that he would not appear in court followed (subject, no doubt, to essoins) by a professional boxer or swordsman, whom you would have to tackle in lieu of calling evidence. And so on. And all this maybe about a claim so clear that you could get it disposed of in five minutes if you could only bring it to the stage of being tried at all!

It would have been a very different matter, so perhaps your counsel would advise you, if only the issue were about *personal* property instead of real property. We could go to a different court with a different form of action. No essoins. No wager of law. No trial by battle. No trial by ordeal. Everything up to date and efficient. What *is* personal property, you might ask. Well, your horse for one thing and your hawk and your clothes and your money—oh! yes, and oddly enough if you were a leaseholder instead of a freeholder and had only a term of years in this precious piece of land, *that* would be personal property too. But can't I get *my* case heard by these people? Don't they understand anything about fee simple? Oh! yes, they understand it all right; in fact they often have to decide the point. For instance, if a leaseholder in possession is ousted by a trespasser—by Jove! I've just thought of something! And then if your counsel had a touch of creative genius, he might perhaps evolve the following device. It *was* evolved at all events, by Tudor times or thereabouts and continued in use down to the middle of the nineteenth century.

Remember the situation: You are the rightful owner of a piece of land of which X, who is in possession, wrongfully claims to be the owner. The device was this: you proceeded to inform the court by your pleadings that you, as owner of the land, had recently leased it to a person whose name was John Doe, and John Doe had been ousted from his possession violently, *vi et armis,* by X, the defendant. *You* were not bringing the action, you pretended: John Doe was; but as X might aver in his defense that the blameless Doe had no title, Doe has joined you, his landlord, in the proceedings to prove that you did have a good title at the time when you leased the land to him. By this means you got your case before the court that had jurisdiction to deal with the action known as ejectment, and were able to take advantage of the simpler and more effective procedure. Sometimes the fiction was a little more elaborate. Instead of alleging that X had ejected John Doe, you said that another gentleman called Richard Roe, or possibly William Stiles, had done so. Richard Roe having subsequently allowed X to take possession now claimed no interest in the proceedings, but he had given X notice that they were pending, so as to give X a chance to defend his title. In this case the first thing X heard of it all was a letter, signed "your loving friend, Richard Roe," telling him what had happened. Needless to say, John Doe and Richard Roe had no existence.

Many thousands of actions of this pattern and using these names must have been brought between the fifteenth and the nineteenth centuries and before long the whole procedure was no doubt so much a matter of course that it was little more than a kind of mathematical formula. There must, however, have been some earlier occasions on which it was a good deal more, and it is upon any one of these — perhaps the first of all — that I want the reader to bend his mind. Picture to yourself the court, with counsel on his feet opening the case. The story of John Doe and Richard Roe is being unfolded. At one point the judge suddenly looks up and looks very hard at counsel, who either winks very slightly or returns a stolid, uncomprehending stare according to his temperament and the intimacy of his acquaintance with the judge out of hours. But counsel knows all the same what has happened. The bench has tumbled to it. The judge has guessed that there is no John Doe, no Richard Roe, no lease, no entry, no ouster. At the same moment, however, the judge has seen the point of the whole fiction, the great advantage in the speedy administration of justice (for the real issue — the validity of X's title and yours — will be heard fairly and in full) and in the extended jurisdiction of his own court. He decides to accord to the pleadings that willing suspension of disbelief which hundreds of years later made Mr. Bumble say that the law was a "hass." The case proceeds. Place this picture before your mind's eye and there I think you will have a slow-motion picture of "tarning."

Has new law been made? It is much the same as asking whether new language has been made when a metaphor disappears into a "meaning." At all events, we begin to understand more fully what Maitland meant, when he wrote of English law that "substantive law has at first the look of being gradually secreted in the interstices of procedure." This is particularly true of an unwritten system like the English Common Law, where the law itself lay hidden in the unconscious, until it was expressed in a judgment, and where rights themselves depended on the existence of remedies. Consider that very important fiction, which is very much alive and flourishing all round us today—the fiction on which the law of trusteeship is based. Anyone who is a trustee will know how absurdly remote from reality is the B interpretation of his position, according to which he is the "owner" of the trust property. Yet this fiction, which permeates the whole of our jurisprudence, which most certainly is law, and not merely procedure, was introduced in the first place by devices strictly procedural, devices and circumstances which had their origin in that same contrast between the genealogical and the personal conceptions of society which gave us John Doe and Richard Roe.

Moreover, this fictitious ownership, which we call trusteeship, has been strong enough to have other fictions erected on it. By the Common Law the personal property of a married woman became her husband's as soon as she married. But by a particularly ingenious piece of tarning the equity judges expressed in the form of law, and in doing so no doubt partly created, a more modern view of the rights of married women. They followed the Common Law doctrine that the husband *owned* everything but, as to property which someone had given to the wife with the intention that she should have it for her own separate use, the courts of equity began in the eighteenth century to say that the husband did indeed own this, but he owned it as *trustee* for his wife; and they would prevent him from dealing with it in any other way.

In the same way a metaphor may be strong enough to support a metaphor, as when Shelley bids the west wind "Make me thy lyre even as the forest is." If Shelley is not a lyre, neither is the forest; yet he illustrates the one fiction with the other. Nor is there anything grotesque or strained in this magnificent line. It is only when we begin to ponder and analyze it that we see how daring it is.

The long analogy which I have been drawing may be expressed more briefly in the formula:—metaphor: language: meaning:: legal fiction : law : social life. It has no particular significance if poetry is to be regarded *only* as either a pleasurable way of diverting our leisure hours or a convenient

vehicle for the propagation of doctrine. For it must be conceded that there
is all the difference in the world between the propagation of a doctrine
and the creation of a meaning. The doctrine is already formulated and, if
we choose to express it by tarning, that is simply a matter of technique or
political strategy. The creation of meaning is a very different matter. I
hope I may have succeeded in showing in the earlier part of this article
that metaphor is something more than a piece of the technique of one of
the fine arts. It is πολὺ μέγιστον not merely in the diction of poetry but in
the nature and growth of language itself. So far we have only considered in
this connection those ubiquitous figures of speech which are, or used to be,
called "tropes," as when we speak of our lives *fluctuating,* of our insight
bearing fruit in deeds, of *seeing the point,* and so on. But if we proceed to
study language with a more definitely historical bias, and look into the
etymologies and derivations of words, then the vast majority even of those
meanings which we normally regard as "literal" are seen to have originated
either in metaphors or in something like them. Such words as *spirit, sad,
humor, perceive, attend, express, understand,* and so on immediately spring
to the mind as examples. Indeed the difficulty here would rather be to find
words that are *not* examples. There is no doubt that they were once metaphorical. The question which a good many people have asked themselves, a
little uneasily, is, Are they *still* metaphors? And, if not, when – and still
more *how* – precisely, did they cease to be so?

What is essential to the nature and growth of language is clearly essential to the nature and growth of our thought, or rather of our consciousness as a whole. In what way then is metaphor or tarning essential to that
nature and that growth? Here we begin to tread on metaphysical ground
and here I think the analogy of legal fictions can really help us by placing
our feet on one or two firmer tufts in the quaking bog. It can help us to
realize in firmer outlines certain concepts which, like all those relating to
the nature of thought itself, are tenuous, elusive, and difficult of expression.

Students of history will have observed that rebellions and agitations
arising out of dissatisfaction with the law tend, at any rate in the earlier
stages of society, to demand, not so much a reform of the law as its *publication.* People complain that they do not know what the law is. They want
to know what it is, because otherwise they cannot be sure that it will be
the same tomorrow as it is today. In fact it is the very essence of a law that
it should apply to every case. It follows that the forms of action must be
limited in number, and they must not change from day to day. If there is a
different law for every case that arises, then what is being administered is

simply not law at all but the arbitrary (though not necessarily unjust) decisions of those who govern us. But that is exactly what the word "law" *means*—something which is *not* such a series of arbitrary decisions or events, something which will be *the same* for the next case as it was for the last. This is where the difficulty arises; for it is the nature of life itself (certainly of human life) never to repeat itself exactly. Phenomena exactly repeated are not life, they are mechanism. Life varies, law is of its nature unvarying. Yet at the same time it is the function of law to serve, to express, and indeed partly to *make* the social life of the community. That is the paradox, the diurnal solution of which constitutes the process called society. One solution is legislation, the other is fiction. Legislation is drastic, *a priori*, and necessary. Fiction is flexible, empirical, and also necessary. "Without the Fiction of Adoption," says Maine in his *Ancient Law*, "it is difficult to understand how Society would ever have escaped from its swaddling-clothes."

In the paradoxical relation of law to social life I think we have a useful picture of the paradoxical relation of language to consciousness. Formal logic is not much studied nowadays, but that does not alter the fact that logic is essential to the very existence of language and the forms of proposition and syllogism underlie all expression. Now logic presupposes first and foremost that the same word means the same thing in one sentence as it does in another. Humpty Dumpty may speak of making his words "mean" what he chooses, and if somebody made a noise never heard before or since he might possibly manage to convey some sort of vague sympathetic impression of the state of his feelings. Yet repetition is inherent in the very meaning of the word "meaning." To say a word "means" something implies that it means that same something more than once.

Here then is the paradox again. The logical use of language presupposes the meanings of the words it employs and presupposes them constant. I think it will be found to be a corollary of this, that the logical use of language can never add any meaning to it. The conclusion of a syllogism is implicit already in the premises, that is, in the *meanings* of the *words* employed; and all the syllogism can do is to make that meaning clearer to us and remove any misconception or confusion. But life is not constant. Every man, certainly every original man, has something new to say, something new to mean. Yet if he wants to express that meaning (and it may be that it is only when he tries to express it, that he knows what he means) he must use language—a vehicle which presupposes that he must either mean what was meant before or talk nonsense!

If therefore he would say anything really new, if that which was hitherto unconscious is to become conscious, he must resort to tarning. He must talk what is nonsense on the face of it, but in such a way that the recipient may have the new meaning suggested to him. This is the true importance of metaphor. I imagine this is why Aristotle, in calling metaphor "the most important," gives as a reason that "it alone does not mean borrowing from someone else." In terms of mixed law and logic we might perhaps say that the metaphorical proposition contains a judgment, but a judgment pronounced with a wink at the court. Bacon put it more clearly in the *Advancement of Learning* when he said:

> Those whose conceits are seated in popular opinions need only but to prove or dispute; but those whose conceits are beyond popular opinions have a double labour; the one *to make themselves conceived,* and the other to prove and demonstrate. So that it is of necessity with them to have recourse to similitudes and translations to express themselves.

If we consider Bacon's position in the history of thought, it will not surprise us that the problem should have presented itself to him so clearly. Himself a lawyer, was he not attempting to do for science the very thing which Maitland tells us those old legal fictions were contrived for, that is, "to get modern results out of medieval premises"?

At all events there is a sentence in the *Novum Organum* which provides one of the most striking illustrations of tarning that it would be possible to imagine. It is a double illustration: first, there was an attempt at deliberate and fully conscious meaning-making, which failed: Bacon tried to inject new meaning into a word by *saying* precisely what he wanted it to mean. But we have seen that what is said precisely cannot convey new meaning. But, since his meaning *was* really new, there had at some point in the process to be a piece of actual tarning. There was—and it succeeded. He did in fact inject new meaning into another word—not by saying, but by just meaning it!

Licet enim in natura nihil vere existat praeter corpora individua edentia actus puros individuos ex lege; in doctrinis tamen, illa ipsa lex, ejusque inquisitio et inventio atque explicatio, pro fundamento est tam ad sciendum quam ad operandum. Eam autem legem ejusque paragraphos formarum nomine intelligimus; praesertim cum hoc vocabulum *invaluerit, et familiariter occurrat.*[2]

2. 'Although it is true that in nature nothing exists beyond separate bodies producing separate motions according to law; still for the *study* of nature that very law and its investigation discovery and exposition are the essential thing, for the purpose both of science and of practice. Now it is that law and its clauses which we understand by the term "forms" – principally because this word is a familiar one and has become generally accepted.' *Novum Organum,* ii. 2.

The "forms" of which Bacon here speaks were none other than the Platonic ideas, in which Bacon did not very much believe. What he did believe in was that system of abstract causes or uniformity which we have long since been accustomed to express by the phrase "the laws of nature," but for which there was then no name, because the meaning was a new one. He therefore tried deliberately by way of a *simile* to put this new meaning into the old word *"forma"*; but he failed, inasmuch as the new meaning never came into general use. Yet at the same time, more unconsciously, and by way of *metaphor,* he was putting the new meaning into the word *"lex"* itself—that curious meaning which it now bears in the expression "the laws of nature." This is one of those pregnant metaphors which pass into the language, so that much of our subsequent thinking is based on them. To realize that after all they *are* metaphors, and to ask what that entails, opens up avenues of inquiry which are beyond the province of this article. Certainly, they may be misleading, as well as illuminating. Long after Bacon's time, two great men—a lawyer who was concerned with the nature of law and a poet who was concerned with the nature of Nature—felt bound to draw attention to this very metaphor.

"When an atheist," wrote Austin, "speaks of *laws* governing the irrational world, the metaphorical application is suggested by an analogy still more slender and remote. . . . He means that the uniformity of succession and co-existence resembles the uniformity of conduct produced by an imperative rule. If, to draw the analogy closer, he ascribes these laws to an author, he personifies a verbal abstraction and makes it play the legislator. He attributes the uniformity of succession and co-existence to *laws* set by *nature*: meaning by nature, the world itself; or perhaps that very uniformity which he imputes to nature's commands."[3]

The introduction of the atheist into this passage does not, I think, weaken its force as an illustration, for whatever the strength of Bacon's religious faith, it is quite plain that the "laws" of which he speaks in the *Novum Organum* have very little to do with the "commands" of any being other than nature itself.

"Long indeed," says Coleridge in *The Friend,* "will man strive to satisfy the inward querist with the phrase, laws of nature. But though the individual may rest content with the seeming metaphor, the race cannot. If a law of nature be a mere generalization, it is included . . . as an act of

3. *Jurisprudence* (1869), i. 213.

the mind. But if it be other and more, and yet manifestable only in and to an intelligent spirit, it must in act and substance be itself spiritual; for things utterly heterogeneous can have no intercommunion."

Perhaps we may supplement the last sentence by saying that an *apparent* intercommunion between things utterly heterogeneous is the true mark of metaphor and may be significant of spiritual substance. If this is so, and if the aptness of a metaphor to mislead varies inversely with the extent to which it continues to be felt and understood *as* a metaphor and is not taken in a confused way semiliterally, then the contemplation by the mind of legal fictions may really be a rather useful exercise. For these are devices of expression, of which the practical expediency can easily be understood, and whose metaphorical nature is not so easily forgotten as they pass into general use.

There is not much that is more important for human beings than their relations with each other, and it is these which laws are designed to express. The making and application of law are thus fundamental human activities, but what is more important for my purpose is that they bear the same relation to naked thinking as traveling does to map-reading or practice to theory. It is not by accident that such key-words as *judgment* and *cause* have two distinct meanings; the practical task of fixing personal responsibility must surely have been the soil from which, as the centuries passed, the abstract notion of cause and effect was laboriously raised. Accordingly it would be strange indeed if the study of jurisprudence were not well adapted to throw light on the mind and its workings.

That study was formerly regarded as an essential element in a liberal education. It was a distinguished Italian jurist, Giovanni Battista Vico, who at the turn of the seventeenth and eighteenth centuries became interested in the figurative element in language and evolved therefrom a theory of the evolution of human consciousness from an instinctive "poetic" wisdom (*sapienza poetica*) to the modern mode of analytical thought.

It is perhaps a pity that this respectful attitude to legal studies has long since been abandoned; a pity both on general grounds and because the vast change in man's idea of himself wrought by the new notions of evolution and development, and by the comparatively recent birth of historical imagination, have opened up rich new fields of speculation both in language and in law. A better and more widely diffused knowledge of the latter could hardly fail to be beneficial in far-reaching ways at a time when the whole theory of human society is in the melting-pot. For instance, a deeper, more sympathetic understanding of the long, slow movement of the human mind from the feudal, or genealogical, way of regarding human relationships towards what I have called the "personal" way would do no harm.

But I have been mainly concerned here with the subject of fictions. Properly understood, are they not a telling illustration of the fact that knowledge — the fullest possible awareness — of the nature of law is the true way of escape from its shackles? "ἐγὼ γὰρ διὰ νόμον νόμῳ ἀπέθανον," 'I, by the law, died unto the law,' wrote St. Paul; and the *nature* of law, as law, is the same, whether it be moral, or logical, or municipal. If it be important for men to get a deep feeling for this process of liberation in general, it is equally important, for special reasons, that they should better comprehend the particular problem of the part played by metaphor in the operation and development of language. Here too the way to achieve liberation from the "confusion" of thought on which metaphor is based is not by attack or rebellion. The intrinsic nature of language makes all such attitudes puerile. It is not those who, like the optimistic Mr. Stuart Chase,[4] set out to cut away and expose all metaphorical usage who escape the curse of Babel. No. The best way to talk clearly and precisely and to talk sense is to understand as fully as possible the relation between predication and suggestion, between "saying" and "meaning." For then you will at least know what you are *trying* to do. It is not the freemen of a city who are likeliest to lose their way, and themselves, in its labyrinth of old and mazy streets; it is the simple-minded foreign nihilist making, with his honest-to-god intentions and suitcase, straight for the center, like a sensible man.

4. *The Tyranny of Words* (London, 1938).

Note. — The author expresses his thanks to Mr. de la Mare and to Messrs. Faber & Faber for permission to quote *The Listeners.* Reprinted with permission of The Literary Trustees of Walter de la Mare, and The Society of Authors as their representative.

The Harp and the Camera

The harp has long been employed as the symbol of music in general, and of heavenly music in particular; just as music itself has been employed as the symbol of heaven on earth. As the English poet Walter de la Mare put it:

> When music sounds, all that I was I am
> Ere to this haunt of brooding dust I came —

In Ireland the harp is the national symbol. It is even on their postage stamps. I remember, when I was young, a popular song that began: "Just a little bit of heaven fell from out the sky one day / And dropped into the ocean not so many miles away." Years later I came to suspect a grain of substance underlying the sentimental drivel. If you travel to Scotland and then go on to Ireland, you see first the Scottish mountains and then the Irish mountains; and they are very much alike in many ways. In both places it is probably raining, or will be in a minute or two; yet there is a subtle difference between them, the kind of subtlety that really needs a combination of Ruskin and Henry James to put it into words. Perhaps you could put it crudely like this. In the Scottish mountains you feel the mountains are somehow being drawn up into the sky. The earth seems to have been raised up to the sky and to have mingled with it; whereas in Ireland it is the other way round. It is almost as if the mountains were actually a part of the sky that had come down and was mingling with the earth.

There is one kind of harp which most of us never have seen. I have never seen one myself. And that is the aeolian harp or, as I shall call it for short, the wind-harp, since Aeolus was the Greek god of the winds. It

sounds a delightful instrument, and I have always meant, but have somehow never managed, to make one. It is simply a series of strings in a box,
which you fix up somewhere where the wind will blow through the strings
and the strings will sound. A good place is an open window; and that might
perhaps remind us that the earliest windows were not the kind we have
today with glass in them. They were designed not for letting in the light
and keeping out the air, but for letting in both of them together. In fact
the word "window" is a corruption of "wind-eye."

The wind-harp has been much more written about than it has been seen
or heard. It had a very special fascination for the Romantics. The German
poet Eduard Mörike speaks of "*einer luftgeborene Muse geheimnissvolles
Saitenspiel*" "the secret string-melody of an air-born muse" (today perhaps
it would be safer to say "wind-born"), and describes how, when the wind
grows more violent, the harp gives out a kind of human cry. The wind
makes a sound of its own, but in the harp's strings it echoes or imitates
itself, with a would-be personal sound that reproduces the cosmic, imper-
sonal sound of the wind itself. William Wordsworth begins his long poem,
The Prelude, by speaking of "aeolian visitations"; and in a later passage of
the poem, where he is describing the crossing of the Alps, although the
wind-harp is not mentioned, he probably has it in mind when he speaks of

> a stream
> That flowed into a kindred stream; a gale
> Confederate with the current of the soul . . . .

Many of the great Romantics were as much interested in the theory of
poetry as they were in writing poetry. So Wordsworth's "confederate gales"
represented to him not just a flight of fancy, but really an avowed part of
his theory of the nature of poetry, or rather of his whole aesthetic theory,
that is, his whole theory of the relation between man and nature in perception considered especially in the realm of art. Now you find in reading
the Romantics that sometimes their theory of poetry is embodied in the
poetry itself. That is the case with Coleridge's poem *The Aeolian Harp,*
where you find these often quoted lines:

> And what if all of animated nature
> Be but organic Harps diversely framed,
> That tremble into thought, as o'er them sweeps
> Plastic and vast, one intellectual breeze,
> At once the Soul of each, and God of all?

But more often perhaps the theory is kept apart from the practice and is expressed in prose. There is Shelley, for instance. The wind-harp, as you might expect, made a very strong appeal to his imagination. You find in his early essay "On Christianity" this passage: "There is a Power by which we are surrounded, like the atmosphere in which some motionless lyre is suspended, which visits with its breath our silent chords at will." He is depicting the genesis of poetry. But if poetry is merely the wind that agitates the wind-harp, what is a poet? Well, Shelley has his answer in the same early essay, and you remember that it was an attack on Christianity. He tells us that poets are "the passive slaves of some higher and more omnipotent Power. This Power is God." Did he really think that? If we conceive of the genesis of poetry in terms of something like "inspiration," as perhaps we must, we are at once faced with a difficult question. What is the part in it played by the poet himself? That always has been a difficult question and remains one now. Whether we speak, as Shelley does, of the "breath of universal being," or of the unconscious, or the id within the unconscious, or whatever terminology we choose to adopt, we still have an extremely difficult question. And so a few years later, when Shelley came to write his "Defence of Poetry," he felt he had to make his wind-harp a little more complicated. He now put it this way:

> Man is an instrument over which a series of external and internal impressions are driven, like the alternations of an ever-changing wind over an aeolian lyre, which move it by their motion to ever-changing melody. But there is a principle within the human being, and perhaps within all sentient beings, which acts otherwise than in the lyre, and produces not melody alone, but harmony, by an internal adjustment of the sounds or motions thus excited to the impressions which excite them.

So we have now a "principle" which acts otherwise than in the lyre. And one feels he has changed the symbol to something more than an ordinary lyre or harp, something more even than a wind-harp, something more like a kind of magic harp that somehow plays itself by being played on. But then again, does it play itself? Later in the same essay we have him saying it is "those poets who have been harmonized by their own will" who give forth divinest melody, when the breath of universal being sweeps over their frame. That is rather different from the "passive slave" we heard of before. You might think it is rather a queer sort of a passive slave who has to have a will of his own. My idea of a slave — and I am pretty sure it was shared by the author of *Prometheus Unbound* – is someone who is just not allowed to have a will of his own.

The title of this lecture is "The Harp and the Camera"; and while I have been talking about harps, you may have been privately wondering when I am going to come to cameras, and what on earth the two have to do with each other. I must first tell you how they became linked together in my mind. The trick was done for me by one very remarkable man. He was a German Jesuit called Athanasius Kircher, and he lived some three hundred years ago. Kircher was a "polymath" if ever there was one. He studied a variety of subjects including – and these are not the only ones – music, Egyptology, Sinology, botany, magnetism. In the course of his life he had himself let down into the crater of Vesuvius and he is claimed as the founder of geology. But besides his book on music he also wrote one on optics, which is called *Ars Magna Lucis et Umbrae.* I must mention here that I am indebted for my acquaintance with Kircher, and therewith for the germ of this lecture, to M. H. Abrams, the author of that truly admirable book *The Mirror and the Lamp,* in which the notes are almost as excellent as the text. Now Kircher is the first writer to have described the wind-harp. Whether he actually invented it is disputed, and indeed there is an old tradition that it was invented by St. Dunstan. St. Dunstan is also the patron saint of the blind, and whether there is any significance in *that* I shall leave you to ask yourselves at the end of the lecture. Anway it was during the hundred or so years after Kircher's death that the aeolian harp became a popular tenant's fixture. Quite a lot of people had one as a normal addition to the amenities of the house. Then, towards the end of the eighteenth century, it seems to have died away as a toy and begun a second life as a symbol. It was adopted, as I have said, as a favorite symbol by the Romantics.

But there is another quite different invention, in the development of which the same man, Athanasius Kircher, seems to have taken a leading part; and that is the camera obscura. Moreover it is agreed, I think, that he *was* the actual inventor of yet a third device, and one which occupies a very important place in what I shall later on be calling the "camera sequence." But let us begin with the camera obscura, which Kircher both described and improved, though he probably did not invent it. It is, as I expect you know, something like a box with one single very, very small aperture. One could perhaps think of the aperture as a tiny window. It is either so small as scarcely to deserve the name – just a pin-prick, in fact – or else, though not quite so small as a pin-prick, it is still very small and is filled with a particular sort of glass which we now call a lens. Inside the box you fix a mirror, disposed I think at an angle of forty-five degrees; and the result is that, by looking through a larger aperture in the top of the box, you receive a picture in miniature of all that the focused light brings with it through the tiny one.

Reflecting on those two very different ploys of Athanasius Kircher it struck me that, if the wind-harp can be seen as a kind of emblem of the Romantic Movement, or the Romantic Period if you like, the camera obscura is no less an emblem of the Renaissance. Only in this case it is a good deal more than an emblem; and it is an emblem of a good deal more than the Renaissance. It points us to something that underlay the Renaissance and came to expression not only in the Revival of Learning but also in such other historical movements as on the one hand the Protestant Reformation and on the other the birth of modern science. In other words it is an emblem of that species of Copernican Revolution in the human psyche which was quite as much the cause as it was the consequence of the Copernican Revolution in astronomy. I mean the revolution, formulated rather than initiated by Immanuel Kant, whereby the human mind more or less reversed its conception of its own relation to its environment. It is more than an emblem, because the camera obscura (considered as the original source of the whole camera sequence) was also *instrumental* in actually bringing about the change of which I have spoken. We may better call it a symbol, since the camera sequence as a whole was part of the change which it betokens or symbolizes. You know it has been said that the proper definition of a symbol is that it both represents something other than itself and is also a part of it. Coleridge defined a symbol as "part of the reality it represents." For that reason he held that a historical event may be a symbol of the historical process of which it is a part. It is precisely in that sense that I am claiming the invention of the camera as a symbol of post-Renaissance man.

Let us now have a look at this "camera sequence." In the world in which the camera obscura was invented, in the sixteenth and seventeenth centuries, there was as yet no such thing as photography. There could not have been, since the camera obscura was itself the photographic camera in embryo. Besides therefore being an amusing toy, the camera obscura quickly came to be used for practical purposes, for the production of reduced-size sketches of larger objects or assemblies of objects, and particularly in the business of sketching landscapes. There on the screen you had the complex three-dimensional real world, in which we walk about on legs, conveniently reduced to a little two-dimensional image which the pencil had only to trace. In other words, this convenient device effected, almost of its own accord, a result which many great painters had been trying very hard for a large number of years to learn how to bring about, and in which they were just beginning to succeed. There you had given to you a picture drawn very accurately *in perspective.* Now if it is true that the painters had been trying for a number of years to bring about the use of perspective — to discover what it was — it is also true that, in terms of the whole history of the art of painting, that number is really a very small one. In fact, the gradual and very late discovery of the secret of perspective seems to me to be a truly remarkable phenomenon. I ask you to consider, in support of that contention, the following five facts. There had been for centuries past many great and skillful painters passionately interested in the technique of their art. Secondly, geometry was a study highly advanced among the Greeks. Thirdly, the Greeks were perfectly well able to apply their discoveries in geometry to the practice of art — to architecture for instance — for if you read about the principles on which the building of the Parthenon was conducted you will find most elaborate geometrical principles embodied in it. Fourthly, Euclid himself actually wrote a work on optics. Euclid, the founder of geometry, wrote a work on optics, although that work is lost. And lastly, the Greek theory of art, whether of sculpture or poetry or painting, was a theory of *imitation,* imitation of nature. Now, keeping all that in mind, recall that nevertheless European painters only began to interest themselves in the comparatively simple rules of perspective in perhaps the fourteenth or fifteenth century A.D.; in perspective, which is the kingpin, one could say, of the whole craft of representing three dimensions in two! When it did happen, not only were they interested but they were wildly excited. There is a story somewhere, I believe it is in Vasari, of an Italian painter who walked about the streets, and I believe also woke up his wife at night, constantly repeating, *"Che dolce cosa é questa perspettiva!"* "What a lovely thing this perspective is!" Leonardo's reflections led him to the conclusion that you should make your picture look like a natural scene reflected in a large mirror. And naturally, when the camera obscura came and he heard of it, he soon went on to it.

It seems so obvious; and yet apparently something had to happen, something quite out of the experience of the Greeks, and of the Egyptians, who were also no mean geometricians, to make it appear even possible, let alone obvious, to imitate nature by that simple trick. And now when it did come at last after all those years, here was a simple mechanical device that brought the fruit of years of technical study and experiment by great painters within the reach of every Tom, Dick, and Harry. All he needed was a pencil and a hand steady enough to trace accurately. The art of imitating had been reduced to the technique of copying. The next step in the camera sequence was to do away with even the pencil and the steady hand. For the camera obscura led to the invention of the daguerreotype and so to that of the photograph. And then the advent of the photograph did something which could hardly have been anticipated by those who had invented it, though it may well be that it would not have worried them if it had. It all took a little time, but one thing that the photograph did was to kill stone dead (well not quite stone dead, for the wound has only proved mortal in our own time) just that leading principle of aesthetic theory, that principle of art, which had held sway at least from the time of Aristotle down to the eighteenth century, the theory that the function of the artist is to imitate nature. The imitation of nature, now that it was being done by applying the sweet rules of perspective, had become altogether too easy; so easy that you could make a little gimmick that would do it all for you.

The camera sequence is not altogether simple to narrate. It betrays a certain leapfrogging element. Long before photography was invented, while it was still in embryo as the camera obscura, the next step, which properly *succeeds* photography, had already been taken. It had been taken in fact by Athanasius Kircher himself. For it is generally agreed that Kircher *was* the inventor of what used to be called the "magic lantern." Perhaps it still is. That particular toy does not receive pictures into itself but, with the help of artificial light inside it, it projects (repeat, *projects*) them back onto the world outside itself, normally onto a blank screen, or a blank wall, or some kind of *tabula rasa.* But even if the wall is not blank, provided the artificial light is bright enough, the picture will be projected and it will either mix with or obliterate for the spectator whatever is actually on the wall. Hastening now to a conclusion, the next step was of course to run a lot of these projected pictures together; it was the step from still to motion, from the magic lantern to the movie. And the last step of all followed quickly; from the movie to television. Only here at last do we reach the toy in which Marshall McLuhan's Herr Gutenberg and his successors probably *have* had as big a hand as Kircher himself and his successors. Only in the technique of television does the art of printing enter the long camera sequence that began with Kircher's camera obscura and his magic lantern.

Let us contemplate for a moment the enormous contrast between the camera and the wind-harp, taken as typifying the process of perception. The process of perception is the means by which what is there outside of us—what is going on "out there—becomes our own experience. The harp's medium is air, on which of course sound is borne to us, and air is something that is itself both inside and outside of us. Apart from its use in perception, it is entering and leaving us all day and all night from the day we are born until the moment we cease to breathe. In order that we may perceive by means of it, it has to enter quite a long way into the body before, within the labyrinth of the ear, it is converted into sensations of sound. The word "inspiration," as doctors use it, means taking physical air — oxygen — into our lungs. But the same word in common parlance always suggests taking something else in along with the oxygen. The sounding harp in fact may be taken as the emblem of *inspiration.* By contrast the camera's medium is light. And light does not enter into the body at all. It is stopped short at the surface of the eye; and you know how often the eye has been compared to a mirror. From that point on, what happens is so to speak our own affair. But as to what actually *does* happen, to give us the experience of seeing, whether there are produced replicas, or internal reproductions, or what you will, of the world outside us — that is something that has been argued about almost since argument began. It is very much easier to shut our eyes than it is to shut our ears. What exactly *is* it that is there when our eyes are open but is no longer there when they are shut? With the different attempts at answering that question you could fill a line or two of a dictionary; you would need as much simply for the different names that have been given to what *is* there. *Forms, phantoms, idols, simulacra, effigies, films,* are some of them. In Lucretius alone you find a whole mine of different synonyms for this mysterious panorama that the eye delivers to us. But they all mean something like, or some part of, what the word *image* means. And *image* is perhaps the word most commonly employed. The camera then can fairly be seen as an emblem, or perhaps this time one should rather say caricature, of *imagination.*

The Italian word *camera* means a room or chamber; and the camera is of course, a hollow box or little dark room. Unlike the camera the harp has no inside, it does not first of all receive into itself stimuli from without and then respond to them. The wind-harp becomes what it is by itself becoming an "inside" for the environing air, by becoming a modulated voice for it to speak with. If the eyes are shut and there is no other guide, it is very difficult to tell where any particular sound comes from, presumably because the air and its contents are all around us. Well, light and its contents are also all around us. But our eyes are so made that they leave us in no doubt where those contents are placed, and how they are disposed. The two sorts of arrangement are very different and that difference is really all we mean by the word "perspective." Light comes to us impartially

from all directions and you might think that our point of view out into it
would diverge from the eye in lines going out in all directions into space,
at least in all directions open to it. Actually the opposite occurs. If we see
in perspective, as we normally do, we have to make those lines converge to
one particular point, which is usually called the "vanishing point." The
farther off from us and from each other things are in space, the nearer they
must be in our picture to the vanishing point and therefore to each other.
Now that is not the way we *think* about space; it is the way we see it. We
vaguely fancy there is a difference between "view" and "point of view";
but in fact there is none. The eye, seeing in perspective, is *projecting* its
own point of view, its punctiliar nothingness as I would like to call it, into
what geometricians call the plane at infinity but the ordinary man has to
imagine as something like the inside of a vast hollow shell. By doing so, the
eye converts that hollow sphere into a tableau that reduces depth to surface and flattens three dimensions into only two. That is the *immediate*
experience so faithfully recorded by the camera. If there were no such
immediate experience, photographs would not be "lifelike." That is also
why the camera is a *caricature* of imagination, although it is a true emblem
of perspective. Imagination is living, perspective only "lifelike." It used to
be said that the camera cannot lie. But in fact it always does lie. Just because it looks only in that immediate way, the camera looks always *at* and
never *into* what it sees. I suspect that Medusa did very much the same.

Well, then along come the magic lantern and the movie, and they project all over again that very projection of punctiliar nothingness, that very
"film" which the camera itself produced by projection in the first place.
Perhaps it is not surprising that "project" and "projection" have become
such very loaded words. What a history they have behind them! A student
of the history of words and their meanings is apt to acquire a rather profound scepticism concerning the shared mental horizon of his contemporaries. He notices that when poets use metaphors, they at least know they
are doing so. But nobody else seems to know it, although they are not only
speaking but also thinking in metaphors all the time. I recall very well,
when I was writing my early book, *History in English Words,* being aston-
ished at the ubiquitous appearance of the *clock* as a metaphor shortly
after it had been invented. It turned up everywhere where anybody was
trying to describe the way things work in nature. Then the clocks stopped—
but the metaphor went on. The student of words and their meanings and
the history of them asks himself uneasily: This Newton-Kant-Laplace
universe, in which the nineteenth century found itself so much at home,
was it after all much more than metaphorical clockwork? But unfortu-

nately he cannot stop there. Coming a little nearer to our own time he finds the psychology of the unconscious, in which the first half of the twentieth century felt so much at home. Strange how squarely it seems to be based on an image of "repression." which is much the same as *com*pression! Was it after all just the steam-engine in disguise? We no longer live in the age of the steam-engine. We live in the age of $E = mc^2$, the atomic age. We have discovered, or have told ourselves, that matter does not produce energy but that matter is energy; and we bestow our eager attention on the smallest possible detached unit of matter, expecting to find there the ultimate, still source of all energy. Yes, and we also live in the age of existentialism.

So it is that, in the age of the movie, the student of words who is unfashionable enough to examine their history as well as their current use, is not perhaps so impressed as some others are by the universal practice of projection not only in movie houses and on the television screen, but also, as a concealed metaphor, in the ingenious fancies of men. Is projection itself being projected? He finds, for instance, scientists and philosophers joining hands to assure us that the familiar world around us is a projection of our own mental apparatus onto a kind of wall of imperceptible realities, not perhaps a blank wall, but it might just as well be blank for all the resemblance it bears to anything we do actually see or hear. Or again, when he turns to the psychologists, he finds projections (or perhaps they might almost be called projectiles) in the form of neuroses, fantasies, mother-images, father-fixations, feelings of guilt, and various parts of the body including its secreta and excreta, flying to and fro among them so thick and fast that he has to duck to avoid them. Or again, when the psychologists join hands with the anthropologists, he sees a whole cloud of these projectiles flying off in the same direction and landing on the same target—namely, the mind of that luckless repository, primitive man. One thing at least is made very clear from what all these informative people are fond of telling us about primitive man and that is that, whatever else he was doing, he was always projecting his insides onto something or other. It was his principal occupation. He must presumably have had one or two other things to do as well, but that was what he majored in. The eighteenth century, you know, used to talk of a "ruling passion"; but there is also the ruling metaphor. Perhaps for reading the signs of the times, it is a good deal more important. Let us assume for a moment that it is, and ask ourselves how much of all this stuff would ever have been heard of if Kircher had never invented his magic lantern? Was he, while inventing it, engaged at the same time in inventing for example the anthropological theory of animism? We might even go on to ask (except that the question is one that is never raised in humane academic circles) how much of it all is true?

After all, it is we who actually have *got* the magic lantern and the camera; it is we who have *got* perspective, both in pictures and in photographs, together with the habit of vision which they have raised and fostered. Could it be ourselves who are doing the projecting, when we talk of primitive man in that confident way? *Was* he a magic lantern? Was he even a camera obscura? Are we so sure that he even *had* any inside to speak of? The punctiliar sort that *projects*? Now I personally am quite sure that he had not. Moreover I am firmly persuaded that we shall never get anywhere with our anthropological attempts at reconstructing the mind of primitive man until we make up our minds to throw away all this projection business. If we *must* think in metaphor (and we must), why not try beginning again on the assumption that primitive man was not a camera obscura but an aeolian harp? Surely it is only by this route that we can hope to understand the origin of myths and of thinking at all. Leslie Fiedler, writing on the myth, noted a distinction between two elements we can detect in it. He called them respectively "archetype" and "signature," the signature being that part of a narrative myth which has been contributed by an individual mind or minds. That is a useful distinction, but its usefulness in the long run will depend upon what we are prepared to mean by the word "archetype." It will depend on our accepting the central truth which no one who writes today on the subject does appear to accept, though I should have thought it had been made clear enough more than half a century ago by Rudolf Steiner; the truth that it was not man who made the myths but the myths, or the archetypal substance they reveal, which made man. We shall have to come, I am sure, to think of the archetypal element in myth in terms of the wind that breathed through the harp-strings of individual brains and nerves and fluids, rather as the blood still today pervades and sustains them. Then, when we have started off on the right foot instead of the wrong one, we may come fruitfully on to the problem Shelley had to deal with from a rather different point of view, the problem of the wind-harp that is nevertheless played on by a performer. Then we shall come properly equipped to the problem of that "principle within the human being," as Shelley called it, which acts otherwise than in the lyre and produces not melody alone but harmony. We shall approach in the right way the problem of beings (to quote Shelley again) "harmonized by their own will."

Did that enthusiasm of the Romantics for the wind-harp signify that they had come to see the history of the Western mind as a kind of war between the harp and the camera—that they foresaw the camera civilization that was coming upon us? If so, they were true prophets, because it certainly has come. The camera up to date has won that war. We live in a camera civilization. Our entertainment is camera entertainment. Our holidays are camera holidays. We make them so by paying more attention to the camera we brought with us than to the waterfall we are pointing it at. Our science is almost entirely a camera science. One thinks of the photographs of electrons on screens and in cloud-chambers and so forth. Our philosophers—it is no longer possible even to argue with most of them, because you cannot argue about an axiom, and it is already becoming self-evident to camera man that only camera words have any meaning. Even our poetry has become, for the most part, camera poetry. So much of it consists of those pointedly paradoxical *surface* contrasts between words and between random thoughts and feelings, arranged in the complicated perspective of the poet's own often rather meager personality. Where, one asks, has the music gone? Where has the wind gone that sweeps the music into being, the *hagion pneuma,* the *ruach elohim*? It really does feel as though the camera had won hands down and smashed the harp to pieces.

Perhaps it is just this defeat which the guitar-loving hippies have somehow got wind of. But I do not myself believe that the way out of defeat lies in substituting the harp for the camera, except of course as an aid to historical imagination. For I do not believe that the root from which the camera sequence originally sprang is an unmitigated evil. I even believe it was a necessity. But then neither do I believe that the existence of separate, autonomous human spirits is an unmitigated evil. I traced the camera sequence from a beginning only about as far back as the seventeenth century. But its root is much older than that. It began, I would say, as soon as signature was added to and interwoven with archetype in the structure and substance of myth. That is the same as saying that it began as soon as poetry began to exist within myth—at first within, and then alongside of it. And that again is to say it is something that lies within our destiny. Is not this a truth which the most penetrating minds among the Romantics themselves came to realize? It is interesting to note that, whereas in Shelley we found only that rather perplexed transition from a wind-harp to a harpist's harp, Coleridge—who lived so much longer and had more time to think out a full theory of poetry—does not omit the camera obscura from the imagery he chooses. In the *Biographia Literaria,* by way of comment on Milton's wonderful description of the banyan tree in *Paradise Lost,* he writes:

This is creation rather than painting, or if painting, yet such and with such co-presence of the whole picture flashed at once upon the eye, as the sun paints in a camera obscura.

Coleridge, you see, converts it from a caricature into a true emblem of imagination. How? By placing the sun, instead of the punctiliar nothingness, at that vanishing point which, as he well knew, was really the point of projection from within the eye of the beholder. After all, however it may have been for primitive man, we cannot in our time get away from projection altogether. "The mind of man is not an aeolian harp." That is another sentence from *Biographia Literaria,* reneging rather sharply, it would seem, from the point of view expressed in the author's youthful poem I quoted to begin with. The mind is at least not wholly an aeolian harp. For us there must be projection, and the question for the twentieth century is whether it is to be a projection of nothingness or a projection of the sun-spirit, the spirit of light. Is not this why, in the same book, we find Coleridge quoting that sentence from Plotinus: "The eye could never have beheld the sun if it were not itself of the same nature as the sun"; the sentence which also meant so much to Goethe, and which he rephrased in the form: "If the eye were not of the same nature as the light, it could never behold the light."

If then the story of the harp and the camera is to continue instead of ending with a whimper, it will have to be by way of a true marriage between the one and the other. Is it fanciful, I wonder, to think of a sort of mini-harp stretched across the window of the eye—an Apollo's harp if you will—as perhaps not a bad image for the joy of looking with imagination? That "joy," as will be well-known here, was precisely the thing which C. S. Lewis spent most of his life discovering more about, discovering in particular that it is by no means the same thing as pleasure or happiness or contentment. In a literary climate, which has already become all camera and no harp, all signature and no archetype, we ought not to forget that little group, if group is the right word, which has sometimes been referred to as "Oxford Christians," and sometimes as "Romantic theologians," and with which this college has, thanks to the devotion and energy of Dr. Kilby, established a very special connection. For they may perhaps have contributed their mite to the continuation of the story. The German poet and thinker Novalis, you know, specifically compared with an aeolian harp the *Märchen* or adult fairy tale that modern variant of the myth, in which signature may mingle fruitfully with archetype, but without swamping it altogether. The passage where he does so was selected by George Mac-

Donald as the motto to his own *Märchen, Phantastes,* which played (as he has told us) such a crucial part in the literary and spiritual development of C. S. Lewis. Besides giving us *Märchen* of their own, both Lewis and Tolkien, and their comrade in arms Charles Williams, thought deeply and wrote well on the place of myth and *Märchen* in our modern consciousness. One way or another, they were all three concerned with the problem of imagination; and there is perhaps no piece of writing that deals more gently and genially with the place of imagination in the literature of the future than Tolkien's essay "On Fairy-Stories" in the volume *Essays Presented to Charles Williams.* At least that is so, if I am right in suggesting (as I have been trying to suggest by my own rather devious route) that the ultimate question, to which imagination holds the key, is the question of how we can learn to sign our own names to what we create, whether as myth or in other ways, but so nevertheless that what we sign as our own will also be the name of Another—the name I would venture to say, without venturing to pronounce it, of the Author and the Lord of the archetypes themselves.

Where is Fancy Bred?

Down to about a hundred and fifty years ago the thought, the cultural life, and the religion of the East and that of the West, flowed, in the main, in two separate streams. Anyone who looks at the previous history of the world from that point of view cannot fail to be struck by a remarkable phenomenon. From time to time, often for historical reasons not arising out of the cultural life itself, the two streams are seen to meet and touch one another for a moment; and when that happens, the consequences for the cultural life of the West are apt to be deep and far-reaching. Perhaps one could use an electrical metaphor and speak of East and West as two sources of potential energy and of the spark that unites, or the current that flows, as a result of their momentary juxtaposition. The older generation may recall the "arc" lamp, once used for the brighter sort of street lighting, as a striking illustration.

The traditional visit of Pythagoras to India is one example. The eastern campaigns of Alexander the Great, who also reached India, and the resulting spiritual ferment in and around Alexandria a century or two later, are another. Much later still, there were the Crusades, which, it is now generally agreed, proved at least as significant because of what the West brought back from the East as for anything the West was striving to carry to, or to achieve in, the East.

One way of looking at the Romantic Movement is to see it as yet another fruitful contact between East and West — the last, it may well be, since it looks now as if East and West are rapidly ceasing to be "insulated" from one another to the extent required to produce the old cultural tension. We seem faced, instead, with such a close and constant interpenetration as may lead to something like a single homogeneous culture over the whole face of the globe—under the predominance no doubt (at least in its early stages) of Western tradition and Western impulse. If so, mere geographical location will no longer help us; and we shall have to look elsewhere for the spark of energy that keeps the spirit of man alive on Earth. But that will only make all the more important the personal meetings and the interior polarities with which this article is mainly concerned.

* * *

As long ago as the sixteenth century some enterprising spirits from England founded a company for carrying on trade with India. The story is a complicated one; but by the second half of the eighteenth century the British East India Company had established a virtual monopoly of the trade with India and the British Government, which had been helping itself liberally to the profits of the trade, stepped in to keep order and take control. The British Empire in India, in fact, was born. We are not now concerned with the social and political consequences, momentous as they were. But one of the side-consequences was, that among those going out from Britain to India there began to appear, in addition to the high-powered executives of the Company, a sprinkling of men of rather a different type. As well by the Company as by the Government, administrators were now required in growing numbers—district commissioners, judges, and a host of other officials—and some of the Englishmen who went out to India, to help in these ways in the civil administration of the country, were very highly educated men. The names of Sir Charles Wilkins and Sir William Jones are probably the best remembered. Sir William Jones, a distinguished oriental scholar, was appointed a judge of the Supreme Court of Calcutta. We know now of course, because we have been told so often, that he must have been a ruthlessly exploiting imperialist, riding rough-shod over all the feelings and the traditions of the native population; but, somewhere or other, Sir William had picked up the quaint notion that the people living in a country are entitled to be governed by their own laws—and that a judge who has to decide a dispute between one Indian and another ought to be in a position to consult the Hindu legal authorities. With this object he began to study the Sanskrit language and, before he died at a fairly early age, he had published the first part of his *Institutes of Hindu Law and the Ordinances of Manu*. The first book of the *Ordinances of Manu* consists of an account of the creation of the world and contains the substance of what

Rudolf Steiner, at much greater length and using a modern idiom, was later to disclose in his *Occult Science: An Outline.*

Thus, the contact between England and India led to a fresh and more intensive study of the Sanskrit language by British scholars. Jones and Wilkins were not the only ones; there was also Sir Alexander Hamilton (known to his Scottish friends as "Sanskrit Hamilton"), who was already a professor, in England, of Persian and other oriental languages, before he joined the service of the East India Company.

It happened that, when the German Romantic philosopher, Friedrich Schlegel, was residing in Paris between 1802 and 1804, Alexander Hamilton was interned there, through some crisis arising out of the Napoleonic Wars. The two men met and formed a friendship; and Schlegel began studying Sanskrit under Hamilton's guidance. It was this (as Schlegel himself says in his Introduction), which led to his writing and publishing a few years later his treatise *Über die Sprache und Weisheit der Indier* – a work which is sometimes described in literary and philological circles as "epoch-making." In the same Introduction Schlegel also acknowledges his debt to the work of Wilkins and Jones.

Now Friedrich Schlegel, according to the *Encyclopaedia Britannica* (11th edition),

> was the real Founder of the Romantic School . . . to him more than any other member of the school we owe the revolutionary and germinating ideas which influenced so profoundly the development of German literature at the beginning of the nineteenth century.

The whole link, especially in its early stages, between Romantic philosophy and the historical study of language is a close and intimate one. Read, for example, von Humboldt's little treatise on the "dual" number of the verb found in Greek and some other tongues, *Über den Dualis,* and you find what begins as a philological – even a grammatical – essay turning into a whole theory of the origin of self-consciousness in human beings. But in the historical study of language there has been no more important landmark than the new discovery (brought about by the study of Sanskrit) that the Indian and Persian languages are derived from the same common ancestor as German, French, English, Italian, and the other Romance languages. Hitherto it had been thought that the languages of the East were altogether different growths, with no common root in the past, or at all events no common root that could be actually perceived and felt. We are

Europeans—yes, but in the mysterious depths of language, where the past lives on transformed as the present, we are also "Indo-Europeans." We are Westerners; but we have our origin from the East—and we now begin to feel that that is so.

The discovery began with language; but it did not end there. You cannot translate the *Laws of Manu* without reading them. A new picture began to arise in the mind of Europe of the whole relation between East and West, a picture of India as "Mother" India, and not only of India, a picture of the East as a whole as the source from which the West had originally sprung, from which the spiritual substance of the West had originally been derived; and from which a stream of light and knowledge could be expected to flow again, as the secrets of the past should be progressively unsealed. To pursue the electrical metaphor (which admittedly has all the disadvantages of an attempt to illustrate the living by the dead), it came to be actively felt that the two opposite forces, which create the tension, or "dielectric strain," between them, are nevertheless derived from a single generator. They came originally from one single source and the spark, or the current when it flows, is a partial restoration of that original unity.

Schlegel did not confine himself to language-studies. He delved also into the philosophy and religion of the East; and so, in his treatise *Über die Sprache und Weisheit der Indier*, we find him pointing out that the very nature of human speech, studied historically, reveals that it cannot have originated from the consciousness of a virtually mindless primitive man . . . and that the doctrine of an ascending "evolution" (which was already beginning to appeal strongly to the Western mind) requires supplementing by the older oriental doctrine of "emanation," or the descent of man from a purely spiritual world.[1] Whereas, according to the theory of evolution, man has attained his present degree of self-consciousness by starting from nothing, and including more and more in his awareness as time went on; according to the doctrine of emanation he started from a kind of universal consciousness, in which he was still united with the spiritual world; and he owes his self-consciousness to a progressive exclusion from that world of the spirit.

This concept of "self-consciousness by exclusion" is in many ways very

1. Schlegel's treatise was published in 1808, Darwin's *Origin of Species* not till 1858; yet already, judging by the amount of space Schlegel devotes to refuting it, the doctrine that human consciousness originated as merely animal consciousness was widely accepted. Had this not been the case, the interpretation placed by Darwin and his followers on the evidence he accumulated might well have been a very different one.

near the heart of the Romantic Movement and the Romantic impulse. It would serve equally well as a rough and ready definition of what Steiner has presented from so many different aspects, in so many books and lectures, as the "consciousness soul."[2]

* * *

At about the same time as the rather momentous meeting between a Briton and a German which we have been considering, two other meetings took place in Europe, leading in each case to a lifelong friendship. One of these was between two Germans, the other between two Englishmen. They arose more out of the gifts and inclinations of the two pairs of friends than from any outward historical circumstances, and we approach them by a different kind of route altogether.

In the last few months of his life Rudolf Steiner dictated a series of aphorisms ("leading thoughts") for members of the Anthroposophical Society, most of them preceded by explanatory "letters." These letters were published after his death with the title of *The Michael Mystery*.[3] One of the latest of them is called "Memory and Conscience." In this letter, which is by no means easy, Steiner gives a condensed account of contemporary man's twofold relation to the spiritual world. On the one hand we are all related to the spiritual world through our thoughts and sense-perceptions, which go on in the daytime, while we are awake. But this relation is not *only* a matter of thinking and perceiving. He takes as the central feature, or as a sort of generic term, for all this side of our nature—or better perhaps say, for this direction of our relatedness to the spiritual world: *memory*. Memory is at the center: sense-perception is simply a modification of memory on one side of it; on the other side memory shades off into, or it becomes, something which Steiner here calls "*Phantasie.*"

There is a great deal more in the letter about "*Phantasie,*" for which the careful English translator has throughout used the English word "fancy." After a good deal of hesitation I have come to the conclusion that he was right to do so. The later forms *fantasy* and *phantasy* bring out more clearly,

2. This article reproduces, with some additions and one or two omissions, a lecture delivered by the author to the Stuttgart Branch of the German Anthroposophical Society during their English Weekend, 2nd–4th June, 1967, under the title: "The Consciousness Soul and the Romantic Movement." The consciousness soul (*Bewusstseinsseele*) is especially related on the one hand to the civilization epoch in which we are now living and on the other to the English nation as its peculiar representative.

3. London: Rudolf Steiner Press, revised edition, 1956.

as does the German word, its derivation from the Greek *phantasia,* but they have been pre-empted by psychoanalysis. An alternative choice would have been "imagination," which has also frequently been used to render both *phantasia* and *Phantasie,* but, for reasons that will appear, this would have been at least equally misleading and probably more so — though in a very different way. The difficulty about "fancy" is the wide variety of irrelevant additional meanings it has acquired in the course of its long history as a proper English word, and the overtone of a sort of airy-fairy sprightliness which these tend to display. Romantic love-longing, the art of pugilism, the breeding of poultry, and the kind of little *je ne sais quoi* that chemists' and stationers' shops sell in addition to the staple articles of their trade — these are only some of them. Nevertheless, misleading as it unfortunately may be (especially to anyone with no knowledge at all of the history of English literary criticism), I believe it is the least misleading choice that could have been made.

The second of our two contrasted relations to the spiritual world is a very different one. It is that relation which we have in sleep, and also in that part of us which is always asleep, even in the daytime — our unconscious will. In the first relation our waking life is *presently* related to the spiritual world (though now it is the spiritual world disguised as the sense-world). But, in the second, we are (while we are physically awake) only indirectly related to the spiritual world, inasmuch as we have a kind of aftereffect (*Nachwirkung*) of a direct relation with the spirit undisguised — an actual union with the spirit, which has been experienced during the previous night's sleep. In sleep we revert to that older, universal consciousness which, for contemporary and mundane purposes, is *un*consciousness. For every time we go to sleep, we travel back through all our previous incarnations, in order to resume, before we wake again, that merged union, or contained identity, with the Divine Spirit, which we had in our beginning, before we were excluded from it, before we began our long journey from the spiritual East into the spiritual (or unspiritual) West. This after-working from sleep, which we experience after we have awakened and during the day, is to be looked for (he says) in *conscience.* But again: not *only* in conscience. Again you have a gamut of manifestations, of which conscience is the keynote. Conscience — will — and again *Phantasie.*

Phantasie, therefore, is a manifestation which the human being can arrive at by two opposite routes. And towards the end of the letter, which I have no doubt oversimplified, Rudolf Steiner, by way of rendering more concrete what he has so far described in abstract terms, points out that there are two different types of human being, organized in two differ-

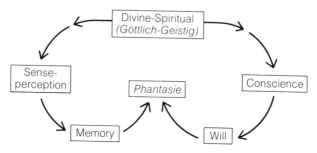

ent ways, one of which arrives at *Phantasie predominantly* by the first route and the other predominantly by the second. Finally, to make it even more concrete, he gives an example of each type. And the examples he gives are the two poets, Goethe and Schiller.

The meeting between Goethe and Schiller had many and far-reaching consequences; but here we are concerned only with the significance of that meeting, and of all meetings and friendships between what we may now call (following Steiner) the "Goethe-type" and the "Schiller-type," for a proper understanding of all that may go on in the realm of *Phantasie*. For the former, his *Phantasie* is something which is so to speak given to him without effort on his part, as part and parcel of his waking experience. Steiner's words are: "With them contemplation of sense-reality turns of itself, so to speak, into pictures of fancy." It is a different matter for the Schiller-type. The Schiller-type is impelled, as it were, into the realm of *Phantasie* out of the working of his own will and conscience. These are they who, "out of inner love for an idealistic world-outlook, vigorously convert their outlook-through-the-senses into forms of fancy."[4]

Yet . . . there is something repugnant to the very nature of *Phantasie* in such a process. Or at least it is so for poetry; we feel afraid that poetic imagery brought about in that way — *voulu* — is likely to be overintellectual . . . lifeless allegory rather than living symbol. This is the quandary of the Schiller-type. His *Phantasie-bilder* are not given to him by Nature herself. He has to *make* them. But *Phantasie-bilder* cannot be "made"; if they are, they have no real content in them. They must *grow*.

How then is the Schiller-type to acquire the *Phantasie* which does not grow naturally? Which it is no use his manufacturing . . . or no use for poetry? What is the way out? Well, there are two ways of getting at some-

4. In this and the preceding quotation I have departed a little from the English translation, which renders *Anschauung* by "conception," *Weltanschauung* by "world-conception," and *sinnliche Anschauung* by "sense-conceptions."

thing you have not got already. One is to make it; the other is to find it. And this is where the meeting and the friendship come in. "To a strenuous will, he was obliged to seek the fancy that should give it content," says Steiner, speaking of what Schiller found in Goethe. One human being is not enough to spark across this gap. It needs a pair. The one reaches out across the gap for the *Phantasie*, or the *Phantasie*-content, which he can find in the other. And of course the intercourse is reciprocal. The second also finds something he needs in the first. But that is not now our concern.

* * *

We will turn instead to the third friendship. In the year 1798 a little volume of poems was published in England, which did not make a very great stir at the time, but which (as the years have passed) has come to be seen more and more as an epoch-making event; as having been, in a sense, the launching-pad for the whole Romantic Movement in English literature. It was the joint product of two poets, who had only recently met, and become close friends; but who afterwards remained intimate friends throughout their lives. This was the *Lyrical Ballads* by William Wordsworth and Samuel Taylor Coleridge. Most of the poems in this little volume were written by Wordsworth, but the three or four that Coleridge contributed include *The Ancient Mariner*, which is perhaps the most superb example it would be possible to find of English poetry in the Romantic genre. Nevertheless, of the two poets Wordsworth was the most *consistently* inspired. The four or five really immortal poems Coleridge produced, during his quite long life, were all written in the twelve months or so following on his meeting with Wordsworth—his "annus mirabilis," as it is sometimes called. Thereafter, as he himself both felt and lamented, Coleridge's poetic inspiration declined. Wordsworth, on the other hand, continued to grow in stature, and in strength, and became England's greatest "poet of nature." It has been said of him that it was he, more than any other man, who restored to English people a *feeling* for Nature, the possibility of experiencing the face of Nature as the countenance of a living being.

Now these two poets, whose fates were so different, and yet who were so closely associated with each other, were both, of course, men of the Consciousness Soul Age, as are all Romantic writers. They both experienced that "self-consciousness by exclusion," to which I have already referred, but they experienced it very differently. To Wordsworth it was a real enough experience, certainly; but not tragically, or bitterly, real. Modern man (he found) as he grows up from childhood into manhood, feels himself more and more cut off from the beauty, the meaning, the life of nature; though, as a young child, he could still feel himself a part of it.

This is the content of what is perhaps his best-known poem – the famous *Ode on the Intimations of Immortality from Recollections of Early Childhood*. It is too well known to require extensive quotation; but the reader will recollect that its prevailing tone is one of gentle melancholy, tempered by a sober joy, rather than of dejection or despair. It is true that "Heaven lies about us" only "in our infancy"; true that "The things which I have seen I now can see no more"; true that "Shades of the prison-house begin to close / Upon the growing Boy." Yet, even now, as full-grown men:

> — in a season of calm weather
> Though inland far we be,
> Our souls have sight of that immortal sea
> Which brought us hither.

And so the poet concludes:

> We will grieve not, rather find
> Strength in what remains behind;
> In the primal sympathy
> Which having been must ever be . . . .

Whereas, for Coleridge, the exclusion from any immediate experience of the spirit that meets us, disguised as the face of Nature, was more even than a tragedy. It was a lifelong agony. The *loss,* at an early age, of his "shaping Spirit of Imagination," as he calls it, was a misery to which he refers again and again, both in his letters and in his poetry – notably in the *Ode to Dejection.* And out of this very agony it was borne in on him that, in the present age, man can really only *receive* from Nature what he himself *brings* to her out of his own *Phantasie:*

> We receive but what we give
> And in our life alone does Nature live.

But Coleridge had a very powerful mind: he had nourished it, almost from infancy, with a quite astounding depth and variety of reading, not only in the poets of all ages, but ranging from Greek, Neoplatonic, and Scholastic philosophy to modern philosophy (especially German philosophy) and modern science. What he *longed* to be able to do was to write great poetry, out of that blissful sense of oneness with Nature, which he had found and which he continued all his life to admire – almost to adore – in his friend Wordsworth. One, though only one, of the causes of his resort to opium was his hankering after just this tranquilizing unity.

This was denied to him. The joys of a happy, inborn gift of *Phantasie* were very largely denied to him. But for that very reason, and out of that very lack, he turned his powerful philosophic mind to the whole *problem* of *Phantasie* . . . so that he is generally accepted today as the greatest, and most creative, of English critics. No theory of poetry, or of the psychology of the poet, in England or America can avoid taking full account, to begin with, of Coleridge's doctrine of the poetic or "creative" imagination.

I have now used the word "imagination," for which the German equivalent would be, not *Phantasie* but *Einbildungskraft*. Could I equally well have said *Phantasie*? Yes. And no. If a history of English criticism which did not mention Coleridge would be *Hamlet* without the Prince of Denmark, there is something that holds as central a place in Coleridge's theory of poetry as Coleridge himself does in the world of English literary criticism as a whole. Every English, or American, or Canadian, or Australian university student of English literature, however poorly equipped, is bound to know *something* about Coleridge's famous distinction between "imagination" and "fancy"; at the very least (if he hopes to pass an examination) he must know that Coleridge did in fact make such a distinction. Very briefly it could be characterized as follows.

Coleridge insisted that what the Greeks called *phantasia* (German *Phantasie*) was not really one thing, but two. It included, in loose association and confusion, two sharply distinguishable experiences, or faculties, of the human mind. He said, moreover, that in order to "drive this home," so to speak, he himself would henceforth give to these two distinguishable faculties – which had hitherto been confused by using both words to convey both of them – two separate English names. Hitherto the words "fancy" and "imagination" had been used indifferently as synonyms – when what was meant was the overall content of *phantasia*. Now he quite deliberately appropriated one of the two words to the one faculty, and the other to the other. And so "fancy" (as Coleridge uses the word) is that which is responsible for, that which produces, the kind of imagery, or combinations of images, that come into the mind ready-made and almost unbidden simply out of the impressions of the senses which the memory has stored and retained. Thus, he speaks of "the law of the passive Fancy and the mechanical Memory." Fancy is predominantly a *passive* thing and its productions (by contrast with those of the imagination) are "fixed and dead."

Whereas the imagination is essentially vital. The images begotten by imagination are alive and creative, and have a sort of germinating power of their own. When true imagination is at work, the same power is operating in man as operated, in the Beginning, in the creation of the world; only now it flows from an individual mind, and in association with what Coleridge calls the "conscious will." Fancy and imagination are both needed for composing poetry (and, in a sense, imagination must work by "irradiating" fancy); but the truly great poet is the poet of imagination rather than the poet of mere fancy. And the greatest of these was Shakespeare. Some of Coleridge's profoundest insights, both critical and philosophical, are to be found in his own *Lectures on Shakespeare*; and every student of the genesis of the Romantic Movement in Europe quickly discovers how intimately it was involved with a new and deeper appreciation of the universal significance, in precisely this respect, of the genius of Shakespeare. Moreover, that is as true, or truer, of German romanticism as of English.

Had it not been for Shakespeare, Coleridge suggests, we might have gone on resting content with the old notion that poetry is born in man out of the sense-perceptions of their own accord, that it is somehow engendered in the eyes by the mere act of gazing. But that is a mistake. If we accept only what the eye transmits to us, then we are under what he was fond of calling "the Despotism of the Eye." The senses alone are not a source of imagination. They are now our tyrants. And it is the task of imagination to rescue mankind from this very "Despotism of the Eye."

There is much more that could be said. Coleridge was a philosopher as well as a critic and indeed many other things as well. And the basis of his philosophy, whether of imagination or of nature, is "the Law of Polarity." It may be compared with the *Naturphilosophie* of Schelling and his followers, though there are important differences. Here however the point is that one seems to see Coleridge reaching out, so to speak, across the gap between what I will loosely call the old *Phantasie* and the new, seizing hold of the *Phantasie* which he found in such rich measure in Wordsworth, pondering deeply on it, taking long walks with Wordsworth and his sister, having long talks with Wordsworth, and – out of that intimate experience – excogitating and propounding what *Phantasie* is, or ought to be, *now* in this age of the consciousness soul. And, here too, of course, the intercourse was reciprocal; Wordsworth's poetry was immeasurably deepened by his contact with the mind and heart of Coleridge.

There is also much more that could be said about the two polarically contrasted types of humanity in general. Rudolf Steiner, for example, tells us in the *Michael* letter referred to how deep is the origin of that contrast in the past histories of the individual souls concerned, the relation in which they stand to a prenatal experience of the spiritual world on the one hand and, on the other, to the individual's own previous earthly incarnations. One recalls Wordsworth's "Trailing clouds of glory do we come / From God, who is our home." But we must not make it a doctrinaire distinction; or, because Steiner has said of the Goethe-type, that "their soul-world appears like waking dreams," go about saying that Goethe in Germany and Wordsworth in England were poets of mere fancy—a sort of survival from the past—while Schiller and Coleridge were poets and philosophers of imagination and the future. It is the very last thing Coleridge himself would have said about Wordsworth, or Schiller (I imagine) about Goethe. In everything to do with polarity, we have to be able to distinguish—without crudely dividing.

Yet there remains a profound significance in the polarity—both that between the two types of genius, and that between fancy and imagination. The very history of language—the sort of thing that is always happening to the meanings of words—shows us how the images of fancy (of the *Phantasie* that is "given" by nature, rather than willed by man; and that is what words are to start with . . . that is how language began), unless they are nourished by the creative imagination of man, "fade into the light of common day" and become mere ideas, notions, *Vorstellungen.*

We have been reminded in the course of this article of the intervention of Shakespeare's reawakened genius in the mystery of the birth of romanticism. Perhaps therefore I may conclude it by returning to him for a few moments. One sometimes has an uncanny feeling that Shakespeare knew all about the birth of the Romantic Movement two hundred years or so before it happened! His "prophetic mind" (to borrow Cecil Harwood's phrase) had a way of just *hinting,* with a feather-soft lightness of touch, at some of the deepest issues that confront mankind in his evolution; and this is nowhere more evident than in the little songs that are scattered like dewdrops through his plays. I have in mind now the song from the *Merchant of Venice,* which is sung at that crucial juncture in the drama, when Bassanio is hesitating between the three caskets: whether to choose the glistering golden appearance that conceals (as the audience now knows) only a death's head behind its luminous glory, or the saturnine leaden box that coffins the radiant likeness of a living and breathing Portia. And I am tempted, at the risk of breaking a butterfly on a wheel, to expand as interpretation what Shakespeare was content to leave as hint:

> Tell me where is Fancy bred,
> Or in the heart or in the head?

> How begot, how nourishèd?
>   Reply, reply.
> It is engender'd in the eyes,
> With gazing fed; and Fancy dies
> In the cradle where it lies.
>   Let us all ring Fancy's knell:
>   I'll begin it,—Ding, dong, bell.
> *All.* Ding, dong, bell.

What is the source from which fancy springs—the head, or the heart? That is, from the nerves and senses alone, or more towards the other pole of the organism, where the breath meets the blood and the heart beats out of the blood into the future? How is it begotten and, when it has been begotten, how is it to be nourished?

There follows the short line that holds us in suspense while we await the all-important answers to both questions . . .

> It is engender'd in the eyes,
> With gazing fed;

That is, in the sense-perceptions themselves. "Engender'd" is only another word for "begot," so the first question is answered. But how is it to be *nourished*? From what source? The poet does not say: he only tells us what happens when it is *not* nourished:

> Fancy dies
> In the cradle where it lies.

It never attains the maturity which was designed for it.

And then (and how typical of Shakespeare this is!)—as though to remove all risk of our taking the whole thing too seriously (for after all we are only men and women)—he finishes with the little jingle:

> Let us all ring Fancy's knell:
> I'll begin it,—Ding, dong, bell!

If we like, you see, we can still take it all at the "airy fairy" level . . . and, if we do, it is still a very sweet and magical little song. But we can perhaps also take even the little jingle at a much deeper level, and with a happier result. "Ding, dong, bell" has a merry rather than a doleful overtone in

English ears . . . it makes us think more of nursery rhymes than of funerals . . . . Yes, fancy has to die . . . and it is well that she *should* die — in order to be reborn as imagination . . . . "*I*'ll begin it" . . . it is, after all, the entry of the ego into the death experience of the consciousness soul, in order to be reborn as individual spirit, as individual-universal spirit, as spirit self, life spirit, spirit man, of which we are, knowingly or unknowingly, speaking, whenever we speak understandingly of a transition from fancy to imagination.

Should I add that, if the stage-direction is properly observed, the whole company finally joins in and takes up the doleful-merry refrain? At all events it is at once a salutary reflection for the temporary isolation in which the consciousness soul of man has its being, and a fitting conclusion to these observations, to recall that the rebirth of the ego through imagination is a matter of vital concern, not only to the individual man in whom it occurs, whether he be of the Goethe-type or the Schiller-type, but to the whole vast company of Heaven and Earth.

The Rediscovery of Allegory (I)

In form this book is a series of brief analytical studies of half-a-dozen well-known "visionary" allegories. Beginning with Boethius, it takes the reader through *De Planctu Naturae, Architrenius,* the *Roman de la Rose,* and the *Divine Comedy,* to bring him finally to rest in *Pearl.* Its substance is harder to designate. The author has a central theme, of which he rarely loses sight; or perhaps better say two themes, one of them historical and the other psychological and ethical, though the two are closely and skillfully interwoven to form a single thread.

It has long been customary, though the practice has lately been questioned by more than one convincing voice, to contrast allegory on the one side with symbol and myth on the other as almost contradictory opposites. "The question of the relationship of medieval allegory to symbolism," says Mr. Piehler, "is not accounted for even in C. S. Lewis's *Allegory of Love,* which still suffers from the misleading effects of Coleridge's remarks." And at the end of his opening chapter on Boethius he sets forth his own view in terms of a *distinguo* within the Coleridge-Lewis doctrine:

It seems appropriate to suggest a modification in Lewis's theory. Allegory is a method of representing states of mind, symbolism of representing an invisible world, of which our experience is but the copy of an archetype. But the distinction between the two modes is not so absolute. In some sense all deities do reside in the human breast. The invisible world exists in the human mind (or perhaps on its deeper levels the

The Visionary Landscape: A Study in Medieval Allegory by Paul Piehler. Edward Arnold, London, 1971. 170 pp. £2.75.

human mind exists in the invisible world). Symbolism represents these deeper levels, whereas allegory, as in Lewis's definition, represents the more conscious processes. But the mind itself functions simultaneously and indivisibly on all these levels, and medieval allegory as a genre at its best represents all these levels. Therefore, it is not only a mode of expression but, more fundamentally, a mode of thought. Poets have been able to employ allegory to express, develop and make judgments on concepts unattainable in their time and circumstances by discursive thought, and attainable now only through the prisms of analysis. Allegory blurs distinctions when they would be unnecessary and distracting, and permits what is discursively complex to be represented symbolically with a directness and a unity of impression that suggests an underlying unity in the 'reality' of the invisible world.

The book then consists of a review in this light of the six major works referred to, with of course incidental references to more recondite ones such as the *Psychomachia* or Andreas's *Art of Love:*

> . . . in much medieval allegorical writing, allegory and symbolism (in Lewis's sense) are in fact inextricably mixed. Lady Philosophy, as we have seen, represents an element in an intellectual process, and is at the same time an embodiment of the universal figure of the lady of wise aspect who comes to us in our troubles, surely a copy of something in the invisible world, a symbol. Moreover, in these instances, as perhaps in all successful allegory, we perceive the two sets of representations as one; they can only be separated by analysis.

Historically the author perceives allegory as a natural development from myth rather than its enemy, and this enables him to penetrate several of its aspects in a new way, or at all events a way that is new to me: notably the device (if it be merely a device) of personification, which has long been regarded in romantic circles as the determining aridity of a hopelessly arid genre. I recall being impressed some years ago by Morton W. Bloomfield's rescue operation in disentangling allegorical from rhetorical personification.[1] Piehler carries it further by distinguishing within the former what he calls "seminal" personification; and much of his presentation is concerned with

---

1. "A Grammatical Approach to Personification Allegory," *Modern Philology* LX no. 3 (February, 1963). The numerous books and essays in English and German referred to in the footnotes constitute something like a bibliography of the subject.

the relation between this particular species of the "seminal image" and what he terms (supporting his choice with a hint from Bernardus Silvestris) the "*potentia animae*" – a relation which consists mainly of the possible transformation of the former into the latter.

The epithet "seminal" has been worked rather hard in the last twenty years or so, but it has perhaps not been generally noticed that the metaphor carries historical as well as genial implications, inasmuch as a seed owes its creative energy to the past no less certainly than it bestows it on the future. The visionary allegories themselves, and also their development by "cumulative tradition," suggest that medieval mentality in general was seminal in this proper sense and that, in allegory in particular, it achieved "a balance of rational and intuitive elements, an acceptance of all levels on which the mind functions." It rationalized and abstracted, but its abstractions were balanced by, or they still contained, the active quality which we have come to associate only with "the intuitive element." In the twelfth century intellect itself was "dynamic," not only imagination; and the allegorical structure of the *Commedia* "makes manifest the dynamic intellectual impulse that underlies the Aristotelian-Thomist categorical method." It can reveal to us that the difference between symbol and allegory, or between a mythical and a rational representation, is not one of kind, but simply one of degree in "the ratio between imagination and intellect."[2]

This achievement of a balance between imagination and intellect is, however, to be seen not only as a historical achievement of mind in general, but also as the very process of healing and redemption, by transformation, through which the medieval allegorist sought to conduct his reader. But "acceptance of all levels on which the mind functions" is also "the goal of those who seek psychic integration today." The following is the first of nine useful "propositions" with which at the start he summarizes the book's argument:

> Medieval visionary allegory offers its readers participation in a process of psychic redemption closely resembling, though wider in scope than, modern psychotherapy. This process typically includes the phases of crisis, confession, comprehension and transformation.

A sufficient sprinkling of psychoanalytical comment and allusion through-

2. Quoted in a footnote from Roger Hinks, *Myth and Allegory in Ancient Art,* a brief work which deserves more recognition than it has received and which is itself a good deal indebted to F. M. Cornford's *From Religion to Philosophy.*

out, culminating in a quotation on the penultimate page from the popular existential psychologist R. D. Laing, is directed to maintaining that proposition.

Such a concept of "applied medievalism" (if the expression may be allowed) entails, as the author presents it, acceptance of history, at all events the history of the human mind, as a single intelligible process—a "goal-directed" one in the sense that the growth of a living organism is goal-directed, since it cannot even begin to be traced and understood except by being so apprehended. That Piehler is familiar with other presentations of this on the whole unpopular view is clear from a number of the books to which his footnotes refer, two of my own (it is pleasant to acknowledge) among them. That he also accepts it is implicit in his whole approach and doctrine. It is the kind of perspective which—as he himself would emphatically confirm if only he were still here to do so—was denied to Lewis by his resolute antihistoricism. Both the process and the "goal" on such a view are what Coleridge, Jung, Piehler himself, and others have termed "individuation"; and this is true not only of the growth of one person's mind from immaturity to maturity, but also of the history of the human mind as a whole. They entail in the first place separation from the paradise of imperfectly differentiated spirit by a "barrier" (in Boethius the figure of Philosophia as a guardian of the threshold, in the *Commedia* and *Pearl* the river). On the farther side of the barrier paradise is still actual, but only as the divine substance of "life" itself, including biological life and thus also unconscious mind. But seen from this side it has become the wilderness, the *selva oscura* full of strange and menacing beasts. "The polarity between city and wilderness" has been established. But *total* individuation—individuation as "goal"—requires the crossing of the barrier. In psychological terms there must be "a synthesis of conscious and unconscious elements in the personality"; in allegorical terms (aside from parodies) the barrier is crossed but not lost, and the world-wide paradise-garden of old becomes (not *shrinks* to) a *hortus conclusus* in the visionary landscape of love. But what, again in psychological terms, does the "barrier" consist of? It consists of that very abstraction—analysis—intellectualism—which is found as a fault in medieval allegory and indeed in medievalism in general. It is "synonymous on the rational level with the category." And yet, as already seen, the category is itself "dynamic." Polar opposites as they are, the energy to erect the barrier and the energy to overleap it are one and the same.

Once the transition had begun from myth into philosophy you had "the start of man's psychic history"; and, at a later stage, medieval allegory (where analysis itself is "carried on predominantly in terms of imagery," and which "switches from mythopoea to conceptual analysis") is directed at once to confirm and strengthen the barrier and to engender measures for crossing it. These measures are its "forces of healing," to which the author more than once draws our attention. The barrier was needed to confine and control the dark forces; the crossing of it transforms them to their original brightness; and the arrived traveler will thus discover that the *selva oscura* was itself a "seminal image." "Jung writes about psychoanalysis, but the *Pearl*, in the deepest sense, is psychoanalysis itself."

Individuation implies internalization — movement inward from nature-centered to self-centered life and spirit. The author casts back to the primitive origins of consciousness, suggesting that, just as the numen in the grove eventually became the *potentia animae* which is characteristic of medieval abstraction, so the grove itself became the *locus animae* which will later on be characteristic of imagination. It is from their origin in a primordial unity of man and nature that both *locus* and *potentia* derive their "iconographic vitality."

It would, however, be a mistake to infer from these bare bones of argument I am laboring to expose that we have here one of those really *splendidly* original books which consist almost entirely of secular and sweeping generalizations advanced with bustling *Schwärmerei*. The "sentens" is there, but it is delicately handled. If there are "undertones of the story of the Fall" in the garden in *Cligés*, "it is an injustice to the subtleties of Chrétien's art to hear them louder than a whisper." Many more paragraphs are expended on subtle analyses of detail than on directly surveying the grandiose perspective — which is more likely to appear focused into some pinpoint appreciation of the niceties of poetic diction. Some of these are of a very high order, and I am tempted to quote in full the comment on Jean de Hautville's use of the word "*lares*" in two passages from the *Architrenius:*

... Architrenius, the 'arch-weeper,' is (like the poet) a young man who, scrutinizing his soul, finds nothing virtuous there, and comes to the conclusion that Nature should have protected him better against the assaults of vice.

> mersosque profunda
> Explorat sub mente lares, nec moribus usquam
> Invenit esse locum, nec se virtutibus unum
> Impendisse diem; 'Mene istos', inquit, 'in usus

> Enixa est Natura parens? me misit ut arma
> In superos damnata feram, . . . ?
> . . . mater quid pignora tantae
> Destituit labi, nec quem produxit alumno
> Excubat, ut nullis maculam scelus inspuet actis?
>
> (I, pp. 247–48)

He explores the hidden abodes within the recesses of his
mind and finds no place there consecrated to morality, nor
can he discover that he has ever remained virtuous for as
long as a single day. "Did Nature, my mother, really bring
me into the world for practices such as these?" he wonders.
"Did she send me out to take up arms against the gods, like a
lost soul? . . . Should a mother abandon her offspring to
such a fate, instead of watching the child she has brought up
to ensure that his actions do not become tainted by sin?"

Since Nature is all-powerful and is able to produce all sorts of monsters,
the train of thought appears to continue, she should be able to protect
Architrenius. He therefore decides to go out and search the world for
Nature's answers to his difficulties.

> . . . profugo natura per orbem
> Est quaerenda mihi; veniam quamcumque remotos
> Abscondat secreta lares, odiique latentes
> Eliciam causas, et rupti forsan amoris
> Restituam nodos, . . .
>
> (I, p. 251)

I must go as an exile through the world to seek for Nature; I
shall attempt to reach whatever secret place it is she has con-
cealed her far-off abodes, and there search out the hidden
causes of sin, and if it may be, join once again the sundered
links of love.

The two passages taken together give us a striking insight into the processes of allegorical creation. In the first passage the 'lares' are 'mersos . . .
profunda . . . sub mente'; in the second they are 'remotos' and must be
searched, for 'per orbem'. A mere hundred lines separate the passages,
so that the transition from seminal image to allegory implies a transfor-

mation of the external world into a new realm of the mind which will obey the laws of the inner life before those of the outer, a realm awaiting the explorations of the mental traveller.

The term 'lares' is used here with particular felicity. It indicates one's dwelling and at the same time the place where the gods make their most personal contact with the individual, as opposed to their relationship with his tribe or city. The transition from the outer to the inner world could not have been suggested to the reader with such evocativeness and clarity were it not for the extraordinary use the poet makes of this term, which for Jean seems to have the meaning of 'shrines' or 'abodes' as well as 'spirits'. For the first time the seminal image of the allegory refers to a feature of the landscape rather than to a personification; in view of this, we shall not be surprised to find that landscapes play a more important role in Jean's work than in that of earlier allegorists. None the less, there is no sharp break away from the use of personifications as a basis for the seminal image. Each time the term *lares* is used allegorically, it is intimately connected with a personification. Apart from the *lares Naturae,* the abodes of *Ambitio* and *Superbia*, both visited by the hero in the course of his travels, are also called *lares* (I, pp. 293–311). The term thus becomes a means of transforming not only personifications into mental forces, but their shrines into allegorized landscapes, often of some subtlety of depiction. Jean provides us with perhaps the most effective statement we have encountered of the fact that the poet turning to allegory is entering the world of the inner life. Thus Architrenius, distantly descended, one might say, from Gilgamesh and Aeneas, becomes the first of the interior pilgrims, wandering over the world in search of his soul, and—like Dante, Bunyan's Christian, and Kafka's Land-surveyor—*profugus,* an exile, searching out the *lares*, numinous abodes of mental divinities, in a landscape at once internal and external.

Here, as it seems to me, we have a combination of sensitive criticism with an underlying metaphysic both firm and profound (the sensitivity deriving from the metaphysic), which Coleridge himself might almost have envied.

There are half-a-dozen or more misprints which could be corrected with advantage in a second edition. For a book so crammed with various matter the Index is on the sketchy side. The last four pages of the Dante chapter, cross-headed "The Figure of Beatrice" and emphasizing her personal as well as allegorical identity, call aloud for some express reference to Charles Williams, but there is none. For both the *Architrenius* and the *De Planctu*

Naturae the text relied on is Thomas Wright's *The Anglo-Latin Poets of the 12th Century* (1872). A footnote to page 60 of *The Visionary Landscape* quotes that part of the *De Planctu* where Natura advocates moderation in the transports of love: "Non enim originalem Cupidinis naturam in honestate redarguo, si circumscribatur frenis modestiae, si habenis temperantiae moderetur, si non geminae excursionis limites deputatos evadet, vel in nimium tumorem ejus calor ebulliat . . ." (*PL* 210, col. 456). It seems odd that the author should have adopted Wright's obscuring (and presumably bowdlerizing?) substitution of *geminae* for *germen* (Wright II, 474), in a note moreover where the name of Freud makes one of its mercifully rare appearances! Lastly it is even odder that, in his fairly full précis of the *De Planctu*, no mention whatever is made of Hymenaeus. Before his appearance on the scene Hymenaeus has already been described at length, and with a string of rhetorical antitheses the contrast has been heavily underlined between the true god of marriage and his raffish half-brother "Antigamus." When he does make his heralded appearance he heads the procession of the Virtues (themselves enumerated in our author's précis) and his countenance and costume are carefully depicted so as to show his application to all ages and all social classes. Moreover at the climax of the work, when Natura decides to send for Genius to come and excommunicate her disobedient subjects, it is Hymenaeus who is appointed her ambassador. If you are going to propound, at the end of your summary, that Alan appears to have "brought off the difficult feat of making a case for the celibate life," surely you ought at least to show some awareness of all this. Fortunately the omission in no way weakens the central argument of the book or its firm structure. The whole of this last paragraph in fact is to be taken simply as a reviewer doing his duty and not as disclosing any at all significant blemishes in this most thoughtful, rich, and, yes, "seminal" contribution to the study of the medieval mind.

The Rediscovery of Allegory (II)

SOME REFLECTIONS ON ICONOLOGY

Last year the Phaidon Press added to its impressive list of art books a volume which differs somewhat from the general run, inasmuch as it is hardly less concerned with literature than with art. Usually the letterpress is strictly subservient to the admirable reproductions of which each book substantially consists. *Symbolic Images,* by E. H. Gombrich,[1] has about a hundred pages of illustrations as against about two hundred of text and another thirty-five of notes. It is a collection of essays published over a period of thirty years or so, mostly in the *Journal of the Warburg and Courtauld Institutes,* several of which are brief and fairly technical studies, such as "An Interpretation of Mantegna's 'Parnassus.' " But more than half of the text consists of two much longer essays, entitled "Botticelli's Mythologies: A Study in the Neo-Platonic Symbolism of his Circle" and *"Icones Symbolicae*: Philosophies of Symbolism and their Bearing on Art." There is an Introduction on the "Aims and Limits of Iconology," and the second and longer of these two essays has been revised and greatly extended beyond the form in which it originally appeared in 1948. Altogether about one-third of the contents of the volume is new.

It is above all this concluding essay, *"Icones Symbolicae,"* more than seventy pages long, and to which the whole volume owes its title, that takes us into the realm of literature and even more perhaps of philosophy and history; since its avowed object is "to arrive at a better understanding

1. London: Phaidon Press Ltd., 1972.

of the conflicting and interacting currents of thought that can be shown to have influenced ideas about symbolism down to our present day." Coming, as it does, from the distinguished author of *Art and Illusion*, that makes you think. Anyone anxious to discern and distinguish one of those interacting currents would be wise to place that book also high up on his reading list. It treated, as is well known, of the relation between the art, and indeed the technique, of painting on the one hand and human perception itself on the other, perception, that is, as it occurs not only in artists themselves but in human beings generally. And in doing so it necessarily raised the whole issue of the ultimate relation between man and nature, between mind and matter, between subject and object. Putting it briefly, the characteristic features of *Art and Illusion* were, firstly, the skillful and entertaining way in which it revealed, almost incidentally as it seemed, the fact that perception is a participating activity and not merely passive reception, and secondly, that its numerous illustrations and its whole approach to the reader were calculated to make him realize that fact not merely as a theoretical conviction but as an actual experience.

Now as theory this view of the nature of perception was of course not particularly new to anyone mildly acquainted with post-Kantian philosophy and psychology and its *sequelae* in the Romantic Movement and elsewhere. Coleridge's "primary imagination" is, it will be remembered, "the living power and prime agent of *all* human perception." Moreover there is little doubt that interaction in one direction began long ago between this psychological principle and developments in the realm of art—impressionism for instance. What appears to be much newer, and what has led me under the stimulus of Sir Ernst Gombrich's essay to try to formulate some reflections here, is interaction in the other direction; *from* the visual arts *to* literature and psychology, *from* iconology *to* typology. In an age when books go on pouring from the press in a kind of weekly Niagara, in spite of the undeniable fact that there are other things to be done beside reading. I always feel ignorant, and at this point there are, I have no doubt, books to which I shall fail lamentably by not referring. It is a field in which the members of the Warburg and Courtauld Institutes have been especially active. Within the ambit of my own limited reading, I think with admiration and pleasure of Edgar Wind's *Pagan Mysteries in the Renaissance.*

It is possible to consider visual art on the one hand and on the other literature, taken in its widest sense as including psychology and philosophy, as alternative ways towards realizing the nature of perception. That is of course not their only function, nor perhaps the most important, but it is fairly obviously one of them. And from that point of view the thing that immediately strikes us about the former is that art — the practice of visual representation — has a *history,* a history moreover which is on record for study and reflection. If it is objected that literature also has a history, the answer is that, as far as perception is concerned, the study of it may indeed give us the history of *ideas about* perception. What it cannot give us is the history of perception itself. Whereas, if it be true that human perception in general is somehow inextricable from human practice in visual representation, then, since representation undoubtedly has a recorded history that can be studied, it must also be true that perception itself has a history; that it has by no means always been the same as it normally is today.

But to say this is also to say that "primary imagination" has a history. (I use Coleridge's term as the one most convenient to English-speaking people for conveying the concept of perception as activity, a concept which was of course extensively developed by the Romantics as a whole, but which is generally recognized today on other grounds — physiological ones for instance — as well.) And that is something of which it seems to me that "literature," again in its widest sense, has not hitherto taken sufficient account, though there are indications that Coleridge, for one, was feeling his way towards it in his later years. It is here, I would suggest, that those "interacting currents" may turn out to be fruitful; and I am inclined to see a certain concentration of interest, which we have witnessed in the last few decades, on such matters as metaphor, imagery in poetry, symbol and symbolic expression in general, as at least a preliminary swelling of the carpel. That the literary use of symbols to convey "meaning" requires, if it is to be understood historically, some understanding of their use in the visual arts was for instance impressively demonstrated by Erich Auerbach in his *Figura.* Conversely we find in Gombrich's *Symbolic Images* not only a number of pertinent observations on metaphor, but also a whole section on "The Personification of Ideas."

It is almost inevitable that an impulse towards understanding figurative expression historically, that is, as an operation which has evolved into what it is today from a different form in the past, should begin by drawing attention to medieval culture, and to the Renaissance as evincing its transition to our own. It will be felt, and I see signs that it is being felt, that the difference between the way in which figurative representation was experienced in and before the Middle Ages and the way it is experienced now has much to tell us. Perhaps, as Sir Ernst suggests, it was Erwin Panofsky who first imported a new, historical meaning into the term "iconology." If so, he has had a good many followers who have been pointing out in one way and another, and without necessarily employing that term, that it is impossible to apprehend medieval imagery without apprehending medieval consciousness as a characteristic whole, and vice versa. This article is concerned with a phenomenon in the realm of literature and art criticism and I am not of course suggesting that nobody ever had such an insight before. On the contrary I have little doubt that, ever since the great cathedrals were built, numbers of quite naive folk, whether primarily responsive to literature or to art, have been quietly absorbing it through a loving acquaintance with their sculptures and their glass; that in their own way they have fully realized, for example, the basic and inescapable significance of that "prefiguring" interpretation of Old Testament history which Auerbach expounded so lucidly in *Figura.* At need moreover they can get help today, whether directly or through some better-class brochure obtainable on the spot, from the thoroughgoing volumes of Emile Mâle.

Within the realm of specifically literary criticism one symptom of the interaction has been, I would say, a marked tendency towards revaluing the whole genre of allegory. One of our legacies from romanticism had been an unquestioning assumption that an allegory is different in kind from a symbol or a myth, and of course greatly inferior to them. Coleridge insisted on it, and on the whole C. S. Lewis followed him in this respect in his *Allegory of Love.* Certainly I myself grew up into a firm conviction that, while myth and symbol are the product of creative imagination preceding or transcending abstract thought, allegory begins with the abstractions, which it then clothes in a system of lifeless figures and personifications. From a man of taste the verdict must always be: symbols yes, allegories no. By contrast with the living gods and nature-spirits of the old mythology or the seminal images of a modern imagination working symbolically, the dramatis personae of the typical allegory were fixed and bloodless lay-figures, as in the case of Kingsley's *Water Babies,* and their activities a thinly disguised moral sermon. Or as Gombrich himself puts it: "The allegory was felt to be translatable into conceptual language once its conventions were known, the symbol to exhibit that plenitude of meaning that approaches the ineffable." Now one of the things the "iconologists," if I may so loosely designate them, have been demonstrating is that, however it may be for literary critics, this comfortable dichotomy just will not do for allegorical *painting.* "It is a strange language," says Sir Ernst, commenting on Botticelli's *Primavera,* "in which there are no dictionaries . . . because there are no fixed meanings."

Whether or no I am right in detecting a relation of cause and effect, signs there certainly are of very similar second thoughts on allegory in literature. I could point for instance to Harold Bloom's essay on "The Internalization of the Quest Romance" and, more pertinently, to Morton Bloomfield's "A Grammatical Approach to Personification Allegory"; since of all characteristic features of allegory, the "device" of personification is for most moderns the hardest pill to swallow. Extensive footnotes to this essay, which appeared in *Modern Philology* in February, 1963, amount almost to a bibliography of recent contributions on and about the subject in English and other languages. More distinguished however by that historical imagination which I have posited as the special characteristic of iconology is Paul Piehler's *The Visionary Landscape* (Edward Arnold, 1971). Piehler develops his argument by examining in successive chapters six well-known allegories, from Boethius's *Consolation of Philosophy* to *Pearl*, including the *Divine Comedy*. It is, very briefly, that "our" symbol was not an additive correction of, but grew naturally and inevitably out of, "their" allegory. The mistake we have been making was to assume that primary, that is constitutive, imagination is simply something that was discovered in practice at about the time of the Renaissance and was expounded in theory rather later by Romantic philosophy. Whereas in fact it was there already. What took place was its development by individualization. More and more it was felt as located in the individual psyche. More and more it was felt as the activity, not of what was being perceived but of the percipient himself. And medieval allegory is ambivalent to interpretation precisely because it reflects the final "moment" of that long-drawn-out metamorphosis.

Viewed historically, allegory was figurative by inheritance from a prerational mode of perception. The mode of personification, says Gombrich, "is still intimately linked with mythology." But prerational *experience* of images had been steadily fading, and allegory *was* also rational; which meant that its personifications could be, and frequently were, abstract ideas in disguise. Not infrequently they were inextricably both at the same time. If personal intelligence had emerged, as it were, from the shell of cosmic intelligence, broken bits of shell were still tenaciously adhering to it. "Medieval allegory at its best," Piehler points out, "achieved a balance of rational and intuitive elements, an acceptance of all levels on which the mind functions," and he goes so far as to add: "which is the goal of those who seek psychic integration today." It is this "ratio between the imagination and the intellect" which we lose sight of when we see allegory through the spectacles of a Romantic Movement, which insisted that intellect and imagination are hereditary enemies. But it is also this ratio which I suggest the iconologists have been bringing into view in their own field of art history. In his earlier *Art and Illusion* Sir Ernst observed:

> We cannot but look at the art of the past through the wrong end of the telescope. We come to Giotto on the long road which leads from the impressionists back via Michelangelo and Masaccio, and what we see first in him is therefore not lifelikeness but rigid restraint and majestic aloofness.

It is otherwise when we came to Giotto not through what came after but through what went before. And so it is with those "rigid" personifications we associate with allegory, when we feel them (as Sir Ernst himself points out in his latest book) as "the joint offspring of thought and imagination." Allegory becomes as important as symbol, and can be as aesthetically satisfying, only when we deeply realize how it is not just a fashion in secondary imagination that has altered since allegory's heyday, but the operation of primary imagination itself; that we must take account, not only of a change of ideas but also of a change of consciousness—or, if it is preferred, a change in "human nature" itself.

Coming to the art or literature of a period from what went before means coming, not from the outside but from the inside of what went before. At least it certainly does, if the quest is an aesthetic and not merely an antiquarian one. And that which went immediately before the late medieval period, and its culmination in and transition to the Renaissance and what came after, was of course the Greco-Roman period; in terms of consciousness it was the whole Platonic-Aristotelian "mind-set" which preceded our own Newtonian-Darwinian one. Maybe it is partly for this reason that I seem to have detected, alongside the critical currents I have referred to, another rather marked feature of the last few decades. I mean an increased and deepened interest in the system of psychology and cosmology (the two were hardly separable) generally called Neoplatonism. It is not a very satisfactory term, and perhaps it would be difficult to find one for an element easily recognizable as the same in such else divergent quarters as, let us say, Plontinus, St. Augustine, the Kabbalah, Johannes Kepler, and William Blake. Once again I instance a selection of books that have come my way, being well aware that I am likely to have omitted others not less significant. But, in addition to the books I have already referred to here, the following are on my list in this connection: Désirée Hirst's *Hidden Riches*, Elizabeth Sewell's *The Orphic Voice,* Kathleen

Raine's *Blake and Tradition,* M. H. Abrams's *Natural Supernaturalism,* Frances Yates's *The Art of Memory* and other books and articles, and, with a slightly different nuance, C. S. Lewis's *The Discarded Image.* What is it that distinguishes these books and others like them from the treatment usually accorded to the same subject matter during the nineteenth and early twentieth centuries? Not, certainly, that the author has come to "believe in" the traditional lore. Lewis incidentally goes out of his way to disclaim any such thing, and yet the very fact that he felt the disclaimer necessary supports my contention. I can only put it that they are characterized by a much warmer sympathy. However it may be with belief, *dis*belief is no longer an ingredient in their response so pungent as to leave the rest of the mixture insipid.

Reflecting on this palpable change of attitude, the adventurous question I find myself asking is this. Does it possibly betoken the dawn of an "iconological" approach, not only to the history of art and literature but also to history in general? Experience in perception, mind-sets, world-structures, cosmologies have altered in the past. Should we rule out the possibility of their altering no less radically in the future? Moreover our *mental picture of the past* is integral to our cosmology. Supposing we have found that the history of art and literature reveals a change in "the ratio between intellect and imagination"; and further that we cannot apprehend that change without first altering the same ratio within our own minds; is it merely fantastic to imagine us going on to discover that a different ratio between intellect and imagination from the one we have just now been living in is requisite for a correct interpretation of *all* historical, archaeological, and indeed paleontological records? Something of the sort, as Gombrich suggests, appears to have been stirring, as far back as the eighteenth century, in the mind of Giambattista Vico; and a renewed interest in Vico, amounting almost to the rediscovery of him, has accompanied the change of attitude to which I have just been drawing attention.

To perceive the true nature of the relation between intellect and imagination in the history of art, and so also of literature, is at the same time to detect the *error* we have made by projecting back into that history our own newly acquired faculty of intellect-excluding imagination. It has entailed our interpreting as inventions of intellect what were in fact operations of primary imagination. What sort of consequences would ensue if the same new, nonprojective perception should be applied to history in general? What sort of errors should we detect there? Inevitably, as it seems to me, we should have to begin by substantially revising the pride of place accorded to "science," or more properly (since hypothetical reconstructions of an unrepeatable past are not verifiable) to "scientism," in constructing our mental picture of the past. The current image, we should find, is analogous to allegory in its late or decadent form. That is to say, it was conceptualized first (on the line that culminated in Darwinism) and then the concepts were clothed in invented images like that of our popular "cave-man." And by virtue of projecting back into cave-man our own psychological mode of intellect-excluding imagination, we were able to assume that, apart from ignorance and bestiality, the world he perceived was more or less identical with the one we perceive today. And so, when it came to such matters as myth and religion, we interpreted as intellectual inventions what were in fact the operations of primary imagination. This was especially the case in the late eighteenth and the nineteenth centuries. In common with Sir Andrew Aguecheek, the heyday of scientific humanism "had the back-trick simply the best of any man in Illyria." But later on, when psychological theory had been complicated by the new concept of unconscious mind, it was still on substantially the same foundation that the historical interpretations of Freud and Jung were erected. The myths, however unconsciously so, were still subjective inventions "projected" upon the same world as our own. Primary imagination was still left out.

The question then is this. If aesthetically historical imagination, meaning by that the practice of approaching the past, not by projection back from the present but from *inside* its own remoter past, is apt to liquify the illusory "rigidity" of allegorical images, will it be found correspondingly apt to liquify the illusory rigidity of our historical image of ape-cave-man and his exclusive preoccupation with bestially struggling for physical survival? Here, it is true, it amounts to something more like a fixation than an image. Very little examination and reflection are required to reveal it as built in to our entire mental world, the structural keystone in our sciences, our politics, and even our religion. So true it is, to quote once more from *Symbolic Images,* that "our attitude towards the image is inextricably bound up with our whole idea about the universe."

But it is still an inferential, and therefore confessedly an invented image. Meanwhile there is an alternative image of primitive humanity which is not confessedly invented, but which claims on the contrary to have been inherited from the very nature of imagery and its sources. There is one discovery which those who are looking to a history of consciousness beyond the history of ideas can hardly help making, and it is this. The doctrine of evolution common to Neoplatonism in all its divergent manifestations is more in accord than the Darwinian one with the increasingly figured richness we come upon, as we journey back in time so far as surviving expressive records can take us. That is something of an understatement. To postulate *Urdummheit*, or mental nullity, as its *terminus ad quem* is to make a mockery of that journey at all its stages. I suspect the presence among us of an as yet obscure feeling that the former doctrine saves the appearances a good deal better than the latter.

In his *Natural Supernaturalism* M. H. Abrams lays his finger on the difference between the two by remarking that we have transformed Plotinus's emanation into evolution. That is to say, we have ceased to conceive of ascent or "progress" as representing in any sense a "return" to the world of archetypes behind the symbols, to the home where with our authentic humanity we belong. It is the difference between supposing the ascent of man to have been a general progress on all fronts from mental nullity to aesthetic and intellectual competence and supposing his ascent as an intellectual being to have entailed and been accompanied by his corresponding *de*scent as a "symbolic" being, in Panofsky's and Cassirer's sense of the word. At this point I can fancy some stubborn spirit among my readers inquiring frostily: are you seriously anticipating a widespread reversion to Neoplatonism and all its fantasies? No, nothing quite so simple and straightbackward as that. But the crucial issue between ascent only and ascent-cum-descent *is*, I fancy, one that will have to be faced before long by all whose interests lie in the directions I have been considering. And I should say that the necessity of facing that issue will bring into focus an even more crucial one. For the concept of a descent of man presupposes the validity of that overall view of the relation between mind and matter—anathema today to intellectual establishments of both Left and Right—which the Scholastic philosophers classified in their succinct way as the doctrine of *universalia ante rem.*

There is after all so much that can really only be taken seriously on that footing. For example, the interpretation not only of works of art and literature, but of historical events themselves, as prefiguring symbols; on which so much of medieval culture depended, and which Auerbach traced so lovingly in that chapter of *Figura.* Or, more generally, consider Panofsky's third "object of interpretation" in the chapter on "Iconography and Iconology" in *Meaning and the Visual Arts.* He calls it *"intrinsic meaning or content,* constituting the world of *'symbolical' values"*; and it requires for its apprehension that "synthetic intuition," which he defines as "familiarity with the *essential tendencies of the human mind."* What are these tendencies, and how did they come to be essential? Is it not one of them to feel that man is a descended, or "fallen" being, as well as (we hope) an ascending one? And is it not our having ceased to think as well as feel just that that has brought about that "artificial antithesis of Pagan or Christian," of which Gombrich complains because it distorts our appreciation of Botticelli? These reflections have lured me a long way from their modest beginning with the advent of iconology. Too far perhaps; but there is one general conclusion, in which even the frostier sort may acquiesce. To the open-minded—a diminishing fraternity—the age we live in, though far from a reassuring, is at least an interesting one.

Imagination and Inspiration

I want to start by drawing your attention to something that stands at the very beginning of perhaps the greatest of all the documents that have come down to us from the literature of the ancient East. I mean the "Divine Song" as it is called: the *Bhagavad-Gita*. You will all, I am sure, have read it, and you will recall how the scene is set at the opening. Two hostile armies are drawn up in battle array and the fighting is about to begin. But in the moment of extreme tension the warrior-prince Arjuna bids his charioteer drive him to a position between the two armies in order that they may talk for a little. It is done, and Arjuna, who is greatly troubled in his soul, reveals to the charioteer the source of his perplexity and his misery. It lies in the nature of civil war, where kinsman is ranged against kinsman and, for that and other reasons, Arjuna finds in himself no desire to fight. It is not because he is afraid. "I do not wish to kill," he says, "though they kill me." Looking ahead, he sees only evils of all kinds coming of the battle. Families will be disintegrated. All sorts of impiety will become rife. The enemy are criminals or tyrants, and yet if he kills them, he will incur sin. "I do not wish for victory, nor sovereignty, nor pleasures, nor even life." Having finished his long speech, Arjuna casts aside his bow and sits down in his chariot overcome by grief.

The charioteer is Krishna, an avatar of the Deity himself; and the song, as you know, consists of the dialogue that ensues between the man and the God. Krishna's immediate response to Arjuna amounts to an endeavor to transpose the thinking of Arjuna to another level or plane of consciousness altogether — to a fresh dimension, within which all the objections he has raised are irrelevant, because unreal or superseded. The wise grieve for

111

neither the living nor the dead. "Never did I not exist, nor you, nor these princes; nor will any one of us ever hereafter cease to be. . . . There is no existence for that which is unreal; there is no nonexistence for that which is real." So Krishna argues, saying in effect that the true, the real self of Arjuna — as well as that of those he will be killing — is to be found only in an imperishable realm beyond action and beyond expression. "He who thinks one to be the killer and he who thinks one to be the killed, both know nothing. He kills not, is not killed. He is not born, nor does he ever die . . ." and so on. "*Therefore*," says Krishna — and now there comes what is perhaps for most Western readers, on a first reading, a dramatic surprise, if not a rude shock. It shocked Thoreau, and later on it shocked Gandhi. Krishna has raised the discourse, one could say, to the level of the Absolute; he is endeavoring to make Arjuna see it from that perspective. It is a point of view from which the coming battle is irrelevant, because the whole of the world as we know it from the everyday point of view is an unreality, an illusion, a mere catenation of appearances. "*Therefore*," he goes on — but he does not go on to say, as we rather expect: "Therefore withdraw from the battle and from the world and cultivate reality, cultivate the Absolute, cultivate the inexpressible." On the contrary, he utters the surprising conclusion: "*Therefore fight on!*"[1]

There are three prominent features that I want to stress here. First, that the main purpose of the *Gita* is, clearly, to raise the thinking, or the consciousness of the protagonist, Arjuna, from the ordinary plane to a higher one, or into another dimension, to which quite different rules apply; secondly, the means by which this is accomplished is a communication and a revelation made by a spirit-being who already lives on that other plane, in this case a temporarily incarnate one: that is, the God Krishna himself; and thirdly, that we are told not to draw conclusions for the lower plane from the higher one, to which the ordinary logical categories do not apply. Whatever we, or others, do or leave undone is from that higher plane or point of view unreal or unimportant; but we are *not*, from this, to conclude, for instance, with the complacent Frenchman: "*Tout comprendre c'est tout pardonner*," to endorse the papers "No action required" and file them away. On the contrary, we are to behave in exactly the opposite way. We are to follow the rules applicable to the lower plane, the ordinary dimension.

And note particularly, before we leave the *Bhagavad-Gita*, the change of atmosphere that immediately precedes, and then accompanies, that mo-

1. *The Bhagavad-Gita*, II. 18.

ment of vision or of direct experience that occurs later in the poem. In the *argument* Krishna has merely indicated the existence of this higher plane of consciousness. Later he raises Arjuna to an actual experience of it. He does this by revealing himself in his universal, divine nature:

> The great Lord then showed to the son of Pritha his supreme divine form, having many mouths and eyes. . . . If in the heavens, the lustre of a thousand suns burst forth all at once, that would be like the lustre of that mighty one. There the son of Pandu beheld in the body of the God of Gods the whole universe all in one and divided into numerous divisions.[2]

It is indeed another dimension of consciousness—a fundamentally inexpressible one (how inadequate, for instance, is that quantitative reference to "many mouths and eyes"!) and Arjuna shows his numinous awareness of the transition. We are told that his hair stood on end and "he bowed his head before the God, and spoke with joined hands."

There are then two different planes of consciousness with what I will call a "threshold" between them. The poem does not say that the threshold is one that can never be crossed. On the contrary, it is essentially the story of Arjuna's being led across it by Krishna. What the poem does inculcate is that, though it may be crossed, it does not cease for that reason to exist. It must not be forgotten; it must not be left out of account. The two opposite sides of the threshold must never be confused with one another. If they are, the result will be only a worse disorder.

And now I will ask you to put the *Bhagavad-Gita,* and everything to do with Buddhism and the whole oriental tradition out of your minds for a time, and to bring before them instead a much later utterance of a very different nature. I am referring to the verse from William Blake's poem, which he included in a letter to his friend Thomas Butts, and in which he stresses that his own "vision" is always a "double" one. It may be more than double, but it is never less. It is:

> Twofold always. May God us keep
> From single vision, and Newton's sleep![3]

You will be surprised, perhaps a little annoyed, when, having quoted

---

2. *Ibid.,* XI. 9.
3. The letter to Thomas Butts is dated November 22, 1802, and is cited in William Blake, *Letters,* ed. Geoffrey Keynes (New York: Macmillan, 1956), p. 79.

this couplet from Blake, with its emphatic distinction between the kind of vision that is only "single" and the kind that is "twofold" or "double," I *again* call on you to leave Blake behind altogether, while I again go on to speak of something quite different. It is my hope that the spasmodic, or at all events disjointed, beginning of this essay will be mended and justified before it reaches its conclusion.

In the fall of this year I listened to a lecture given to the graduates of Brandeis University by a professor from the Department of Electrical Engineering at M.I.T. His more recent researches had been directed to the theory of optics and the neurology of perception; but he had also, at some stage in his career, practiced as a psychiatrist. He told us that he was much troubled about the behavior of neurons; and more particularly by the kind of intercommunication that appears to go on between them, which he said is both "direct" and "universal." He went on to say that his own science of neurophysiology was in a most unsatisfactory state, and he compared it unfavorably with the science of physics. The physicist had something he could teach; but he, as a neurophysiologist, had literally nothing he could teach—indeed, it was because of this difficulty that he found himself addressing a humanities department, in the vague hope that he might get some useful comment from them. The trouble was, what he called the "mind-body" problem. Physics had come up against this problem, also, but only at a late stage in its development—only now—so that the long history that had led up to it could at least be usefully taught and learned. But neurophysiology came up against this same problem at the very outset. One neuron incorporates the mind-body problem as inexorably as the whole system does; and it is a problem to which no answer has even begun to be found. The problem is that no satisfactory transition has been achieved from a context in which you are talking about what is called "matter" to a context in which you are talking about "mind." He threw out a number of suggestions—conclusions he had felt tentatively inclined to adopt, but in which he felt no confidence. Perhaps, after all, "neuron" is only a kind of word. Perhaps we ought to think of it as a "point of view" rather than as an object. Should we assume that there are two kinds of science: (1) the ordinary one, and (2) a science that is more like an art, where you find out about what you are doing by doing it, rather than by thinking about it? And so on. I should add that, towards the conclusion of his lecture, he told us that, because of its total failure before this problem, he considered that the science of psychology (at all events the psychology of perception) had made no progress whatever in the last hundred years. It had been dead since 1864, the date of Helmholtz's work on optics; and the science of physiology had been equally dead since 1877. Finally, he confided in us that he had been chuckling a good deal to observe his colleagues in the biology department laboriously reaching the same foregone checkmate in their researches into genes and chromosomes.

Now, of course, all this is only a particular example, though I found it a striking one, of something the wide-awake have been aware of for a long time. I mean the existence, in the whole structure of Western thought, of an impassable barrier between what we call "mind" (or what we in fact think of as "mind," whether we call it by that name or by some other) and what we call, or what we in fact think of, as "matter." It remains a barrier that is only masked by determined attempts to ignore it, and is again masked, but not penetrated, by the invention and use of portmanteau terms like "psychosomatic."

The first question I want to raise, then, is this: Is there any connection between this impassable barrier that we are familiar with today and that "threshold" between two planes or dimensions of consciousness on which, as we saw, the message of the *Bhagavad-Gita* and much of the traditional wisdom of the East is based? My own conviction is that the connection is a close one, though it can only be traced historically. In other words, although it would be superficial and indeed inaccurate to identify the one unreflectively with the other, it would not be difficult to show, as a matter of historical development, how the later has grown up out of the earlier.

It would not be difficult, but it would be quite a long business. For instance, the *Bhagavad-Gita* was concerned with the threshold between the self on the one hand and what is ordinarily regarded as "not-self" on the other. But the barrier between mind and matter, in the form in which it has been a problem for natural science, is not obviously identical with this, though it may remind us of it. Tracing historically the mind-body problem with which my M.I.T. professor was so concerned, we are led back not (or not immediately) to the ancient civilizations of the Far East, but rather to the origins of Greek philosophy. And the Greek philosophers did not begin by formulating the problem in terms of a dichotomy between self and not-self. I believe it was not until the time of the later Stoics that there were expressions and ideas for the translating of which we should need to pray in aid such terms as "subject" and "object." What they were concerned about was the apparently unresolvable cleavage between other pairs of opposites, pairs such as "being" and "becoming," "rest" and "motion," "one" and "many." It was through this line of investigation, culminating in Aristotle's treatment of it, that they succeeded in establishing the principle of identity, and of mutually exclusive identities, on which the subsequent thought and life of the West have been based. It was through this line of investigation and this way of thought that a clear distinction between mind and matter first came about.

But we should be careful to note that throughout this time, and for many centuries after the schools of philosophy were closed by Justinian — that throughout the whole of the Middle Ages the logic that is based on the psychology of mutually exclusive identities (and that is therefore so closely involved with the self's awareness of its own identity) was by no means coincident with a distinction between mind and matter. To realize this, one has only to think of Aquinas's elaborate angelology, which is closely integrated with his whole psychological theory, while, in the unphilosophical world of general cultural life, the popularity of the allegorical vision as a literary form, as well as a large number of other features, testifies to the fact that what you got, so to speak, when you had eliminated matter from your considerations, was not the bare isolated self, the pure subject, to which all else that was real was counterposed as object, but something like a nonmaterial world in which the self had its place along with other selves, incarnate or discarnate, other nonmaterial beings, forces, influences, with which the self was in direct and universal communication.

Moreover, all this nonmaterial "other" (if I may lump together in this inelegant expression all that was conceived as nonmaterial, but also as notself) was not necessarily limited in its operations either to the individual psyche of the person concerned or even to his own particular physical body. It included the hierarchy of imperceptible beings that constituted the process of nature itself at the prematerial stages of that process. If *natura naturata* was only accessible through sense-perception, there were other channels of communication between the self and *natura naturans.* It was of course on this whole conception that the highly inaccurate sciences of astrology, alchemy, medieval physiology, medicine, and so forth were largely based.

I do not perhaps need to remind you that natural science as we know it — the science that dates back to the Scientific Revolution and no further — is based above all on one important modification of scientific method. It is that modification which brought it about that what are called "occult qualities" are by definition, or at least by way of axiom, to be altogether excluded from the field of scientific inquiry. But of course all that I have just been speaking of, all that can be called *natura naturans* as distinct from *natura naturata,* all that is not either objectively observable "matter" on the one hand, or simply the observer himself perceiving and thinking on the other, comes under the heading of "occult qualities." And so we reach the dichotomy that was formulated by Descartes, according to which all that is not a human self is matter; and by the time the Scientific Revolution was accomplished, our Western distinction between mind and matter had come, by its own route, to coincide with that much older Eastern one of self from not-self.

You get, in other words, a new awareness, and a greatly enhanced one, of that threshold before which, when he was invited to cross it, Arjuna experienced such overwhelming terror that every hair of his head stood on end. And I believe *our* terror at the thought of being called on to cross it is no less than his. Indeed, I would say it is greater. Only in our case it is disguised from us—or rather its very intensity has led us to conceal its true nature from ourselves. Something of this terror I detect, for instance, in the emotional overtones that accompanied the rejection of the so-called occult qualities from the field of scientific inquiry and which still often accompany any reference to them. It is a commonplace that violent hatred generally has fear somewhere beneath it.

But, rather than expatiating on this, let me try to record some of the responses this new and sharper awareness of an impassable threshold between self and not-self has evoked in Western thought. I have three particular ones in mind.

The first is the simple one with which we are all familiar. It is that view of the world that divides, more sharply than anything else does, the fundamental outlook of the West from the fundamental attitude of the East; and it amounts to a denial that the threshold is a threshold at all. This is perhaps more often an implicit rather than an explicit conviction, and it has been well summed up in the maxim: *De non apparentibus et non existentibus eadem est ratio* (the nonphenomenal is the nonexistent). Coleridge sometimes called it "the despotism of the eye." On this view what I have been calling a "threshold" between two dimensions or planes of consciousness is not a threshold but a terminus. It is the edge of things. If it can be called a boundary at all, it is the boundary between existence and nothing. This was the response of the whole of natural science down to the end of the nineteenth century; it is still the working assumption of most scientists and of course of popular scientism. It does not make much difference whether you call it materialism, or positivism, or by some other name. Followed to its logical conclusion, it will be found to involve denying the existence of the self also. (It is not often thought through so clearly; but I feel the corollary should be mentioned, though it cannot here be pursued.)

In the realm of literature and criticism perhaps the most notable manifestation of this one of my three responses has been the critical theory of
I. A. Richards,[4] based on a dichotomy between referential language on the
one hand, that is propositions *de apparentibus,* and on the other hand the
emotive language, which is all we are in fact uttering when we purport to
be propounding *de non apparentibus.*

Before I go on to my second response, I must say something of a further development that took place in the status of what I am calling the
"threshold." It is as if more and more matters were being drawn into its
sphere of influence, to be split between one side of it and the other. We
have seen how the threshold between mind and matter has become also a
threshold between self and not-self. With the coming of Immanuel Kant
and the almost universal acceptance of Kantianism it becomes, in addition,
a threshold between two more pairs of opposites: namely the knowable
and the unknowable. From one point of view this represents a fortifying
and strengthening of the barrier, since that becomes in theory even more
impassable. But note, on the other hand, that acceptance of Kantianism
also rules out the first response. For those who accept it, Kantianism rein-
states the threshold as being in fact a threshold, that is a boundary, between two worlds and not simply the terminus of the only world there is.
As far as science is concerned, this perhaps made little difference—though
it was otherwise with the *philosophy* of science, so far as there is one—because for the practicing scientist the distinction between the unknowable
and the nonexistent is not important. In philosophy it led to the whole not
ignoble development of subjective idealism. In literature and art and criticism I seem to detect, as the result of this further modification of the
threshold, what I can only call the mood of withdrawal, irony, sometimes
defeatism, which has enthralled the culture of the West for the last hundred years or so—the kind of romanticism, for instance, that is called
"negative," an ironical acceptance of human limitations being substituted
for any endeavor to expand them.

To one or other of the two responses I have outlined I suppose we also
owe, in the realm of theology, the rise of ethical secularism, and more lately, its modified form of the demythologizing principle. Myths all sprang
from the illusion that the threshold can be crossed by the human mind, or
could at one time be so crossed. But the threshold is in fact immutable and
eternal, so the myths must be scrapped. So runs the tale. It only remains to
add, as touching these first two responses, that both of them also lead in-

4. Cf. I. A. Richards, *Principles of Literary Criticism* (New York: Harcourt, Brace,
1928); and *Coleridge on Imagination* (New York: Harcourt, Brace, 1935).

evitably to the scientific *impasse* I referred to some while back, that is, the intractableness of what my lecturer called "the mind-body problem." The difficulty here is that it is not simply scientific theory, but the scientific *method* itself that rules out any approach to the problem. It cannot be otherwise, so long as that method continues to assume as given the proposition: *De non apparentibus et non existentibus eadem est ratio.*

I come, then, to the third response, and with that to the real subject of my essay. For there has been yet another alteration in the status of the threshold, and one which is characteristic most of all of our own day, though it began to show itself here and there many years ago. And what I have in mind now is a growing suspicion—at first no more than a suspicion, a hint here, a speculation there, an actual discovery somewhere else—all of which go to suggest that this threshold is not after all so utterly impassable as we in the West had been led to suppose.

It seems to me that quite a number of events, or developments, have joined together in bringing about this last alteration, but I shall mention only three of them. The order in which I have placed them is not significant. The first was the reluctant recognition by the Western intellect that mind and consciousness are not synonymous; that there is a realm, or a sphere, or a mode of being, or a dimension, in which events and activities occur that can only be classified as "mental," notwithstanding the fact that they are unconscious. (It will be recalled that, on a strictly Cartesian view, anything which is not self-conscious must be classified as "matter.") We associate this development with the name of Freud, and it is Freud who has made "the unconscious" a household word. But the admission was forced from us before Freud was born, when even so staunch a positivist as Herbert Spencer was obliged to concede that: "Mysterious as seems the consciousness of something which is yet out of consciousness, we are obliged to think it." Incidentally this mysterious category (a consciousness of which we are not conscious) had formed an integral part of Coleridge's concepts of *genius* and of *imagination* and of the fundamental distinction he divined between the *understanding* and the *reason*, of which I shall have a little more to say at the conclusion of this essay. Coleridge's positive intuition was largely ignored; but the hesitating admission of the same truth that was afterwards forced on an honest Victorian intellect by the facts of life, has of course grown in our time to a general acceptance, one could say a taking-for-granted, that there is a dimension of mind, a reaction to experience that we can only describe in terms of conscious mind, but that is sharply cut off from our self-consciousness and yet is not entirely irrelevant to it. It is a realm that is governed by quite different laws from those which we recognize and obey in our conscious waking lives. There is a threshold between the two worlds, but we cross it in sleep, and in our remembered dreams we even bring back, though usually in an unintelligible form, something of the goings on upon that further side of it. That the being called man spends about one-third of his time asleep is a fact that for centuries had been simply ignored by Western philosophy and psychology, though the business of that philosophy and especially of that psychology had been to determine the nature of man. Now at last that omission has been, in a measure, rectified.

The second event was itself a kind of crossing of a threshold – a threshold that had existed and remained largely impenetrable, at least since the separation of the Western Church from the Eastern. From the moment when Sir William Jones of the British East India Company made up his mind to learn Sanskrit the epoch began in which actual acquaintance with the immemorial religious and philosophic thought of the East more and more took the place of the thoroughgoing ignorance that had hitherto prevailed. We have seen something of the different nuance with which the threshold between conscious and unconscious, between self and not-self, has always had in that tradition. I believe it would be difficult to exaggerate the importance of this new direct impact of the Eastern mind upon the Western, though I have no time to trace its variously ramifying consequences.

The third event, or development, was the gradual recognition of *imagination* as the most indispensable factor in the production of works of art, and particularly perhaps, of poetry. And here I would emphasize that the essential, the distinguishing feature of imagination, as such, is that the whole concept of it is founded on the assumed intransigence of that threshold between mind and matter of which I have previously spoken. Of course there are images or copies in the phenomenal world of objects also in the phenomenal world, but these are not aesthetically significant. When we think of an image or a symbol, we think of something that is impassably divided from *that of which* it is an image – divided by the fact that the former is phenomenal and the latter nonphenomenal. The mystery resides in the fact that we also assume an all-important relation between the two. Imagination is, in this respect, entirely correlative to post-seventeenth-century scientific method. It depends for its existence on the exclusion of any so-called supernatural operation. Perhaps this is brought out most clearly when we contrast it with its predecessor in the terminology of aesthetics: *inspiration.* For inspiration implies, in a greater or less degree, the actual possession of the poet by a nonphenomenal being other than himself. I am not of course referring to the watered-down tradition, in pursuance of which an eighteenth-century poet would still invoke his "muse," but to the deadly serious doctrine of *mania* (divine frenzy, divine possession, *enthousiasmos*)—of which the drawing-room "muse" was not more than a faint echo—the doctrine that prevailed, as E. R. Curtius puts it in his book *European Literature and the Latin Middle Ages,* "through the entire millennium which extends from the conquest of Rome by the Goths to the conquest of Constantinople by the Turks."[5] *Mania* amounted of course to the advent of an actual visitant from the farther side of the threshold to the hither side. If we want to understand the concept, the idea of inspiration, we must think, not of the eighteenth- or nineteenth-century poet decorously invoking his muse in the seclusion of his study, but of something more like what happened to the Cumaean Sibyl before she began to speak to Virgil. And perhaps the best way of observing the gradual process by which the concept of inspiration disappeared and that of imagination entered to take its place, is to study in some detail the histories of some of the technical terms that comprise the uncertain vocabulary of aesthetic discourse; to trace, for example, the progress of such a word as *genius* from its original meaning of "a tutelary spirit," parallel, but by no means identical, with the human personality it accompanied, down to its modern meaning.

And what is its modern meaning? This is a thing about which there is perhaps no very general agreement. But all, or nearly all, seem to be agreed on this: that it is proper nowadays to think of genius as something that functions "within" the man rather than in any sense outside of, or separable from, him. Yet there is still a noticeable reluctance to identify the genius wholly with the personality, and indeed there are great difficulties in doing so. It is almost as though the problem for the theorist of imagination is to retain the concept of inspiration, while at the same time rejecting it! Thus Coleridge spoke, in connection with Shakespeare's genius, of his "possessing the spirit" instead of being "possessed by it," and elsewhere he refined his notion to "the genius within the man of genius." "There is," he writes in his "Essay on Poesy or Art," "in genius itself an unconscious activity; nay, that is the genius in the man of genius."[6]

Today I suppose we tend to identify, or at least to connect, a man's genius with his unconscious being rather than with his self-conscious personality, and we are very ready to locate that unconscious as "within"

5. Trans. Willard R. Trask (New York: Pantheon, 1953), p. 474.
6. Samuel Taylor Coleridge, "Essay on Poesy or Art," in *Biographia Literaria,* ed. (with his aesthetical essays) J. Shawcross (London: Oxford University Press, 1962), p. 258.

rather than "without" him, though what we mean by "in" and "out" in such a context is never very clear. The point I wish to make is that, whatever we mean, there is still, by the very nature of the unconscious, that forbidding threshold between the two dimensions of his being. When a man speaks or acts as genius, his unconscious is operative at least *as well as* his self-conscious personality, if not sometimes actually instead of it. You will note that I have said "his" unconscious, though it could well be argued that I was not justified in doing so. Whether that other, that unconscious side of the threshold, is indeed to be included under the heading of "self" and, if so, whether wholly or only partially, would appear to be just the sort of question around which those who are interested in image and metaphor and symbol and meaning (myself among them) are apt to buzz like flies around a honeypot, or wasps around an intruder.

Now very different considerations apply to the exercise of imagination, on the one hand, and, on the other, to any attempt to *investigate* its nature. The poet remains content with the fact of the threshold, whether it is regarded as fixed between self and not-self, or between conscious and unconscious, or between mind and matter; indeed he works with it, avails himself of it. It is the force of gravity to the overcoming of which his athletic power of jumping is directed, but *without* which he could not exercise that power at all. It is different with the theorist. *He* is obliged, however much he may dislike the idea, to apply his ratiocination not only to this side of the threshold, but also to the other. For, in investigating the working of imagination in symbol and image, he is almost by definition investigating the relation between the two sides; and it is simply a fact that you cannot consider the *relation* between two things or states unless you know something about *both* of the two things themselves.

The existence of this very great difficulty renders all the more surprising a cultural phenomenon that I seem to myself have been noticing for some time now: namely, that the general level—I would even say the general level of achievement—of philosophical criticism (that is of talk *about* such things as poetry, images, and metaphors, and much that is related thereto) has for some time been considerably higher than the general level of the poetry itself that is being written in our time. But since that kind of talk is precisely the kind we are all engaged in, and lest it should be thought that I am inculcating an unbearable complacency, I hasten to ask the question I have all along been leading up to: namely, Can we nevertheless feel that the directions that kind of talk has been taking, and the features of the problem on which it has been concentrating, are really the most fruitful ones? "The talks continue," as we so often read in political bulletins when some high-level conference is in progress. Can we really feel that the talks are in a very satisfactory state?

I do not personally feel that we can. And it is here I believe that Krishna's warning to Arjuna and Blake's aphorism may both be relevant considerations for us. The *Bhagavad-Gita,* you remember, emphasizes that the two sides of the threshold must be kept distinct from one another. Blake insisted that "single vision" is disastrous. And here let me interpose that imagination and a faculty of "double vision" seem indeed to be almost inseparable. When Blake supposed someone asking him if, looking at the sun, he did not see "a round thing somewhat like a guinea," he replied: "Oh no, no, no, but an immeasurable Company of the Heavenly Host crying Holy, Holy, Holy is the Lord God Almighty." He did not in my view mean by this that he was incapable of *also* seeing something like a guinea. Had that been so, he would have been mad. Imagination, in fact, presupposes "double" vision and not simply the substitution of one kind of single vision for another. It requires a sober ability to have the thing both ways at once. May it not be that, if we have reached a stage at which both sides of the threshold are now to be found "within" us, instead of one side being within and the other without—if what was once inspiration is now imagination—nevertheless we must not lose sight of the fact that there is still that threshold between them?

If we do lose sight of it, as I suggest we have been tending to do, if for instance we endeavor to speak, or even to think, of the further side in ideas formed only on this side, in categories of thought and modes of speech, which are almost by definition only applicable to this side, then an unhappy consequence seems to follow. I venture to nickname this unhappy consequence "the curse of Babel" because the Tower of Babel may be seen as the symbol of an endeavor to penetrate a threshold—the threshold between Earth and Heaven—by using materials exclusively manufactured on the hither side of it. And I am thinking of the danger (when some of those concrete inklings from beyond the threshold are seized hold of and converted into abstract propositions) of our getting more and more involved in a kind of spider's web of increasingly abstract, increasingly contentless, and increasingly sesquipedalian jargon, of which the final effect is only to fatigue and bewilder ourselves and our readers—and perhaps to provide an array of new and legitimate targets for the prowling hosts of linguistic analysis.

If, on the other hand, we fall into the opposite error—if we remain vividly aware of the threshold—but at the same time overlook the fact that it is now within ourselves—then there appears to ensue an unhappy consequence of a different kind. This is perhaps the curse of Zacharias (who, you will recall, was stricken dumb on coming out of the Temple—that is, on recrossing the threshold). Here the threshold, in spite of its being within us and thus under the ultimate jurisdiction of our own wills, is still treated as though it were the old Kantian one between the knowable and the forever unknowable. According to this attitude, though we may have inklings of eternity and moments of ecstasy to which we can refer, we cannot *speak* of, we cannot *express* the nature of, the further side at all. All we can really do therefore is to place that very impotence on record. Personally I believe this view embodies a deep and all-important truth and I believe that it is well that this truth should be expressed, well moreover that it should be expressed both discursively and poetically and by different people, and more than once. But further than that I cannot go, and I cannot, in particular, see any future for it. Because, whatever melodious cadences or cunningly emphasized absurdities the message may be wrapped up in, I believe there is a limit to the number of times a man can profitably inform his neighbor, or be informed by him, that the inexpressible cannot be expressed.

You see the dilemma in which I suggest we tend to find ourselves. Either we strive to discuss metaphor, symbol, image, and meaning in the ordinary terms of logical discourse—in which case, because imagination almost by definition transcends logic, we become entangled in a more and more complicated mesh of thinner and thinner intellectual abstractions; *or* we cut through that Gordian snarl by proclaiming that meaning is something that cannot be talked about at all. But if that is indeed so, and if it also applies to the robes of meaning, her images and her symbols, then the outlook for further books of this nature is presumably poor!

It is true that, as an alternative to falling silent altogether, I have sometimes heard it said that the meaning of a poetic symbol can indeed be spoken of, but only in other poetic symbols. This would mean one point of view on the subject still being confronted with another, but not by way of dialectical exchange—only by way of contrast or competition. If *this* is the correct view, it would seem that future discussions about metaphor, symbol, image, and meaning will be much less like symposia and much more like what the Welsh call an eisteddfod, or like what used to happen from time to time at Nuremberg in the time of Hans Sachs—a competition between rival Meaning-singers.

Personally, I only see one way out of this difficulty. Since it is not an easy or an obvious way, my attempt to adumbrate it is, I fear, going to in-

volve me in all sorts of sins of omission and commission, in reckless assertions, rash prophecies, provocative heterodoxies. To begin with an example
of the last—and thus to get it over and done with—I have been coming to
feel for some time that imagination, *as an end in itself,* is a vein that has
been, or very soon will be, worked out. I am in doubt whether much more
that is really significant can be done with it.

Professor Kathleen Coburn, in her introduction to the edition of Coleridge's *Notebooks*[7] that she has in hand, commits herself to the statement
that "interest in the theory of imagination has now become almost synonymous with interest in Coleridge." In the belief that she may be right, I have
thought fit to put what I now have left to say in the form of an exposition
and interpretation of some of the principles and conclusions arrived at by
Coleridge in that long period of his life that elapsed after he himself had
passed from the exercise of imagination in poetry to the business of thinking and talking about imagination in general.

In the first place we must be clear that poetic imagination was only one
aspect of the imagination in which Coleridge was interested. I am not here
referring to his distinction between "primary" and "secondary" imagination, but to that concept of what he calls the "philosophic imagination,"
to which is devoted practically the whole of the long preparatory chapter
that immediately precedes the chapter of his *Biographia Literaria* in which
that other famous distinction is made.

In the second place Coleridge was acutely aware of that "threshold" of
which I have been speaking here and aware of it in its most highly sharpened Western form, that is to say, he was aware of it as being fixed at
once between self and not-self, between mind and matter, and between
conscious and unconscious. That was why the words "subject" and "object" occurred so frequently in his vocabulary. "Subject" to him meant the
self as active mind. "Nature" was "all that is merely objective." "Matter"
he defined as "that *of which* we are conscious but which is in itself unconscious."[8]

Thirdly, he was interested in imagination as the best-known means of
preserving a right relation between the two sides of the threshold. And it
was precisely because the threshold is also a threshold between conscious
and unconscious that imagination could perform this function. It could do
so because, as he puts it, there is a "consciousness which lies beneath or (as

7. S. T. Coleridge, *Notebooks,* ed. Kathleen Coburn (New York: Pantheon, 1957).
8. S. T. Coleridge, *Biographia Literaria,* I, 174–75.

it were) behind the spontaneous consciousness natural to all men" or, as he also puts it, because the mind "can be rendered intuitive of the spiritual in man (i.e., of that which lies on the other side of our natural consciousness)."[9]

What did this becoming "intuitive of the spiritual in man" signify? Some moment of ecstasy, some inexpressible, unrepeatable high spot of generally enhanced awareness, such as LSD without meaning, as well as poetic symbolism without meaning, can probably supply? By no means. It was a form of *knowledge,* but of knowledge that is to be won only *with the help* of imagination. And this involved the whole being of the knower, not, as in logical discourse, of his brain only. It is well enough known that Coleridge held that poetry involves "bringing the whole soul of man into activity." It is much less well known that he held the same view about what he called "the knowledge and acknowledgment of ideas."

What then does he mean by ideas? He has told us in many different ways in many different places. In what follows I shall have to content myself largely with a series of quotations.

Mere impressions and notions are not "ideas"; Why? "Because they lack the activating power of the will." "Ideas correspond to substantial being, to objects the actual subsistence of which is implied in their idea, though only by the idea revealable. To adopt the language of the great philosophical Apostle, they are spiritual realities that can only be spiritually discovered." And again: "There is a gradation of ideas, as of ranks in a well-regulated army."[10]

What it is that Coleridge meant by the word "idea" can only be grasped when we have also grasped his distinction between understanding and reason. The understanding is the isolated intellect of each one of us, but the reason that irradiates it is superindividual. It was because Coleridge was psychologist as well as philosopher, and it was because the superindividual reason is also the unconscious (of which we normally become conscious only as "matter"), that he could develop his concept of the philosophic imagination as the organ by which that irradiation is accomplished. Again, it is because the threshold between unconscious and conscious is now also the threshold between matter and mind that he could see in the ideas of reason the true link between the hither and the farther side of the threshold. For the idea is neither subjective nor objective. What in its subjective aspect is idea, in the objective aspect may, for instance, be a law of nature.

9. *Ibid.*
10. Cf. *ibid.,* II, 259.

To identify, as he did, the unconscious self with superindividual reason involves the transference of "the unconscious" from the category of the unknowable to the category of the specifically knowable. Thus, he affirms in the *Biographia Literaria* that, just as "all the organs of sense are framed for a corresponding world of sense," so "all the organs of spirit are formed for a correspondent world of spirit, though the latter organs are not developed in all alike."[11] When the two sides of the threshold are neither prudently distinguished in the mind nor truly united in the will, the result is either the confusion of Babel or the *O Altitudo!* of an impotent silence. When the two opposite sides of it are run together in the understanding, with the insulating membrane between them rudely torn and shattered, they explode in the resulting short circuit into a chaotic pus of the meaningless or the absurd. It is otherwise when the two are held separate, yet united, in the tension which is polarity. And this is what happens when the idea, which is neither objective nor subjective, is intuited or realized by the philosophic imagination. Then it is that the threshold becomes like Aladdin's ring, yielding new meanings for old and giving birth to a future that has originated in present creativity instead of being a helpless copy of the outwardly observed forms of the past.

There remains the question of terminology. It may be argued that this so-called philosophic imagination, supposing it is admitted, is something so different from poetic imagination that the same label ought not be applied to both. I think that is very likely so. It may well be that a *generalized* awareness of the farther side of the threshold is the ultimate goal, the *ne plus ultra,* of anything that can, with due observance of linguistic usage, be signified by the term "imagination."

A particularized awareness, an advance from excited inkling to sober knowledge, could be another matter. The task of imagination, as Coleridge himself has defined it, is to apprehend the "unity in multeity" of the objective world. When his further researches led him on to approach the further task of apprehending the multeity in unity of the subjective world, it may be that he would have done better to draw his distinction, not between poetic imagination and philosophic imagination, but between imagination in general and something else. I want in conclusion to suggest that the proper name for this something else would have been "inspiration"—but an inspiration very different from the old type of inspiration—the *mania,* or "possession," which was the historical predecessor of imagination. I would suggest that the inspiration that Coleridge dimly divined as the *successor* of imagination is to be a transformed inspiration, an

11. Cf. *ibid.,* I, 167.

interiorized one. Yet I would give it the name of inspiration, because it involves the notion of some communication with individual entities, individual beings beyond the threshold; and this was also characteristic, though in a different way, of inspiration in its former sense.

Such a faculty, such a development of epistemological method, will of course reach out far beyond the realm of literature and of talk about literature. It would, for example, be as indispensable to my M.I.T. professor and his associates as to the creative writer. The planners of the future shape of society need it no less urgently. That does not trouble me, for I feel that literature, like many other things, is most itself when it is reaching out beyond itself. *Within* the realm of literature, and particularly of the use of imagery and metaphor, I seem to see it leading to many changes. Indeed, the final prophecy I shall hazard is perhaps my greatest heterodoxy of all. For I am inclined to see any advance from imagination to inspiration as entailing the sort of change that sounds at first more like a retreat than an advance—like a retreat to some of the types of semantic usage we generally regard as superseded.

Thus, one of the outstanding characteristics of all kinds of "tensile" language, as opposed to "steno-language" (if I may adopt Professor Wheelwright's useful terminology)[12] is that it has many meanings, or potential meanings. The vehicle of a metaphor, for instance, may be fixed enough, but the tenor is polysemous—and thus ambiguous also. I think we may now have to find terms and phrases of which the *tenor* will be monosemous—though it will still be the tenor of a vehicle, and not a piece of steno-language. That was also a characteristic of the mode of personification, and of allegory as opposed to myth or symbol. Personification is monosemous and it is not ambiguous, yet as long as it continues to be uttered and apprehended with "double vision," it functions as a metaphor—even (as Professor Morton Bloomfield pointed out in February, 1963, in an article in *Modern Philology*) as a metaphor with especially vigorous potentialities. I do not see us profitably returning to the rhetorical devices of personification and allegory as they were known in the past, but I do hazard the prophecy that, if imagination advances towards transformed inspiration, it will be accompanied by something like a transition from metaphor to transformed personification and from myth and symbol to transformed allegory. It will be a question of finding a kind of tensile language that is not merely polysemously suggestive, but of which the

12. Cf. Philip Wheelwright, *The Burning Fountain: A Study in the Language of Symbolism* (Bloomington: Indiana University Press, 1954), and *Metaphor and Reality* (Bloomington: Indiana University Press, 1962).

words convey reasonably identifiable and repeatable meanings – the kind of meanings that we can hold, so to speak, between our lips, and taste and explore them with our tongues while we do so, though if we attempted to seize them with our teeth they would collapse into dust . . . "soft-focus" meanings.

One of the things that images, metaphors, and symbols do is to develop and strengthen our faculty of imagination. For without that we soon find that we can make nothing of them. It could be that, in a time still to come, this faculty, once it has been so developed, will be valued, not primarily as an end in itself, but rather as a preliminary training in a whole new way of using language – a way that will be neither vague and inaccurate on the one hand nor rigid and definition-ridden on the other. Language so used would be the true utterance of "double vision" inasmuch as it would embody a simultaneous, and yet not an *intermeddling,* awareness and acceptance of both the two opposite sides of the threshold. And it could be that it is only in some such language that effective and badly needed inspirations from beyond the threshold that is fixed between the subjective potency of humanity and its objective perceptions can ever be either uttered or apprehended.

Language and Discovery

The last forty or fifty years have witnessed a rapid and accelerating growth of interest in philosophical problems connected with the nature of language. When I was a boy, people turned and stared if they saw an automobile; when I was a young man, they stared at anyone who used the epithet "semantic." They don't stare any longer.

It is noticeable that this attention paid to language, which has expanded so rapidly, has done so in two sharply divergent directions. There is the analytical school, for whom the study of language is a department of symbolic logic or of information theory, and sometimes also of physiology. On the other hand there is a more nebulous body of thinkers, for whom the word "symbolic" has quite a different meaning and for whom, if it is a department of anything, the study of language is a department of psychology, mythology, ontology — or of poetics.

As far as I can see, intercommunication between these two schools is very slight, if not nonexistent, though they are occasionally heard abusing each other. Nevertheless a bird's-eye view of both of them (if such a thing were possible) would, I believe, reveal *one* tendency they have had in common. Logical positivism and its successor in title, linguistic analysis, have both stressed the dubious propriety, if not the impossibility, of distinguishing the "meaning" of language from language itself. And, from the opposite direction, the other school — those who (like myself) are mainly interested in the *figurative* aspect of language — have, rather more lately, been showing a pronounced tendency towards reaching a similar conclusion, although on different grounds.

The people I have in mind as constituting this second group are those who, with all sorts of internecine differences of approach and emphasis, share a common concern with such matters as metaphor and simile, and thus of parabolic utterance in general—all those rhetorical practices, or more purely linguistic phenomena, by virtue of which "more is meant than meets the ear." It is a wide field. Even if we exclude such extensions as myth and confine ourselves to poetry or literature, it is a wide field. One has only to think of the different ways it has been handled by such writers as the French symbolists or the Anglo-Saxon imagists—Valéry, Mallarmé, Amy Lowell, T. E. Hulme, Ezra Pound—and later by such critics as I. A. Richards or William Empson, apart from a host of less well-known writers, to be reminded just how wide it is. And I ought not to omit the striking figure of Susanne Langer, with a foot in both camps, inasmuch as her first publication was a primer of symbolic logic, whiler her later work has given us *Philosophy in a New Key, Feeling and Form,* and *Problems of Art.* They remind us that the field is by no means limited to literature. The issue of, for instance, the true function of metaphor in poetry raises the whole question of image and symbol in general and the part they play at almost all levels of human consciousness. Such names as Eliseo Vivas, Merleau Ponty, Joseph Campbell come to mind, and there are many others. And again we are led through the wider question into that vast structure of imagery and symbols, the traditional myths; and thus into the history of human consciousness itself: Ernst Cassirer, C. G. Jung, Mircea Éliade will serve for examples.

It is not less obvious that the topic of symbolism, and particularly of symbolism in language, will be felt to have an important bearing on the interpretation of religious documents including the Old and New Testaments. This has in fact been the case. For example, we have seen, over the same period, a rather novel view of the nature and function of parable in the New Testament and in Christian experience; a view very different from the older allegorical definition of "an earthly story with a heavenly meaning." The names of Fuchs, Ebeling, Van Buren will come to the minds of any who have concerned themselves with it, and the field was very fully explored and expanded by Dr. Robert O. Funk in 1966 in his book *Language Hermeneutic and the Word of God.*

Last but not least there has been the distinctively philosophical approach: those nonanalytical philosophies of language, in which I suppose the outstanding names are Heidegger and the later Wittgenstein.

Now there are two observations I want to make about the subject matter of this hurried survey. The first concerns a *tendency* and the second a *difficulty.* As to the first, I have already suggested that the tendency all these developments have in common has been an increasing endeavor to find the meaning of language confined within language itself; without, that is to say, looking beyond it to something other than language, to which its words are to be taken as "referring." More technically expressed, there is evidence of a strong desire to integrate meaning with the linguistic structures by which the meaning is revealed, to treat language as an end in itself rather than as a means to an end—to classify it as an *event*, rather than as a means of reference, or of imparting information. Thus, just as the imagists told us that in our poetry "the object is the image," and as we hear of "symbols without meaning," so the parables in the Gospels are to be received, not as allegories pointing beyond themselves, but as veritable happenings. Whether Marshall McLuhan's doctrine that "the medium is the message" is to be regarded as the culmination, or the *reductio ad absurdum*, of the tendency will depend on how formidable we feel to be the *difficulty,* to which I now turn.

I suspect the difficulty is already obvious enough to all who are not deeply habituated to the line of thought I have been trying to advocate. It is that language, by definition (that is to say, by virtue of its very nature *as* language) *does* point beyond itself. When a man talks, we are affected by what he says precisely because we assume that he is talking about *something*—and that that something is *not* simply the effect he hopes his talking is going to have on us. He may want to get at our ganglia, but he will succeed in doing so only as long as we are convinced that he is not talking *about* our ganglia. Thus, when I. A. Richards long ago distinguished the "emotive" language of poetry from the "referential" language of science, and insisted that the semantic function of emotive language is not to make statements but to arouse emotion, he overlooked the fact that emotive language arouses emotion precisely *because* it is taken to refer to something; and to something other than the emotion. For talking about an emotion will neither express nor arouse it; rather the opposite. Lovers do not intend to talk about the emotion of love; they intend to talk qualitatively about each other, and a speaker's intention *is* his meaning; indeed it is another word for it.

This difficulty is, for me, so fatal that I cannot find any more profundity in the proposition that "a poem must not mean, but be" than I could in the proposition, say, that "a satellite must not orbit, but stop still." Alas, it is by virtue of orbiting that it *is* a satellite at all. In the same way, it is by virtue, not of orbiting but of leading, or pointing, or hinting, or referring—what you will, but certainly of relating in *some way*—to what is other than its own syllables that a word is a word at all. Words are only themselves by being more than themselves. Perhaps the same thing is true of human beings.

This, then, is the difficulty which the operators within the tendency are always up against, and which they seek to evade by inventing various new and cautious formulations of a depressingly self-contradictory nature. We hear them fastidiously manipulating such terms of art as "nonobjectifying language," "symbols without meaning," "self-reference," and so forth. But it is a difficulty which, as far as my understanding goes, not even Heidegger or Wittgenstein ever really surmounted or even faced, and I become painfully aware of it the moment I get around to reading their works or those of their exponents and commentators.

Perhaps all this may have suggested that I consider I have simply refuted all the distinguished people I have been talking about and proved that they have nothing important to tell us. On the contrary I have a strong feeling that they are trying to tell us something very important indeed, and even that the tendency I have outlined may one day prove to have evinced a sort of turning point in the history of ideas; or (which I think more important and a more likely place for turning points) in the history of consciousness. That is just why I feel so uncomfortable. I am *im*pressed by the tendency and *op*pressed by the difficulty; and I oscillate uneasily between the one feeling and the other—rather as those who go along with the tendency seem to oscillate between a somehow pregnant conviction that language does not "refer" and the necessity, which arises as soon as they open their mouths, of assuming that it does.

When you find yourself caught in a tangled and frustrating situation, so that the mind seems to be grinding to a stop from the friction generated by the rapid motions of its attempts to escape, it is sometimes a good thing to step clean off the particular track, on which you have been shuttling to and fro between one horn of a dilemma and the other, and approach the situation from a different direction altogether. On that principle I want to cease now from looking at the approaches to the problem of language made from an initial standpoint of poetry, etymology, semantics, psychology, theology, philosophy, and look at another one altogether: an approach from the initial standpoint of natural science. I emphasize the term "*initial* standpoint," because the relation between language and science has, of course, also received consideration from those other standpoints. One recalls, for example, Max Black's *Models and Metaphors* or Colin Turbayne's *The Myth of Metaphor.* But these authors, and others like them, approached language from *within* the language tradition itself, or certainly from within the humanities. As against this it is interesting, and it might be helpful, to watch someone approaching language from within the scientific tradition. And in this context science means, above all, physics. Not only do we see most of the other sciences busy trying to resolve themselves into physics, but physics alone is the fundamentally epistemological science, because only physics today seeks to investigate, not just the *behavior* of matter or of nature, but the *nature* of nature. A physicist may for that reason be less out of sympathy than the rest with a topic so ontological as the nature of language.

We should however expect a scientist, trained as such, by virtue of his whole habit of thought, to start with an even heavier bias in favor of "reference" than the ordinary user of language, let alone poets, theologians, and philosophers. When he makes a discovery, he certainly does not consider he has made a discovery about language. How could there be anything in common between his intellectual adventures and those of a Wittgenstein or a Heidegger?

Apparently it is not so impossible, since it was a physicist who remarked a few years ago that:

> One of the most remarkable characteristics common to the developments in modern physics is the revolutionary change in fundamental notions which has been brought about by the recognition of *new forms* of language in physics rather than by the introduction of new physical *content* into previous language forms.

Professor David Bohm, the physicist to whom I am referring, on one occasion illustrated this contention with the examples of Albert Einstein and Niels Bohr, the principal exponents respectively of relativity and quantum theory. Thus, Einstein resolved the confused situation concerning the relation between mechanics and electrodynamics, which prevailed towards the close of the nineteenth century, but he did so by showing that the old language had become irrelevant:

> His insight was based on the perception that it was no longer fruitful to continue with efforts to change the content of physics, as described in terms of the older language forms (for example, by making new assumptions about the properties of the ether). Thus, room was made for thinking in terms of a different language form, one that allowed a new kind of description of space and time as mutually related and dependent on general physical conditions, such as velocity, acceleration, gravitational fields, etc.

Similarly Niels Bohr

> perceived the uselessness of the efforts to change only the *content* of
> these classical laws (for instance, by looking for mechanical explana-
> tions of the "quantum"). And, as happened with Einstein in a different
> context, room was then made for a new kind of language form that al-
> lowed for novel modes of description (which for example did not con-
> tinue the traditional description in terms of separation of the observer
> from the observed).

Out of such initial considerations Bohm has been developing an interesting critique of the coexistence, among modern physicists, of what he terms
"formal language forms" on the one hand and "informal language forms"
on the other. Formal language forms comprise mathematical formulae; informal language forms comprise the language of ordinary discourse—which
however is always required for the general *description* of any subject of
scientific enquiry. Total diremption of the informal from the formal language would reduce physics *to* mathematics.

The system of mental constructs called mathematics is, I suppose, about
as "self-referring" a language form as could well be imagined—and *yet* it is
also effective outside itself, effective both in discovery and in operation.
So much so, that it has given birth to our present technological civilization.
But it is only by returning from time to time from the informal language
to the formal language of description that this connection with natural
process can be maintained. Bohm maintains moreover that the unresolved
duality between the two language forms has been operating to *conceal* the
revolutionary change in language form which has in fact been taking place.
There has been a steadily increasing tendency to assume that informal
language forms no longer matter much, and that all the real business of
physics is transacted in formal language—its informal brother being confined to those invented "models," whose sole function is to give to the
poor layman with no mathematics some sort of fanciful picture of what is
being (or perhaps is not being) talked about. He denies this and insists that
the presumed sharp distinction between formal and informal language cannot be maintained. The reason for this is not that their edges overlap, so
that there are borderline cases. The formal language is *born from the womb*
of the informal. The distinction between the two is contained only in the
latter.

In the same way one could perhaps point out that the very term "self-
referring" owes any significance it could possibly have to the fact that lan-

guage is *not* merely self-referring. Or will it be suggested that the term "self-referring" is itself self-referent? Such reflections, we are sometimes assured, usher the speaking soul of man into an ultimate resort of "Silence." They may indeed do so, but if there is a silence of sublimity, there is also a silence of idiocy.

It was because Einstein introduced new *in*formal terms of description, such as "signal" and "field," that he also became able to develop new formal laws, laws which gave effective content to his notions. Niels Bohr, in the same way, perceived the irrelevance to his message of a presumed existential disjunction between the observer and what he observes—which presupposition is built so firmly into the present structure of our informal language. By contrast, the "quantum description" is a form of unanalyzable wholeness: and this entails that the description of experimental results is not separable from the general experimental conditions which provide their context.

This last needs emphasizing, and I shall be returning to it. Meanwhile I remark that the bringing into account of *experiment* is naturally one of the features that mark off a scientist's approach to language from that of all the others we have looked at. And I find this especially interesting because, in other respects, his approach need not, as we have seen, be so very different. When he starts talking about "unanalyzable wholeness," when he undercuts, or undermines, any absolute distinction between observer and observed, the physicist comes up against a problem, which is clearly recognizable as the problem of linguistic reference in another costume. If the linguistic theorist sometimes feels forced to conclude that his language has nothing to refer to outside of itself—and if that raises a difficulty, because, as I have sought to emphasize, it is the very nature of language to refer—correspondingly, when the physicist feels forced to conclude that there is no absolute distinction between observer and observed, and thus nothing to be observed outside of his immeasurable self, then his science has nothing to *measure*. And *that* raises a difficulty, because it is the very nature of science (at least as we have it up to now) to measure. This difficulty is now recognized, and is sometimes referred to as "the measurement problem."

Bohm himself relates the two problems by tracing the provenance of this measurement problem to the fact of our being *imprisoned in our own language*. But, unlike Wittgenstein (for whom it was apparently coextensive with eternity), he finds that that imprisonment arose from a particular disjunction, which became built into the languages of the West at about the time of Descartes and was made explicit in Descartes' adoption of two reciprocally isolated descriptions of the world: one in terms of "matter," or extended substance, and the other in terms of "mind," or thinking substance. The disjunction was of course modified and elaborated by Kant; but by him and his followers it was not removed; it was rather riveted more firmly; and it has remained with us to become at once the basic maxim of natural science and the central problem of philosophy.

Seen in this light, quantum theory is one instance of an attempt to organize an escape from imprisonment in language, instead of sitting still and contemplating the inside of the prison wall. For it is fairly clear that quantum theory, since language-games do not launch rockets, is more than just one more language-game. Yet at the same time it really is "nonobjectifying language." For "the description of quantum theory *is* quantum theory." It is the discourse itself rather than the object of discourse; and if you raise the question "whether the theory fits the facts," you are already assuming a disjunction which the theory itself denies or supersedes. You are really only asking whether one description fits another description. This difficulty is inescapable, because the *form* of your theory (its language) connotes a disjunction between observer and observed; while its *content* is the *wholeness* of observer and observed. Thus, the form in which quantum theory is described is quantum theory. In this case at least the form in which knowledge is communicated is knowledge.

There is that in men's minds to which the abandonment of a distinction between form and content is intensely repugnant. It is to this obstacle that Bohm attributes the difficulty Einstein and Bohr experienced in understanding one another's language. And, it was this which brought about that regrettable feature of modern physics—the adoption of two distinct language forms—which has been previously referred to. This device however has concealed the confusion without disposing of it; for, if formal language has given up the attempt to "describe," yet the formalizing itself is still treated as a kind of "content," which is capable of being talked about in the informal language of description. "The only way out of such confusion," says Bohm, very wisely as I think, "is, at a certain point, just to drop the issue altogether and go on to something new." The fashionable distinction between two language forms will have to be abandoned, if any further progress is to be made in physical discovery. We need a new concept of theory itself, a new definition such as, let us say, "a language form that gives insight." From now on real scientific discovery (not just the hardware improvements we call "technology," but any radical advance analogous to the advance from classical to modern physics) will be inseparable from the development of new forms of language. It is on this development that Bohm himself is at present working.

One reason why such new developments are needed is that "the *infor-*

mal language of physics plays just as important a role with regard to experiment as it does with regard to formal theories . . . our present way of doing experiments in itself constitutes a very strong commitment to continue the *current* informal language of physics (and of science in general) into the indefinite future." Physics had to develop a new language when Copernicanism replaced the Ptolemaic system; and the consequential experiments ensued. So too, when the underlying presupposition of mechanism was replaced by that of the electrodynamic field; and so, again, now that physics has begun dealing with subject matters in which the velocity of light is a consideration. The *selection* of the experiments to be made, and of the machines to be constructed to make them possible, is imbedded in the language form. Indeed the machines themselves are "an extension of the current language forms of physics," and they provide us accordingly only with "the kinds of data which can readily be described in terms of those very forms." Only a full *realization* of this intimate relation of experiment to language forms will lead both to new forms of language and to new forms of experiment. As it is now, experiment and theory are treated as quite separate and "the ball is tossed to and fro from theory to experiment and from experiment back again to theory" as in a kind of game. But the *fact* of its being a kind of game has not been recognized, and therein lies the tragedy. Why was the concept of "game" so attractive to Wittgenstein? In a game the rules are known to have been voluntarily adopted by the player himself; there is thus "a wholeness of form and content, so that in each new move the *form* of the game is a whole with the content of each transaction." To recognize the relation between experiment and theory as being *in that sense* a "game" would be a first step towards escape from the prison of our fragmented language and our fragmented science — and ultimately from the fragmented civilization they have produced.

But only a first step. Penetration of the categorical barrier between theory and experiment is not in itself so novel an idea as it may sound. Goethe's scientific writings, for example, include a brief essay entitled "Experiment as Mediator Between Subject and Object"; and it was Coleridge's view that "an idea is an experiment proposed; an experiment is an idea realised." But Professor Bohm adds: "To see the wholeness of theory and experiment as extension of common language is not only to open up the possibility of changing *science* in a fundamental way, but it also opens up the possibility of corresponding changes in the scientist." And I find it very significant that, just within this practical issue of experiment, a finger is laid upon a truth of which I for one have long been firmly convinced: namely that, although one may learn to *talk* eloquently enough about it, he cannot really and serious-mindedly adopt a different view from the conventional Cartesian one of the relation between mind and matter, without at the same time beginning to become a different kind of human being. To renounce the heterogeneity of observed from observer involves, if it is taken seriously, abandoning the whole "onlooker" stance, upon which both the pursuit of science and modern language-use in general are based; it means advancing to awareness of another relation altogether between mind and matter. If we had actually made the advance, we should have become naturally, unforcedly, and unremittingly aware that the mind *cannot* refer to a natural object without at the same time referring to its own activity. And this in turn would require an equally unforced awareness not only that scientific discovery is always a discovery about language, but also that it is always a discovery about the self which uses language. Or, putting it another way, "the measurement problem" is also the general problem of objectivity in science.

Here I shall allow myself a brief digression. When natural scientists are called upon, as spokesmen, to address the world on the topic of themselves and their discipline, they commonly spend part of the time orating, if not boasting, about their objectivity. And it is quite true that science does demand objectivity first and foremost, and that the good ones among them endeavor to eliminate all personal bias from their judgments of fact. But I sometimes wonder: Is there any need to make quite such a song and dance about it? After all, it is not so very difficult to eliminate all personal considerations, all subconscious bias, when the matter or process you are investigating is, by definition, one in which you could not possibly have a direct personal concern; when from beginning to end it is assumed to be absolutely other than yourself. To put it rudely, any reasonably honest fool can be objective about objects. It must be a different matter altogether, should we be called on to attend, not alone to matter, but to spirit; when a man would have to practice distinguishing what *in* himself comes solely from his private personality—memories, for instance, and all the horseplay, of the Freudian subconscious—from what comes also from elsewhere. Then indeed objectivity is not something that was handed us on a plate once and for all by Descartes, but something that would really have to be *achieved*, and which must require for its achievement, not only exceptional mental concentration but other efforts and qualities, including moral ones, as well. The self which uses language is indeed the personal self; but the self which *utters* it—which has made utterance possible at all—is a something more *within* the personal self; and this is a distinction about which it is not to easy to become objective.

Moral qualities have hitherto been regarded as the province of the humanities rather than as a department of scientific training. But to my mind the most promising developments both in science and in the humanities are to be looked for there, where there are signs of a new interpenetration between the two. If so, it is no bad thing that they should both be concerning themselves with language. We have heard it suggested that the most satisfactory definition of a scientific theory is "a language form that gives insight." The language philosophers and oracles, to whom I began by referring, are also concerned with language forms that give insight; and in their case the notion that a new insight involves a change of character is probably not so unpalatable. As against this however, they seem little concerned with knowledge in any accepted sense; and certainly not with the new knowledge that is called discovery. Perhaps that is why they give the impression—at least they give *me* the impression—of operating each in his own island of subjectivity (real, if you like, and whatever that means, but still *mere* subjectivity), while science is left respectfully alone to go on altering, and incidentally polluting, the outward face of nature, as it thinks fit. They talk of language existing in its own right, and tell us that we must not think of a word as "standing for" something. But in fact it soon becomes apparent that they themselves mostly do think of language as "standing for" something, and that what it stands for in their view is the feelings, or other internal responses to external stimuli, of a physically isolated psyche: Richards and Langer, for example, explicitly so, the others implicitly by the very texture of their diction.

Here, it seems to me, the opposite approach from the standpoint of science may come as a useful corrective. A scientist also may tell us that we must not think of a word as standing for something, but must look instead for language forms that give insight. But he will differ from the language philosopher, because he *is* interested primarily in knowledge, and particularly in the new knowledge which is discovery. The insight in which he is interested is going to be primarily a heuristic insight; while those islands of subjective feeling will be precisely what he is *not* much interested in. Perhaps each needs the clasp and support of the other in his half-blinded staggering towards the light. Perhaps there is not one prison cell, but two: the "nonobjectifying" subjectivity, in which the humanities are immured, and the adjoining cell of subjectless objectivity, where science is locked and bolted; and maybe the first step towards escape for the two prisoners of language is to establish communication with one another.

Part Three

MAN, SOCIETY, AND GOD

Matter, Imagination, and Spirit

There are certain words in common use which appear plain-spoken enough, but the meanings of which turn out to be extraordinarily vague and indeterminate. Two such words, for instance, are "materialism" and "spiritualism." I have a suspicion that a great deal of mischief would have been avoided if more people, who are happy to make use of them, stopped more often to think about their meaning, and it is that suspicion which led to my choice of this topic.

In the first place, if we are to use the terms "material" and "spiritual" intelligently, it seems clear that we must know — or at the very least must have tried to find out — firstly what we mean by the two words "matter" and "spirit" themselves, and secondly (and it is here that the other word in my title will become relevant) what is the relation between them. Afterwards, in the space left to me, I shall be drawing one or two conclusions which I hope will prove to be of more than theoretical interest.

If, then, we take the word "matter" and look at it squarely, the first thing we notice about it is its extreme abstractness. Of all the abstract terms in the language it is very nearly the most abstract one can find. Perhaps that sounds as if I am being paradoxical? No. I don't mean it that way at all. To say that "matter" is a very abstract word is not the same as proclaiming that matter does not exist, or anything of that sort. It is abstract in the way that a word like "insect" or "bird" is abstract. We never perceive a bird with our senses; what we do perceive is some particular starling or thrush. "Bird" means a number of elements or qualities which all starlings and thrushes and other species have in common (the habit of flying through the air is one of them). Consequently it is something we cannot

143

perceive, but can only *think*. If this is what is meant by an "abstraction," one will see at once how much more abstract is "matter." For "matter" means something which starlings have in common not only with all other starlings, not even only with all other winged creatures, but also with lions and tigers and motorbuses and the Eiffel Tower and . . . well . . . and so on.

Now the element which all these things indubitably have in common is that we apprehend them through the senses. So we shan't be far wrong if we define "matter" as some element or ingredient common to all that is perceivable with the senses. But as it is the actual meaning of the *word* that we are considering, that is, the sort of thing most people have in their minds when they use it, I think we must add (in view of popular interest in physical science) that "perceivable" here means either *actually* or *theoretically* perceivable. Even in that particular starling we do not, we are assured, actually perceive the particles of which it is composed. But we are also very definitely assured that those particles are, in their nature, perceivable as well as thinkable; not only so, but even that they are the basis of all perception, inasmuch as it is only *their* presence, outside of our minds and independent of ourselves, which provides us with something to perceive. It is their presence or absence which distinguishes an actual perception from a hallucination or a fancy. They are the world we are conscious *of*; the rest (that is, the familiar macroscopic world of mountains, mice, and motorbuses), however objective and independent of ourselves it may appear to be, is in fact only the form our subjective consciousness takes, owing to our physical organisms and to our conscious and unconscious psychic activity.

Now all this begins to raise an issue into which I do not wish to be drawn, because it is not really relevant to what I shall be trying to say. I mean the vast difference between the modern theories of physics and those of the eighteenth and nineteenth centuries, which are sometimes distinguished from it as "classical" physics. If it is true that the ordinary man's notion of "matter" is still closely associated with the notion of solidity — so that the expression "solid matter" is almost a tautology — it is now also true that the steadily increasing emphasis laid by physical science on *energy* as a basic factor in material solidity places even the ordinary man in difficulties as soon as he stops and begins to think what he means by "matter." Perhaps it is also true — as I often hear mentioned — that the world-picture of modern physics is therefore more "spiritual" than that of modern physics. But I do not want, on this occasion, to be drawn into all that. And I think the best way of finding a shortcut that will take me past it is the following.

Let us begin by assuming straightaway not merely that matter is a form of arrested physical energy, but that Leibniz was right when he propounded that matter is *coagulum spiritus* — a kind of coagulation or concentration of spirit — that the material is formed from and within the immaterial, rather as ice is formed from and within water. I may add that I personally have no doubt that he *was* right. Very well: we are still left with the question I raised at the beginning, and my answer to it remains unshaken. We are still left with the *word* "matter" — a very useful word we cannot do without — and with the question of what we mean by it. And it still remains true that it means the quality common to all that we could perceive through the bodily senses. Perhaps it began life as spirit, and only coagulated or materialized later. Perhaps the process was a very gradual one. Very well: but it is still precisely at the point at which it *became* perceptible to the senses that we are entitled to dignify, or, if you prefer, to vilify it, with the name of "matter."

I come now to the word "spirit," of which I have already been making free use. I think I said I would first consider the meanings of the two words, and secondly the relation between them. But it is not really possible to serialize in that way, because the question of their meanings and the question of the relation between them turns out to be one and the same question. That is one reason why we cannot do without the word "matter." What do we mean by "spirit"? The question I am asking is what the word means today — *not* (all-important as that is from another point of view) what it once meant, or what its Latin predecessor "*spiritus*" meant, and so forth. Do we not mean precisely that which is *not* matter? If it is a *definition* we are seeking, our answer will be an accurate one to the extent that, whatever else the term may mean, it always means that. And that does seem to me to be something about which everyone agrees, as soon as he begins to reflect, from those at one end of the scale who hold that spirit is the only reality, to those at the other who only use the word for the purpose of denying that whatever is meant by it *has* any reality at all. In logical parlance, whatever attributes we assign to the term "spirit," it must always be the contradictory of the term "matter." Or, more briefly, spirit is, by definition, immaterial.

To make this clearer, let us look at it once more from the Leibnizian point of view (although of course it is not peculiar to Leibniz; indeed it is common to nearly all oriental philosophy and religion). Matter is *coagulum spiritus*. Ultimately, therefore, spirit includes matter as part of itself. But, if so, what does the *word* "spirit" mean? As was the case with matter, we have the word, and it is apparently a very useful one, and we shall no doubt go on using it. But, with the help of Leibniz, we now seem to have succeeded in making it mean . . . what? Well, nearly *everything*! And a word that means everything is not much use to us anymore. It is about as much use as a word that means nothing.

From all this it seems clear to me that by "spirit" we must mean "that which is not matter," and by "that which is not matter" we mean that part of the totality which is not perceptible through the senses. If the totality is ultimately one, as I hold (with Leibniz), then it is perhaps better to speak of one *phase* of the totality rather than one *part* of it. But the definition still holds good. If matter is, after all, spirit, then it is spirit so far transmuted as to have become perceptible by the senses. That must be so, because, if what is perceptible by the senses were *also* to be called "spirit," then we should have no good name left for all that is *not* so perceptible.

But now suppose that we want not merely to talk about spirit, by defining the word and so forth, but to *have to do* with spirit? I purposely use a vague phrase. Having to do with spirit might mean trying to prove its reality; it might mean investigating its workings and that of units or beings who comprise its totality; it might mean striving to live in the light of it. It will cover every shade of mysticism. How do we *get at* spirit? There is one sense of course in which a Leibnizian need not worry. He knows he is *always* having to do with spirit, because matter itself is spirit. But we have already looked at and rejected that rather meaningless meaning of the term. I am asking not. "How do we have to do with everything?" but: "How do we have to do with spirit" What means of access have we to spirit, as the term is normally used, that is, as the contradictory of matter?

The first thing that is clear is that we have no percipient access to it, for the simple reason that anything we perceive through the senses is, by definition, matter. To say therefore that we have perceived, or could perceive, spirit or a spirit is a misuse of words. And this must be true not only for you and me, but also for the most gifted and the most dedicated medium in the world. It will only *not* be a misuse of words if the words are uttered metaphorically—if they are being used by way of legitimate metaphor. And by legitimate metaphor I mean one in which the speaker is *aware* that he is speaking in metaphor; I mean that what is ostensibly being affirmed materially is in fact being affirmed (*and the speaker knows it is being affirmed*) spiritually. With that proviso, what is literally a misuse of words may be a good way, it may well be the *only* way, of speaking at all about the spirit we are having to do with.

But the proviso is a very important one. Thus, if we choose to speak of a "spiritual body" (and I see no reason why we should not), then we must either mean an organism, but an organism not perceivable through the senses, or else we shall be meaning literally nonsense—just as we should be meaning nonsense if we talked about a sharp kind of bluntness or a blunt kind of sharpness. To put it another way, we should be mistaken if we supposed that a spiritual body could ever *be* a phenomenon. For, just as "matter" is the common word for everything that is perceivable through the senses, so "phenomenon" is the common word for any particular thing, or complex, that is so perceived.

Now of course there are paranormal phenomena as well as normal ones. Incidentally I hope nothing I am now saying will be taken as insinuating some kind of contempt for the investigation of paranormal phenomena. I shall be saying a little more on that subject later. At the moment the only point I am making is that the same conclusions apply to paranormal phenomena as to normal. For even if through the senses we perceive a paranormal phenomenon, what we perceive is matter. Only to the extent that we are aware of something without supposing that we have literally "perceived" it can it be spirit.

Therefore, if we are asking: "How do we have to do with spirit?" the first question that arises is: "What sort of things are we aware of without supposing that we have perceived them?" Well, there is *one* thing we *never* suppose we have perceived, one thing of which we are aware during most of our waking lives, and of which we are perhaps aware most of all when we are in the act of perceiving other things. I mean of course ourselves, who are doing the perceiving. We come back to the definition of matter. Just as we cannot really think of spirit, *as* spirit, unless we are also able to think of matter, so we cannot think of matter, *as* matter, unless we are also able to think of spirit. Matter is always that *of which* I am conscious; but correlative to it, and at the opposite pole, is the "I" who am conscious. Or we may say, as Coleridge said on one occasion, that matter is "that *of which* there is consciousness, but which is not itself conscious." Spirit, on the contrary, is not that which is perceived, but that which *is*. It is not what we perceive, but what we *are*.

I have so far been thinking about matter and spirit almost exclusively from the point of view of perception in general—of the philosophy or psychology of perception. It is a rather unsocial point of view—so much so that I fancy practically everything I have said so far, if it is true at all, would be equally true if I were the only conscious individual in the world. In fact of course each of us knows very well that he is not the only pebble on the beach. So let me go on now to consider an important particular instance of perception. Suppose that the phenomenon we are perceiving

happens to be not a mouse or a car or the Eiffel Tower, but a fellow being.
The same conclusions necessarily apply. All that I am perceiving through
my senses is matter. But in this case I know very well that the particular
matter I am perceiving (the particular phenomenon) is especially associated
with—if you like, it is the *expression*—of another individual being. I know
that there is the same relation there between matter and spirit as there is
here. And I know equally well that what is important is not the relation
between two phenomena as such—between his body, which is my "matter," and my body, which is his "matter"—but the relation between the two
individual spirits, of which those bodies are reciprocally the vehicle and the
expression. I said "another individual being" rather than "a fellow man,"
because it can make no difference from this point of view whether the
phenomenon is normal or paranormal. There must still be the same duality
between matter and spirit in my experience (if it is an experience of sense-
perception at all), whether it is a man I am seeing or hearing or touching,
or whether it is—let me use the old-fashioned word—a ghost. The ghost
may well be the means to a relation between myself and another spirit . . .
but so may every fleshly body I meet. As far as the possibility of a relation,
via sense-perception, between two spirits is concerned, it can make no
more difference that one of them is a man and the other a ghost—than it
can make that one is a fat man and the other is a thin man.

Well, now I have used that word "expression," and I did so in trying to
point out that there is another very different relation between matter and
spirit. The one we began by looking at is the contradictory one. By virtue
of it at any given moment matter is always the negation of spirit. And that
still remains the case even if, historically, it is the product of spirit. If I was
right in saying that we are never more aware of ourselves as immaterial
than when we are in the very act of perceiving, we must also say that matter is the *occasion* of spirit or, at all events, the *occasion* of the spirit's
awareness of itself as spirit. I will shorten this and say that it is the occasion of spirit. But this word "expression," and some others that are often
associated with it, reminds us that there is another relation between spirit
and matter that we have not yet looked at at all. It is a fact of immediate
experience that, besides being the contradictory of spirit, besides being for
that reason the occasion of spirit, and besides being the finished product
of spirit (if we so hold), matter can be the present *expression* of spirit. The
material can become an image, or picture, of the immaterial. Whether or
not it does so for us will depend on ourselves. *When* it does so, we may call
the resulting experience "imagination." Imagination, then, also is by its
very nature a relation between matter and spirit; but it is a special kind of

relation, a relation which at once maintains and transcends that contradiction between the two, to which we have so far been giving our attention.

Mere perception – perception without imagination – is the sword thrust between spirit and matter. It was the increasing predominance of that kind of perception within Western humanity that enabled the philosopher Descartes to formulate his partition of all being into the two mutually exclusive categories of extended substance and thinking substance – which is another way of saying: between matter and spirit. But mere perception is not what normally occurs when we look at, or listen to, a fellow being. When we do that, we see his body, or hear his voice, not only as matter, but also as expression. We see his body and his countenance as a material picture of the immaterial. I say that is what normally occurs, and I think it does normally occur to *some* extent every time one human being observes another. But of course it may occur to a greater or lesser degree. And the extent to which it does occur will depend a good deal on ourselves. We may – or we may not – make up our minds that it shall occur, in our case, to the maximum degree of which our imagination is capable. 'Tis not in mortals to command success, and the result will be uncertain. What seems certain is that something very important will depend on the extent to which we *are* successful. For what will depend on it is precisely what I suggested just now is the most important thing in a meeting between two human beings – that it should be not simply a relation between two phenomena, but a relation between two spirits.

Now it is possible to look not only at a fellow being, but also at the world of nature in that way, that is to say, not merely as matter but also as expression. It is possible, but for most people it is no longer normal and instinctive, to do so. It has been becoming less and less normal in the course of the last three or four hundred years. And the great discovery made by the poets and philosophers of the Romantic Movement was just this: that, although it is no longer normal, it is not impossible. This is the discovery that found expression and became embodied in the aesthetic and philosophical concept of imagination, as it was developed especially in England and in Germany in the second half of the eighteenth and the first half of the nineteenth century – that it is to imagination, in the first place, that we must look for the healing of that Cartesian sword-thrust between matter and spirit.

Thus, for all these reasons I have long felt that, whether by way of the so-called inanimate world of nature, or whether by way of our fellow beings, a strengthening and deepening of the faculty of imagination – or better say the activity of imagination – is the only way in which we can really begin to have to do with spirit. I think I would put it this way: we *live* in that abrupt gap between matter and spirit; we exist by virtue of it as autonomous, self-conscious individual spirits, as free beings. Often, in addition, it makes us feel lamentably isolated. But because our freedom and responsibility depend on it, any way that involves disregarding the gap, or pretending it is not there, is a way we take at our peril.

Now imagination does not disregard the gap; it depends on it. It lives in it as our very self-consciousness does, in this case not as a small helpless creature caught in a trap between the two, but rather as a rainbow spanning the two precipices and linking them harmoniously together. The concern of imagination is neither with mere matter nor with pure spirit. It is thus a psychic, or a psychosomatic, activity. On the other hand, if we are seeking to have to do with spirit, it is worse than useless to try to approach it by way of scientific investigation—at least as the word "science" is used today, for science is avowedly based on *mere* perception, and in mere perception it will always be matter we are having to do with and never spirit. Indeed *mere* perception *is* itself the gap between matter and spirit and, whatever else one can do with a gap, one cannot use it as a means of crossing itself.

Spirit, as I have said, is not what we can perceive, but what we are; and experience of spirit must depend not on what we see, but on the manner in which we look. It seems better therefore to take the other course: so far from attempting to disregard the gap—or, if you prefer, the wound—between matter and spirit, to realize very fully that, as human beings on earth, we can only live in it. We can only live there *today*; however it may have been in the past, when the word "spirit" (or "*spiritus*," or "*pneuma*," or "*ruach*") had a rather different meaning. It seems better to realize the gap and live in it not as a creature caught in a trap, but as the rainbow that spans it. Then, within the rainbow, or spectrum, of imagination we shall find ourselves free to move sometimes in one direction and sometimes in the other, either towards the one extremity—let us say the red one—of matter and perception, or towards the violet extremity of pure spirit. We shall be free to turn either outward towards what we perceive or inward towards what we *are*.

I have mentioned the Romantic Movement. It will be in the former direction that we shall turn, as Goethe did, when our primary concern is to have to do with spirit through nature, and, by perceiving nature as expression, to realize for ourselves that matter is after all spirit. It will be in the latter direction that we shall turn, as Hegel did, when our primary concern is to have to do with the human spirit. And note that what I said about being able to turn in *either* direction is well illustrated by these two examples. Goethe's primary concern, both as a poet and as a scientist, was with nature, but he was also a student of Spinoza and an intimate admirer of Hegel. Hegel's primary interest, on the other hand, lay within; but he was the author not only of *The Phenomenology of Spirit,* but also of a long work, containing much scientific detail, on *The Philosophy of Nature.* It must be said that both Goethe and Hegel had been given the freedom of the spectrum of imagination, and the same is true of Coleridge, whose mind could turn so easily in either direction.

It is of course in the second direction, that of the human spirit, that we must turn if we are seeking to have to do with spirit in one special sense. This is the sense which many people feel to be the most important of all; I have a suspicion that they are right, though I would wish to emphasize that I mean important not merely for the two human beings I shall be referring to in a moment, but for the whole future of humanity. The issue of survival after death today has, I believe, that kind of importance as well as the personal one. But I am not very fond of the word "survival" in this context. It has too strong a suggestion of a mere prolongation of the life we are so familiar with. I prefer "immortality" as suggesting transition to a new and very different kind of life.

Perhaps I may recall for a moment what I said earlier about the relation between two human beings, when I distinguished a relation between two phenomena from a relation between two spirits. The latter relation is achieved only when we experience another in the same mode as we experience ourselves, when we experience him not across the gap between spirit and matter, but as being on the same side of the gap as *we are.* It is of course possible to hold—and there are those who hold it—that, when we perceive the body of another human being, we merely perceive matter, and we then go on to draw the inference that, because his body is something like our body, there must be something like us within it. But I see no evidence that anyone has in fact ever syllogized in that way, and I believe it to be nonsense. What *is* true is that the extent to which we perceive his body as mere matter, and the extent to which we experience it as spirit, will depend on the degree of imagination with which we are perceiving. We may call this "moral imagination," to distinguish it from the aesthetic imagination which is concerned with the perception of nature. To the extent that we experience another's spiritual activity in speech, in gesture, in the mobility of his countenance, and so on, in the same mode as our own— and thus as if it *were* our own—we are exercising moral imagination.

Now it follows, I think, from all I have been saying that, if the word "spirit" means anything real, then spirit depends on matter, or on body, not for its being, but for its expression. Incarnation is the way in which spirit becomes evident through the senses to imagination. To the extent, then, that we shall have succeeded in traversing the spectrum of imagination in the direction of the human spirit, we shall have diminished the use we make of the body of the other for our relation with his spirit. It will have become less and less essential. Indeed, because we are not of imagination all compact, and our perceptions of matter cannot all be transfigured by imagination, the phenomenal relation may well prove in some respects a positive hindrance to the spiritual one. But the point I want to make first is that we can experience another spirit *as* spirit only in the same mode as we experience ourselves.

This, I believe, is a truth that holds irrespective of life and death, but it is the death of the body of our friend that brings it home to us with especial sharpness. For there is after all much else in the relation between two living human beings, and much else that we value dearly and long to preserve, besides the relation between two spirits. What death does is to force us to concentrate on that most important relation of all, by taking all the others away from us. In particular it takes away that part of our relation that was based on *expression* – at least as I have been using the term. For I have been using it to mean a function of incarnate spirit. And we may feel this to be the most important – the most desperately important – of all, since expression is, between incarnate spirits, the normal means of communication between the one and the other. Does death, then, take away all possibility of every kind of communication between the one and the other?

I think not, but we must remember what kind of communication it is we are speaking of. We are speaking now of the experience which one spirit may have of another spirit directly *as* spirit – therefore of a very close and intimate experience indeed. Furthermore, I have sought to demonstrate that we can experience another spirit only in the same mode that we experience our own, that is, in the mode that we experience ourselves. It follows that the communications of the dead can only come to us from within – not by the long and bumpy road through matter, expression, and perception, but arising within us as events occurring within ourselves. This is in fact the only form in which I myself can recognize, or even (I think) desire, communication with some of my friends who have died before me. It can be a very real, but also (no doubt because I am a very limited person) a very limited, experience. Here the problem is that it is a very subtle form of communication, and one that it is very difficult to discern. This follows,

I would say, from the very fact that it takes place without the aid of ex-pression, without the sturdy confidence we are given by the gap between matter and spirit, because it occurs wholly on the spirit side of the gap. We have thus to learn to distinguish between subject and object, not just in the field of commonplace experience, where "object" means matter and "subject" means ourselves. We have to distinguish between subjective spirit and objective spirit, or between spiritual experience that is merely subjec-tive and that which is also objective, or between that which is *merely* our-selves and that which is another being *in* ourselves. And here let me hasten to add that I for one owe virtually the whole of such understanding of the problem and its possible solution as I possess to the writings of Rudolf Steiner.

Perhaps "problem" is too dry a word for what must really be an ardu-ous endeavor. Natural scientists have to be "objective" about a natural world which is by definition devoid of spirit, and they are often rather proud of being so. But after all, it is not so very difficult to eliminate all personal considerations, and all subconscious bias, when the matter or process you are investigating is one in which you could not possibly have any personal concern, when from beginning to end it is assumed to be ab-solutely other than yourself. It is a different matter altogether when we are called upon to attend not to matter, but to spirit; when one must learn to distinguish what *in* oneself comes solely from oneself—memories, for instance, and prejudices—from what comes also from elsewhere. Then in-deed objectivity is not something that is handed to us on a plate by the very framework of our inquiry. It is something that has really to be *achieved,* and which requires for its achievement not only exceptional mental concentration, but other efforts and other qualities as well.

I said I would return to the subject of paranormal phenomena and I have left myself very little space in which to do so—which is perhaps just as well, because it is not a part of my topic on which I should wish to lay undue stress—if only for the excellent reason that I know very little about it. It seems to me to follow from all I have been saying that, if I am right, the endeavor to have to do with spirit, and in particular to communicate with the dead or with otherwise discarnate spirits, by way of attending to paranormal phenomena, is open to certain objections. It is analogous, I would say, to an attempt to botanize, or to cultivate, a love and under-standing of nature by investigating fungi. This is not to condemn it. A lov-ing study of fungi may well throw a special light not only on fungi themselves, but on the whole working of nature in her more normal mani-festations. In fact I believe it has done so. Nevertheless, it would be a bad thing if we became so obsessed with fungi that we could no longer conceive of any other approach to natural history—if, even, in our vocabulary the word "biology" gradually became just a synonym for "fungology." In the same way I should expect a sympathetic understanding of paranormal phenomena to illumine some of those spiritual truths that underlie all phenomena; but I should find it deplorable if there came to be many people about to whom such words as "spirit," "spirits," and "spiritualism" suggested paranormal phenomena and nothing else.

Self and Reality

The question "Do I exist?" is seldom uttered and is probably not very often explicitly formulated in the mind. Here and there, it is true, there is evidence of its having been both formulated and answered in the negative. When we find a linguistic philosopher objecting to the word "consciousness" being used, or when we read a few pages of some kinds of behaviorist sociology, or of the psychology on which it is based, we quickly come upon that evidence. Within the fold of Marxism the straight answer "yes" would be deviation, if not rank heresy. But what is more important for the free world is the evidence all round us that precisely that unspoken question, or doubt, is present as a subconscious undercurrent in so many different fields of contemporary thought and feeling. We doubt pretty well everything, because we doubt ourselves.

It sounds an unlikely question to have become almost part of the air we breathe. But so it is, and it may be as well to begin taking it out of the air by putting it soberly down on paper and answering it. That is what the following pages attempt to do, and it is with that object that they begin by examining how the question came to be asked in the first place.

The basic assumptions concerning man and the universe underlying the mental and emotional attitudes of the many will be found for the most part to have been taken over, unexamined, from the more sharply defined philosophical or scientific thinking of the few; and in this context "the many" includes also the few who are productive in the domain of art and literature. In our time these basic assumptions are no longer those of a violent and avowed positivism. The term "reductionism" is in fairly common use as a pejorative label for the doctrine, now often considered old-fashioned, that nothing is "real" except physical stimuli and physical responses. Mind has no distinct reality; but all the same, man is not a mindless machine; he is a psychosomatic organism.

This descriptive epithet (*psychosomatic*) was of course borrowed from medicine with the object of excluding an outmoded distinction between the "mind" or "soul" (*psyche*) of man on the one hand and his "body" (*soma*) on the other. It may sometimes be necessary for practical purposes, but it is considered strictly unscientific, to distinguish mind from body or body from mind.

Here it must be observed that we are examining one of those pieces of semiscientific terminology which are wielded much more confidently by the laity than by responsible scientists themselves. At all events I have myself heard a neurophysiologist with an important academic appointment devote the greater part of a lecture to what he himself invariably referred to as the "mind-body problem." Research disclosed this problem as already (and, according to him, insolubly) present at neuron level, and reduction to the neuron merely pinpointed the dichotomy it was aimed at solving. If this is so, the reason is not very far to seek, and it is clearly this. Suppose we adopt the concept "psychosomatic" wholeheartedly, and employ it uncritically—to the extent of refusing to distinguish *at all* between something like mind and something like body—we are still left with a fundamental distinction which we shall never be able to ignore. We shall never be able to ignore it, because it is a distinction presupposed by anyone who writes, speaks or thinks "about" anything whatsoever—so that to go through the motions of denying it as theory is at the same time to exemplify, and thus affirm, it as fact. This is the distinction between "I" and "not-I," or "self" and "not-self," or (if these formulations are rejected) between anyone's consciousness and *that-of-which* he is conscious.

It was the transition from the second of these to the first that the lecturer was referring to when he spoke of the "mind-body" problem and it was this problem with which he insisted (rightly or wrongly) that no progress whatever had been made since neurology and psychology first became sciences.

Since our language, in common with the other languages of Europe, already possesses two words that signify: (a) "that which is conscious" and (b) "that of which (a) is conscious," I propose to adopt them. They may sound a little forbidding in some ears today; but *some* terms or other we must have for the simple reason that, long before we reach the sophisticated point of questioning the ontological status of either of them (in plain English, doubting whether it really exists), there are all sorts of interesting things we certainly do observe, and may well want to say, about them. And these particular words have the advantage of denoting what is to be talked about precisely, unemotionally, and without any kind of limitation or question-begging.

The two words in question are "subject" and "object." Subject, then, means that with which this essay is mainly concerned and which normally calls itself "I." Object includes anything to which a subject can attend (or of which he can be conscious) whether a tea-table, a mountain, or an idea. And I want to begin by pointing out that prominent among the multifarious objects upon which subjects in general are wont to bestow their attention are: ideas of past, present, and future *time*. For the less reflective, these ideas are restricted to the present, the immediate past, and the immediate future; for the more reflective they include the subject's own relation to past and future; for the still more reflective, they include the relation to past, present, and future of the human race as a whole. We find moreover that the whole range of ideas which a subject habitually entertains, the sort of questions he consciously or subconsciously asks himself — and often the vocation in life which the whole psychosomatic organism ultimately adopts — are apt to depend on the relative emphasis given to one out of the three.

For instance, the type whose attention is attracted more by the past is likely to concern itself with such fields of study and enquiry as, say, history or anthropology; while the type more interested in future time tends to gravitate towards empirical science and technology. For the former the underlying question that fascinates is: How did I get here? — or how did humanity in general become what it now is? For the latter the question is rather: Where do we go from here?

What is however common to both types of person in this age is, that any explicit answer found or given to the key question is almost certain to lay heavy emphasis on the "somatic" aspect of the psychosomatic nexus called man. We speak of "psychosomatic." It would be more honest to reverse the order and say "somatopsychic." A simple illustration of this is our invariable recourse to the term "sex," which automatically expresses the speaker's, and induces the hearer's, concentration on the somatic component, in artificial abstraction from the whole delicate complex of masculine-feminine polarity. But to feel the full significance of this emphasis we need to contrast present basic assumptions with the older, and simpler, religious view of man's relation to past and future — the view that obtained as long as it was generally held that the soul *could* be considered apart from the body. Then the answer to the first question was: I was created by God at or shortly before the birth of my body; and to the second: I shall go either to Heaven or to Hell for all eternity. Here the point is, not whether these answers were better or worse than the current ones (in one respect at least the current ones are "better," as being less self-interested — since the issue is the future of mankind rather than my own particular fate or that of my immediate connections). The point is only that they were different.

Today the first question is commonly answered in terms of historical determinism, Darwinian or neo-Darwinian evolution, genes, amino acids, and so forth; while the second is answered by technology in technological terms. If some sciences (biology for instance) do contemplate an altered future for the mind of man as well as his body, the technique envisaged is a somatic one, operating through applied genetics or in some similarly physical way. Such at least are the answers given by vocational specialists and experts. Between the two groups of experts, the uninstructed laity or "general public" is left to do the best it can. The general public is on the whole unreflective, but that part of it which does reflect most often interprets the first answer in the terms of a vaguely scientific humanism or of historical inevitability, whether Marxist or otherwise; while it transmutes the second answer into pipe dreams of a "brave new world," or perhaps a strained existentialist ethic or a "God is dead" theology.

2

There still remains the third type of subject — the type which is moved to interest itself mainly in its own *present* relation to objects. It is this type that is likely (insofar as it is at all reflective) to turn its attention to art (including literature) and the theory of art. Here what I have called "the underlying question that fascinates" is neither "How did we get here?" nor "Where do we go from here?"; but rather: "What *am* I?" or "What is man?" And here also the slant of contemporary answers has been decided by the heavily somatic bias of the basic assumptions of the age.

In this case, too, if we wish to feel the full force of these, we must endeavor to look at them from outside. For the purpose of contrast, we must abandon for a moment a whole catena of concepts within which we live and move and have our being, in order to take up and look through those of another age. If, for example, we take up the medieval, and premedieval, background picture of man as a microcosm within the macrocosm, we are at once struck by the violent contrast between this "anthropocentric" view of man's relation to the universe and the "prosopocentric" one that has become current since the Scientific Revolution. An anthropocentric outlook is a "man-centered" one; whereas a prosopocentric outlook is "person-centered"; but the distinction requires expanding a little.

The *anthropos* (man) who was at the center of the medieval and premedieval cosmos differed from the psychosomatic organism which an individual human being is deemed to be today in somewhat the same way that the elementary particle of modern physics differs from the atom of nineteenth-century physical theory. It is only necessary to read attentively *The Divine Comedy* or any one of a host of books, to discover that both the somatic and the psychic components of the "self" were assumed to be, and felt as if, connected by invisible and immaterial threads with the world of "not-self" that lay outside them. The whole organism was one of many points of concentration of a field of forces, and of the beings from whom the forces emanated, rather than one object placed among other objects in a void. The modern view of it as essentially an object among objects entails totally different assumptions and different feelings. It entails in fact two basic assumptions, which appear at first sight to be opposed to one another but turn out, on closer inspection, to be complementary. The first is, that the dichotomy we commonly experience between the "public" world of objects outside us and existing independently of us, on the one hand, and the "private" world of our thoughts and feelings, on the other, is a kind of illusion, or at all events, that the former is "real" in a way that the latter is not. The second assumption is that, from its own point of view, each individual "subject," each individual psyche, is isolated in its own private world of subjectivity, of which one is as good or as bad as another. "There is nothing either good or bad, but thinking makes it so." Insofar as the subject exists at all, it is largely cut off from the world outside it and from other subjects; and what it makes of these depends on the network of thoughts and feelings, neurally and perhaps neurotically determined, which it spins out of itself as time goes on. We could perhaps call the first assumption "reductionist" and the second "projectionist." But each really implies the other. Projectionism springs inevitably from reductionism and would have been impossible without it.

It is hardly too much to say that contemporary art and literature are almost wholly based on the projectionist assumption. Most explicitly so, perhaps, in surrealism and its offspring movements; but it is equally implicit in the stream-of-consciousness type of fiction that has been with us now for some decades and in the more recent tendency, already commented on, to treat all *values* as purely subjective manifestations, any one of which is as interesting and important as another. The two assumptions can also be traced, and have even sometimes been made explicit, in aesthetic *theory* — as in the popular distinction (based on behaviorism) between "emotive" and "referential" language, on which much modern poetics is based, and which even more modern criticism takes for granted.

Here however — owing to the fact that emotive language is only emotive (indeed, is only *language* at all) because it is assumed to refer to something other than the feelings it is intended to arouse — we are brought perilously near to a *reductio ad absurdum*. And it could even come about that future generations, looking back on the present period, will find that one of the principal functions of art and literature, and still more perhaps of aesthetic and literary *theory*, was precisely the exposure and correction of the confused mess of reductionism and projectionism that constitutes our contemporary feeling for the relation between self and reality, and of the whole prosopocentric picture of each human person as a merely spatial center, psychically as well as physically isolated from the outside world and from its fellow units.

For it so happens that both the conscientious practice of, and reflection on, art (including literature or certainly including poetry) differ in one important respect from the kind of mental activity that is normally begotten by a predominant interest in the past or in the future. Art and literature, it has already been suggested, are more likely to be pursued where the predominant interest of the subject is in its *present* relation to objects. Almost inevitably their pursuit concentrates attention on that relation; and we find that to concentrate attention on it, instead of taking it for granted, is to be led to question some of the otherwise unquestioned presuppositions of a psychosomatically based cosmology.

The basic distinction between subject and object is clearly not the same as the distinction between mind and body, though we have seen that the latter distinction points us towards the former — especially when it is probed. Still less is it equivalent to the distinction between man and nature, as those words are ordinarily understood. It is a fact, however, that today most people make only this third distinction and, when they mentally contrast themselves with all that is outside themselves, form a vague picture of "me" (this body) confronting all other objects.

It is this distinction which the practice of art, and still more perhaps the habit of reflecting on what happens when it is practiced, forces us to examine more closely, as the history of the last hundred years or so has shown. Whether we look into the function of imagery in poetry; or whether we probe the psychology of visual art, as Gombrich for instance has done in his *Art and Illusion*; whether we are led towards the concept of what Coleridge called "primary imagination" and Susanne Langer much later called "formulation," or whether we find ourselves concluding that, with the help of the painters, the human "mind-set" has been projected upon the outside world, the result in this respect is the same. We are forced to realize that the portmanteau distinction we normally make between man and nature is not rooted in the objects as such, is not in fact fixed and unalterable, but is on the contrary based on the shared perceptual habits, or "coenesthesis" of subjects. Or, to put it another way, it compels us to discover for ourselves that what we call "nature" is largely man himself reflected and by the reflection disguised.

I used the expression "what we call" nature only to make it clear that what I am referring to is nature in the ordinary sense, that is to say, qualitative nature, the familiar and macroscopic world we actually perceive and experience—not any purely quantitative substratum that is *inferred* (in the science of physics, for example) but is never directly experienced. The difference between these two is something to which we shall have to return for a moment shortly, but at present the point is that interest in the psychology of art and poetry, by forcing our closer attention to the present relation between subject and object, has been leading a good many people, not merely to infer, but to *experience* this truth that the habitual portmanteau distinction we make between man and nature does not march with the break between self and not-self.

To experience this truth, to experience it with the same directness that characterizes our "ordinary" experience of nature herself, is a very different matter from arriving at it as a logical conclusion based on scientific or philosophical thought. That is why it seemed worthwhile to dwell a little on the aesthetic aspect. For the last hundred and fifty years have also shown that such a conclusion, however ineluctable, if it is not matched by actual experience is quickly forgotten.

3

I am in fact not seeking to establish this truth, but merely to point to it. The establishing has been done long ago. Simply as theory, the notion that macroscopic nature exists independently of man was already largely abandoned by Descartes and today its falsity is common knowledge among all specialists concerned in any way with perception. The physicist, the neurologist, the cerebral anatomist, the psychologist, all agree that the objects we perceive and experience are at least mainly effects or constructs of a subject or community of subjects.

It is not, then, this hoary fact itself, but what follows from it with which this essay is concerned; and one thing that follows is this. Since all parts of the human body, perceived or assumed to be perceivable, are themselves natural objects among other natural objects, it is not enough to describe only *the organism* as "psychosomatic." In other words, we ought not to say, as we look out into the world and then down at our own bodies: "The behavior of this organism is psychosomatic"; but rather: "Nature as a whole (including this organism) is psychophysical."

Why is it then that we say the former so often and the latter so seldom—in spite of its being agreed (when they come to think of it) by all our experts? We have proved beyond a peradventure that nature is psychophysical, but we are determined to forget it as quickly as possible. Even our experts themselves, even science forgets, whenever it is not at the moment actually engaged in investigating perception, or otherwise bypassing nature's macroscopic objectivity. We know, but our basic assumptions remain opposite to what we know. They arise therefore, not from clear thought but from force of habit; and they are all the less easily eradicable and all the more compulsive because they are only half-conscious.

Yet we shall have to eradicate them, if we do not mean to slide deeper into the morass of self-deception that is paralyzing our wills.

To eradicate is first to find, and then to extract, the root. In this case I believe the root is to be found in a certain pernicious habit of thought which has been growing on most of us during the last two or three hundred years. I mean the habit of refusing to *distinguish* what we cannot *separate*. A very little reflection, it is true, suffices to show that that is the very operation which our reason exists to enable us to perform. But then it is just that little bit of reflection which we withhold. A little further reflection, as I have sought to demonstrate in the first section of this essay, discloses that it is upon that very operation that our self-consciousness depends. Whatever theory we may adopt concerning the nature or the origin of self-consciousness, this unavoidable truth will peep through it. The term "psychosomatic" itself, for instance, derives all its meaning from a notional distinction between the two halves of the word. If only that is real, which can be physically divided off from the rest, we must abandon the word. We cannot pronounce indivisible what we have not first, in thought, divided.

The long-current scientific principle of seeking to explain a whole only from its parts ("reductionism") springs from the same root. For the obverse of a refusal to distinguish what we cannot divide, is the impulse always to divide where we seek to distinguish. We assume that systematic investigation consists in the reduction of whatever we are investigating to its minimal physical units, because we have come to believe we must separate physically in order to distinguish mentally.

To sum up: all the facts, if we choose to look them squarely in the face, are compelling us to regard objective existence as one correlative aspect of a perfect reciprocal relation between subject and object—the one inseparable, but not therefore indistinguishable, from the other; and the same thing is true if we speak, instead, of "mind" and "world." But, instead of accepting this, we have been led to set up a factitious objectivity and to reify a world of objects fancied existing independently of any subject.

As the result of our doing so, we have been left, at the opposite pole, with a ghostly subjectivity which we do not know what to make of, which we suspect of being unreal, and which some extremists would like, even in practice, to get rid of. It is the intrusive presence of this awkward residue of subjectivity which has led to the invention of such a term as "psychosomatic," as it is used today; that is, with the tacit assumption that the somatic component of the organism came first in time and was determinative in the evolution of the whole.

We have been led into this aberration by an inveterate habit of refusing to distinguish what we cannot physically separate. For it so happens that the *body* can very conveniently be separated (is, in fact, separated by the skin) from the rest of the world. Since, however, not the body alone, but the whole of nature is psychophysical, the break that is crucial for establishing the reality of the self (and also, incidentally, of the not-self) is not—violent as that appears to be and is—the break between the epidermis of *Homo sapiens* and the surrounding air, but the break between the act of thinking and the product of thought or of perception and thought. The more, therefore, my thinking is my own act and the less it is mere "externally" induced, passive reverie, by that the more am I an independent and responsible self.

In short, all the facts point to the truth that reality resides in an ultimate, irreducible polarity between subject and object, such as would naturally lead us to say: "Because I, and other I's exist, the familiar world around me exists." But what we mostly do say is: "The familiar world around me exists, and therefore I, too, seem to exist."[1]

1. It is sometimes argued that either one of these two positions is a valid conclusion from the premise of an irreducible polarity between subject and object. This argument, express or implied, underlies philosophical pantheism, and its superficial attractiveness accounts, I believe, for the increasing popularity of Buddhism, particularly Zen, which we have recently witnessed. Its fallacy lies in the circumstance (already emphasized here) that the familiar world dissolves under analysis, or as the

In one of his prose writings, *The Statesman's Manual* (Appendix E), Coleridge speaks of the "obstinacy"

> of opinions that have always been taken for granted, opinions unassailable even by the remembrance of a doubt, the silent accrescence of belief from the unwatched depositions of a general, never-contradicted, hearsay; the concurring suffrage of modern books, all pre-supposing or re-asserting the same principles with the same confidence, and with the same contempt for all prior systems;—and among these, works of highest authority, appealed to in our Legislature, and lectured on at our Universities; the very books, perhaps, that called forth our own first efforts in thinking; the solutions and confutations in which must therefore have appeared tenfold more satisfactory from their having given us our first information of the difficulties to be solved, of the opinions to be confuted.

In any period of history, it is only a few so-called original minds (though I could think of better and humbler epithets) that go to the uncomfortable length of questioning what everyone is positive about. Yet history has shown more than once that what everyone is positive about may be a ghastly aberration. The validity of plenary indulgences is one example, and in the fifteenth century the logical necessity of witchcraft trials was taken for granted by most of the intelligent men living at the time.

It was impossible to comment fruitfully on the question here at issue without first seeking to expose and eradicate an almost universal aberration of our own day; and the obstinacy with which it is persisted in must be the excuse for the space I have devoted to it.

4

As was pointed out in the first section, the basic assumptions of the many concerning man and the universe are taken over, unexamined, from the more sharply defined philosophical or scientific thinking of the few. Through the channels of literature, art, drama, journalism, and the pulpit the latter imparts its coloring matter to the former. But can there really be

---

result of reflection, whether philosophical, aesthetic, or scientific. We cannot therefore, without absurdity, treat it as the *source* of that very analysis and reflection. Whereas, at the conclusion of any process of analysis, reflection, or investigation, however prolonged, the self remains what it was at the start: namely, that which is *doing* the analyzing, etc.

an aberration in "scientific" thinking? Not, I would say, in that of a scientist who remains at all times aware of the openness of mind and the caution over conclusions which the strict discipline of science demands. But in the whole community loosely recognized as "scientific" such figures are comparatively rare; and they are rarest precisely in those areas of scientific theory that have the widest popular appeal. Among these the science of psychology has come to occupy a prominent position.

Its territory is fairly sharply divided between behaviorists and nonbehaviorists, and it is the nonbehaviorist psychology, stemming from Freud, or from Freud and Jung, which has had the most far-reaching influence on the public mind. The all-out behaviorist psychology associated with such names as Pavlov, Eysenck, and Skinner has so far penetrated not very far beyond the specialist fringe. The psychoanalyst repudiates it, as they repudiate him. But the question arises whether the "double-think," which I believe I have shown to underlie the whole position of behaviorism, is not as firmly, though less conspicuously, built into the original framework whereon the whole edifice of psychoanalytical interpretation has been erected. I underline the word "interpretation," because the clinical use of psychoanalytical method is distinguishable from the philosophical and historical interpretations that are frequently deduced from it.

Such interpretations will be found especially indebted to Freud's later theories. When he became dissatisfied with the hypothesis of traumatic causation in infancy as a sufficient explanation of adult neuroses, he did not abandon the theory, but carried it, instead, further back into the past. It was not the child, it was more likely to be his ancestors, and indeed his remote ancestors, who had experienced in their bodies the fateful trauma. The Oedipal complex was more a phylogenetic than an ontogenetic phenomenon, and the "trauma" in the life of an individual, though still so referred to, is less often an actual event than it is the "inherited memory" of an actual event, and of the anxiety associated with it, occurring far back in the past. Freud found that ontogenetically the cause lay "within," in the psyche rather than the soma. Nevertheless he continued to take it for granted that the *root* cause must lie in an actual event, a physical event — that it must, in fact, be somatically determined.

If one goes on to ask why, in revising his original hypothesis (which first-hand observation had obliged him to do), he ruled out a more obvious inference (that the neuroses might not be somatically determined at all) and preferred to erect an elaborate network of supplementary hypotheses about the nature of primitive civilizations and inherited archaic memories, the answer can only be that it was because he accepted as beyond question the overall picture of a somatically determined psyche and a somatically determined evolution.

And this is a good example of the sort of result the aberration brings about, in the way of glaring inconsistencies, not only in the popular mind or in the aesthetic or sociological domain but within the domain of "science" itself. For you have, first of all, the basic axiom of somatic determination, and this axiom is itself squarely based on the biological (Darwinian) theory of evolution. Later, in order not to have to abandon it, you introduce the concept of inherited memory, regardless of the fact that an exclusively biological theory of evolution is itself as squarely based on the principle that *acquired characteristics cannot be inherited*; so that, as a theory, it must stand or fall with that principle. It does not apparently occur to you that, if a *memory* is not an "acquired characteristic," it would be difficult to say what is! Or that if you are obliged to jettison the rule against inheritance of acquired characteristics, you must also be obliged to look outside Darwin for your starting point in the descent of man.

Yet the impulse to seek the provenance of the objects of our world by going back into their past history is in itself a healthful one—if only for the reason that it obliges us to overcome our reluctance to distinguish what we cannot now divide. At least it obliges us to do so, if we will not remain content with glaring inconsistencies nor refuse to look facts in the face because they upset our foregone conclusions. For instance, it is perfectly true to say that written or printed language cannot be separated from its meaning without ceasing to be language and becoming mere squiggles. Nevertheless the history of the alphabet is a different study from the study of language and cannot be profitably pursued until we have accepted that fact. Again, in a successful work of art—say a statue—the nature of the material is inseparably fused with the form of the work and the quality of the expression achieved. But the history of marble, or of that particular piece of marble, is widely divergent from the history of sculpture, or of that particular sculptor and his art. However far back you trace the history of sculpture, you will not find it emerging from the geological adventures of marble. So it is with the history of the psychosomatic organism called man. If you wish to seek its history, you must distinguish its components, because they have different histories and different kinds of history. At least you must do so, unless you can remain happy after you have removed the ground from under your own feet by introducing the self-contradictory notion of a phylogenetic "memory."

In our time the received picture of the evolution of the earth prior to the appearance of *Homo sapiens*, or at all events of the higher animals, is one of an evolution of somatic units with no psychic component. After the appearance of *Homo sapiens* it is an evolution of psychosomatic organisms somatically determined. As against this, I believe I have shown that in fact it must have been, *and we really know it must have been*, at all times the evolution of a psychophysical whole; and that after the appearance of *Homo sapiens* it became also the story of a changing reciprocal relation between the psychic and the physical components. We can, if we choose, focus our attention on that changing reciprocal relation; and it is the business of anthropology, and some part of biology to do so. But we shall get nowhere in the end if we are not prepared to accept that the two components have distinguishable histories which can be separately traced.

These are some of the reasons why I have long found credible an account of evolution such as Rudolf Steiner gives, in his *Occult Science: An Outline* and elsewhere, but not the theory of an exclusively biological evolution. To go so far, it is not necessary to judge, or even to examine, the method underlying Steiner's spiritual science. We can very well entertain his findings as hypotheses and, as Karl Popper and others have pointed out, the validity of a hypothesis is determined not by its psychological origin (which is irrelevant for the purpose of testing it), but by the degree of its congruence with the general body of previously ascertained facts and of *verified* theory.

5

Before however pursuing this any further, it will be relevant to mention that a good deal of recent thinking of and around the subject of evolution *has* been tending to pay more attention to the psychic component than had hitherto been the case. The later stages at least of the vast process are now not infrequently seen, even in Western thought, as comprising the gradual emergence of self-consciousness from an originally communal consciousness. Such at least appears to be the interpretation placed on it by the followers of Jung, Durkheim, and others. A picture has also been forming itself in a good many minds (the names of Ernst Cassirer, Nicholas Berdyaev, Mircea Eliade, Erich Neumann, occur to me in this connection) of an earlier or overlapping process of emergence, through the phase of "mythic" consciousness, from a condition in which the consciousness of men and the processes of nature were one single process after a fashion it is difficult for us to imagine. It is not always easy to divine from their writings how far such thinkers continue nevertheless to accept the basic assumption (which I have called an aberration but will henceforth refer to as an "axiom") of an initial world of subjectless objects. It is fairly clear from some passages in his *The Meaning of History* that Berdyaev did not, whereas Jung and Eliade could perhaps be taken either way. They seem to me not always consistent with themselves upon that issue. By others who certainly do pay firm allegiance to the axiom—Sir Julian Huxley for instance, and in a very different way, Teilhard de Chardin—evolution, taken as a whole, tends to be conceived as a kind of physical, biological, and finally psychological "*nisus* towards individuality." Where the basic assumption *is* retained, as it very definitely is by Huxley, this idea of a *nisus* towards individuality does seem to involve, as already noticed, the smuggling into a fundamentally Darwinian framework of the fundamentally un-Darwinian notion of something like an inherited or phylogenetic "memory."

The question whether such an interpretation of history and prehistory will prove to have been a passing fashion or whether it will gather strength and become in the end generally accepted by those among us who are deeply interested in the past is, I suggest, highly relevant to our ominous predicament of self-doubt; and it is relevant in this way. It has been pretty well proven that modern man must believe of anything that exists, that it has come gradually into being, that it has "evolved." By and large, he can no longer accept a hypothesis of instantaneous creation; and there is little doubt that, consciously or subconsciously, he applies this as much to his own individuality—"himself" as such—as to anything else he makes the object of his thought. If belief in his own existence is to involve believing that he was created at, or immediately before, his physical birth, he will abandon that belief, and he will have good reasons for doing so. It could however be quite otherwise, indeed it must be quite otherwise, should he ever be satisfied that this individuality is (like so much else he is familiar with) the end-product of a long process of evolution.

This is why it is particularly unfortunate that a viable and convincing picture of an evolving self-consciousness is strangled at birth by the axiom. Any idea that we must *from the outset* distinguish the evolution of the mind from that of the body and, inseparable as they now are, pursue them separately towards their origin in the past is ruled out in advance.

If it were not so ruled out, Chardin for instance could never have divided his book *The Phenomenon of Man* into three sections entitled respectively *Matter, Life,* and *Thought*. Between *Life* and *Thought* he must have inserted a section entitled *Speech*; for the origin and development of speech are, both ontogenetically and phylogenetically, the phase of emergence of human process from natural process ("consciousness" from im-

pulse and instinct) and of the individualized consciousness, which
"thought" presupposes, from superindividual consciousness.

The name to be given to this superindividual consciousness – *Spirit,
Logos, Creator* – is not here in point. The point is that a true account of
evolution would have to show the evolution of our psychophysical cosmos
for what it actually is, and not simply as a fancied evolution of objects
without subject. Moreover, after incarnate subjectivity had taken root in
Homo sapiens, the evolution of the psychic component of the nexus would
have to be treated as respectfully as the somatic. That is to say, the somatic would have to be, distinguished indeed from the psychic, but not fanci-
fully divided off from it. For precisely that incarnate subjectivity is today,
as we have been reminded, an integral part of the nature of the object – of
the nature of "nature."

The relevance hardly requires stressing of these considerations to any
possible, realistically and responsibly conceived program of "planned" or
"controlled" evolution in the future.

6

If the idea of evolution as a *nisus* towards individuality, culminating in
the individual human being's present-day wide-awake awareness of himself,
has become attractive to many minds, there is nevertheless one awkward
obstacle in the way of its acceptance; and particularly of its acceptance as
a ground for believing in my own existence. It is this. If self-consciousness
can truly be said to have "evolved," it must have increased *gradually*, even
if not regularly, towards its present status; it must have emerged gradually
out of a less individualized consciousness.[2] That is, it must, if we really
mean what we say – and are not simply supposing an evolution of external
conditions, or of instruments making self-awareness momentarily possible,
such as more complex brains, accumulated linguistic and cultural records
and the like. If self-consciousness can truly be said to have grown, or
evolved, from what it was in, say, 4000 B.C. to what it is in, say A.D. 2000,
then the same self must be assumed as present in both periods. In grammatical terms (which, if they prove nothing, are nevertheless sometimes useful
for driving a point home) when the verb "to evolve" is predicated, it re-

2. Jung, Berdyaev, and Eliade have already been selected for reference in this
connection. The process is more closely demonstrated in Bruno Snell's *The Discovery
of Mind,* R. B. Onians's *The Origins of European Thought,* and in many of the writings of Ernst Cassirer.

quires a univocal subject if it is to mean anything. In existential terms the process of evolution entails the continued presence of what is evolving. Thus, it makes sense to speak of the species *horse* evolving through the ages, though individual horses may have perished utterly. But when it is *individuality* itself that is conceived as evolving, this clearly will not do. For individuality is by definition not a species. In fact it is its converse. There can be a species of vehicles for individuality, but not of individuals as such; because now the very assumption we start from is, that something called "individuality" has taken the place of a "species" in the process of evolving. In this case, then, it is not the same species, but the same individual that must have persisted through the successive embodiments that reveal its evolution to an observer—becoming, in the process of transformation, gradually more recognizable as its present self. At this point a biological severance of ontogenesis from phylogenesis can no longer be maintained.

For these reasons the postulate of successive embodiments of one and the same individuality is, in my view, not merely compatible with, but indispensable to any hypothesis that a *nisus* towards individuality constitutes the law of the direction of the evolutionary process. It is principally because what is commonly called "reincarnation" is integrated in that way, and on that basis, into the evolutionary process as a whole that I attach to the treatment of reincarnation by Steiner an importance far beyond that of any other approach with which I am acquainted.

Reincarnation is primarily the name, not of a modern hypothesis but of an ancient and very widespread tradition. The coloring of that tradition, as it has come down from the past, is predominantly oriental; and the whole "set" of oriental philosophy and religion has been not towards, but against any such concept as a *nisus* towards individuality. Individuality is seen there, not as something to be striven for but rather as the characteristic human failing to be striven against; and successive reembodiments are the evidence of that failing. They are leftovers from the past, not earnests of the future. It is the aim of a wise and good man to avoid them.

Few things are more striking than the contrast between this attitude and that of a Western mind, such as that of the German philosopher Lessing, when he wrote on the same topic:

Why should not I return as often as I am capable of acquiring fresh knowledge and further power? Do I achieve so much in one sojourn as to make it not worth my while to return? Never!

The one, surely, is itself a "leftover" from the infancy of humanity, while the other looks forward (brashly, if you will, but still forward) to an adult status. It is, like a good many other Western utterances on the subject, no more than a speculation, but in the work of Rudolf Steiner the Western, and modern, concept of reincarnation came into its own. Can we doubt that the transition from the one attitude to the other is itself a part of the evolutionary process? Judging by the noise they make, infants do not much like being born, and we have good modern authority for the view that their principal desire is to get back to the unindividualizing womb from which they came. But a time comes when those at least who become really "adult" adopt a different stance and begin to think more of entering fully into life than of withdrawing to prenatal bliss. It would perhaps have been surprising if the primordial birth and initial growth of self-consciousness had not followed a similar pattern.

So much for the difference between the oriental and the occidental concepts of reincarnation. But of course there are difficulties for most people in the way of accepting *any* concept of reincarnation. Here I shall consider only the one that is perhaps most often advanced: if we have really lived before, why do we remember nothing of it?

It could not really be otherwise. I must refer the reader again to the fact that the ultimate break between "I" and "not-I," or between "I" and "world," is the break between the *act* of thinking (here) and the *product* of thought and perception (over there). I am able to perform that act, not because I am a complex personality—a mix of memories absorbed and qualities perceived—but because I am a single spirit. The *product* of thought is indeed, as we are so often reminded, psychosomatic, and so therefore are the contents of our memory. They are also, as we have seen, part of the whole psychophysical cosmos. But they are that because they *are* psychosomatic; they are that because, in the product of thought, the act has already become inseparably united with the brain, nerves, and senses, which are not the ultimate "we," but are parts of the world. I acquire a memory and a personality by uniting myself, somatically, with the world. It is not (and here East and West are quite in accord) the personality that persists, as a biological species does, through successive embodiments but the individual ego. To distinguish between the act of thinking and the product of thought is at the same time to distinguish between the two components of the psychosomatic organism—and to realize that, however inseparable they are during embodiment, the somatic component is not "I" but is part of the world. The personality is the psychosomatic unit.

If it could survive the dissolution of the body, it would not be that; it would be purely psychic. But neither would it be that, if *nothing* survived the dissolution of the body; it would be purely somatic.

7

Such is the analysis, and it was necessary for reasons already given to go through with it. But most people are likely to be less interested in an analysis of the concept of reincarnation than in its practical consequences. It will still seem to them rather pointless to be told that they have "been here before," when they have no recollection of it, or that they will be here again, but will remember nothing of their here and now.

A good deal however of our prescribed life as persons is rather pointless until we look into it more closely than we usually reckon to do. There is, for example, the circumstance that we "waste" about a third of our time in apparently ceasing to exist, as persons, at all. There may well be no better way of familiarizing ourselves with the thought of repeated Earth-lives than to reflect on this other abruptly but rhythmically recurring alternation of emphasis, which we know characterizes, and even constitutes, the actual nexus between the psychic and somatic components of our organism. The time spent by that organism is divided between two sharply contrasted phases of experience, the second of which, during adult life, has a total duration of about half as long as the first; and as long as each of these phases endures, the other is forgotten. During sleep the personality ceases, or ceases to manifest, but the individuality does not cease to exist. Not only so, but modern psychology discovered, or rediscovered, long ago that experiences undergone during sleep may well be as much, or more, important in the *formation* of personality than ordinary waking experience; and more important, not despite but because of the fact that we are "unconscious" of them. The truth is, it is hardly open to an educated man of today to maintain that I only exist because and so long as I am aware of myself as a personality.

Let us remind ourselves once more that a psychosomatic organism, and thus the personality, does not cease at the epidermis. If we suppose it does, it is because we were not really thinking of it as psychosomatic after all (see section 3). In actual fact it is built into the whole psychophysical cosmos. In sleep the unit thus built-in does not cease to function, but it does cease, or virtually cease, to function as psyche. Presuppositions apart, there is no particular reason why after death, that is between one life and another, it should not cease to function as soma.

If that is so, we might on the analogy of sleep expect this period of existence to be at least as important, if not more so, in the formation of a personality as is the period of bodily life. And this is another respect in which the findings of Steiner on the subject of reincarnation differ so markedly from any teaching on the subject that I have come across. It is common, in discussing or expounding reincarnation, to lay all the emphasis on incarnate and to say little or nothing about the discarnate periods of existence. There are even some who exclude the latter altogether, surmising that rebirth follows instantly on death. For Steiner, in almost all respects except that of the developing individual *will*, the latter period is the more influential; and is likely to endure more than ten times as long as the former.

There is however another point of view as well, from which the experiences of forgetting and remembering ought to be considered. If we observe the growing up of a child, or when we recall our own childhood, we have a process by which a chain of disjointed and for the most part quickly forgotten experiences gradually link themselves together, particularly on the thread of language, to form a human personality, for which memory then becomes the indispensable unifying factor; though without the forgotten experiences the personality would not be what it is. Here I think we have a useful analogy for the chain of forgotten lives and forgotten personalities, which successive embodiment involves and which we can suppose to be threading together to form the ultimate transbiographical individual.

The question of course arises: What in this case is the indispensable unifying factor, of which at some later stage of the process we must expect to become aware, if the analogy is to hold? In the case of the developing personality it is memory; but memory is part of the built-in psychosomatic unit, and we need for it a particular brain and nerves and senses. It is not transbiographical but only biographical.

To go into this would be beyond the scope of the present essay; for it would involve establishing the possibility of that very "sense-free" thinking on which the findings of Steiner on this and other matters claim to be based. Or to put it another way, it would involve establishing, not simply that there *is* such a thing as the act of thinking (which perhaps I may claim to have done) but also that it is possible, given certain conditions, to become conscious of the act of thinking to the same extent that we are normally conscious only of the product of thought. For this I must refer the reader to the philosophical, or more properly the epistemological, part of Steiner's own writings, the substance of which I once endeavored to summarize briefly in an essay entitled "Rudolf Steiner's Concept of Mind."

Meanwhile it may be possible to answer, for the present and not only for a presumed future, the teleological objection tentatively raised by the complaint just now imagined: that it is "pointless" to have had experiences we do not remember.

It was once remarked by someone who did not estimate the scholar's vocation very highly that the ideal scholar is one who remembers everything he reads and understands nothing. If he does not remember everything, he is less than a scholar; if he understands anything, he is more than a scholar. The epigram points to a truth that is a matter of common experience, namely that a too retentive memory, like Macaulay's, may be as much of a curse as a blessing. If we can retain and reproduce too easily, we may have no time or energy left for producing. Producing is our own act in a way that reproducing is not, and even understanding, as every schoolteacher knows, is an act. It can be assisted and "called forth," but it cannot be imparted. How much then of our own capacity to act depends on the gaps and interruptions (including the interruptions of sleep) that break up the smooth flow of memory? Lessing continues as follows in the passage on reincarnation quoted a few pages back:

> Or is it that I forget my former sojourn? Well for me that I forget. The recollection of my former estate would enable me to turn my present condition to but poor account.

If our felt existence as persons depends on our remembering, our ability to act, to *initiate* action, to be, in whatever sense of the word, "creative," depends on our forgetting.

This really brings us back to the point we started from. We find ourselves beings who perceive and remember. Thoughts, perceptions, and memories light up in us and then quickly vanish again. They are dependent on our brains and nerves and senses; and today we are aware of this dependence as perhaps never before in the history of humanity. But it is because of the consequently *fleeting* nature of our thoughts, perceptions, and memories that we are not determined by them, but free. But this freedom is rapidly becoming useless, and even menacing to us, because, overtly or covertly, we draw from the fleeting nature of conscious experience the conclusion that we have, as individuals, no real being. But this real being, in spite of the fleeting experiences of the personality, is precisely what is secured to us by our having already existed as units in the past. It is because of this that we are and can, if we will, remain more than pieces of stimulated behavior. It is because of this that we are, whether we like it or not, not merely spirit (as the Buddhists for instance maintain) but individual spirits. The sense of not-being from which we suffer in our present selves, and which gives rise to the anxious question "Do I exist?" is the indispensable foundation of our freedom. This is the orchestral *motif* we have just been hearing clearly and vigorously stated by the horns of existentialism. But this freedom gives us no assurance of reality. That is because we should in fact *have* no reality, we should be mere bundles of stimulated behavior, if the self had to rely on present experience for its being. But it does not have to. It experiences its freedom in the fleeting present; it is a real being because it has an immemorial past and has slowly evolved to become what it is.

Much, if not everything, may depend on how soon the generality of mankind comes to recognize this fact.

But if we remembered all that past, then, like the "ideal scholar" we should "know" too much to be free to understand what we have known, and to act on it. Freedom depends on the break between being and knowing; and so does transition from instinct to understanding.

To remember an experience is one thing; to recognize a fact is another. The moment we can recognize the fact of previous lives without the memory of them, the rudderless and drifting "Do I exist?" is converted into the very guarantee of our freedom and our competence to steer; we become, not the free nothings of Sartrian existentialism, but free spirits deep-rooted in the past and responsible to it, growing thence towards the future and responsible for it. I do not believe the one is possible without the other. For, like the two components of the psychosomatic organism itself, the question "Where do we go from here?" and the question "How did we get here?" though they are readily distinguishable in thought, will be found to be inseparable for practical purposes.

Science and Quality

Modern science is inseparable from the voluntary decision out of which it arose three or four centuries ago; namely, the decision to exclude what were called "occult qualities" from its purview. Modern scientific *method* remains based on that rule, and technology owes all its strength to a rigid observance of it.

The word "occult" means hidden, and "occult qualities" means qualities or forces which, although regarded as causally effective in the natural world, are not even in theory observable by the senses. These were to be firmly excluded from all scientific hypotheses. But what about nature's nonoccult qualities? I do not need to remind you of their fate as far as science is concerned. First there came, as early as Galileo himself I believe, an important distinction between "primary" qualities, like extension in space, on the one hand and "secondary" qualities, like color, scent, sound, beauty, ugliness, etc., on the other hand — the latter belonging (it was held) not to the world which is perceived but to the being who is perceiving it. The distinction no doubt seemed fairly obvious to those who first made it, but it grew less and less meaningful as, with the further advance of science, it was followed by the progressive withdrawal of *all* qualities from the primary into the secondary class, from the world perceived into the perceiving mind of man, or onto the subjective side of the line between subject and object. *Objective* nature is, for modern science, only the microscopic and submicroscopic processes which physics investigates. The rest is subjective. It is not the actual world, but a something which the mind and senses of man "project" into or upon that world.

Some materialists, or extreme behaviorists, go on to affirm that, be-

176

cause qualities are not inherent in objective nature, they are not "real" and it is better to think of them as "values." But we need not concern ourselves with them. Because whether we call them qualities or values, whether we classify them as objective or subjective, they are what the macroscopic world in which we consciously live and move and have our being is in fact largely composed of. They constitute the *life* of nature. Perhaps for that awkward reason it is more common to draw a distinction between the world of physical particles, or waves and particles, on the one hand and something like the "world as experienced," that is the macroscopic world, on the other. I will not pause to consider whether this is or is not a very satisfactory philosophical position, because my concern here is with *method*, and with philosophy only as incidental to it. And, from the point of view of method, it is a manifest fact that the macroscopic world *is* the world as experienced, and further that it must always have been so. Once we have admitted that, we may then, if we choose, go on to ask the question: How much of it is objective and how much subjective? But if we do, I think it will be found that the question we are really asking is: Experienced *how* and by *whom*?

It may be instructive at this point to compare our stance with that of enquirers who lived before the Scientific Revolution. Their whole world-picture was of course a different one. They had no philosophic or scientific doubts as whether such simple terms as "red," "blue," "loud," "silent," "warm," "cold," "moist," "dry," etc., betokened qualities inherent in nature; but neither did they have any doubt that these terms *also* betokened subjective experience. What they called "elements" for instance were not conceived as exclusively objective, and what they called "humors" were not exclusively subjective. The pre-Copernican, or Aristotelian, world-picture was a very subtle and complex one of man as a little world, a microcosm, imbedded as it were, in the macrocosm, and linked to it by an elaborate network of interpenetrating forces—forces which were neither exclusively physical nor exclusively psychic; and this was of course reflected in their cosmology, with the Earth as the center of the universe.

We reject that cosmology on the ground that it was "anthropocentric." But let us now, without ceasing to reject it, compare it from just that point of view with our own. We have just been seeing how the qualities formerly treated as inherent in nature have, as far as any scientific theory is concerned, disappeared from it, and how they have reappeared on the hither side of the line between subject and object, within the experiencing human psyche; how we conceive ourselves as "projecting" qualities onto nature rather than receiving them from her. Is that any *less* anthropocentric than the Aristotelian world-picture? I would have thought it was more so. The world as experienced. Experienced by whom? The Aristotelian microcosm, at the center of all things, was at least man, humanity as a whole, Rousseau's "*l 'homme général,*" anthropos. But our supposedly projecting psyches are to be found only in the separate head of any one particular man. We should have to find a new word for our own cosmology—something like "prosopocentric" (person-centered) rather than anthropocentric (man-centered). My object however is not to contrast our own world-picture unfavorably with the Aristotelian one. It is simply to emphasize the undoubted fact that, as far as the world is qualitative, it is an extremely anthropocentric world-picture.

It is from that point of view, as I see it, that one must approach the kind of question with which this conference will be mainly concerned. For it follows from what I have said that the method which has become traditional since the Scientific Revolution could never by itself achieve more than external and peripheral cognition. If you wish to investigate qualities, you will not get very far with a method which by definition has excluded all qualities from its purview; which has relegated them, as we saw, to the limbo originally reserved for the so-called occult qualities; and for the same reason: that they are unobservable in terms of measurement and quantification. Moreover, if you set out to investigate phenomena which you have admitted to be anthropocentric, you will inevitably find that your investigation of the world cannot be divorced from investigation of the bodily constitution, and still more the mind, of man himself. That is why the kind of science which Rudolf Steiner was seeking to establish is called "anthroposophy." *Both* the considerations I have advanced are essential to it: the inclusion of man *and* the development of a method. It will not, for instance, help us to accept the first alone and start investigating the mind and constitution of the human being by the traditional method. You can never by that means arrive at the anthropocentric source or focus of qualities, because your very method will have ruled out qualities in advance. Scientific investigation asks questions of nature and awaits her replies. If it asks only questions that can only be answered in terms of relations between quantities, whether statistical or otherwise, the answers it gets will be only in those terms. This last observation may seem rather pitifully obvious, but, as the late George Orwell remarked of the times we live in: "We have now sunk to a depth at which the re-statement of the obvious is the first duty of intelligent men."

If then we are obliged to look for a different method with which to supplement the traditional one, a method that will apply to qualities as well as quantities, what sort of method could that be? Another way of putting what I have been saying would be to affirm that qualities are "inward" as well as "outward"; whether we choose to mean by that an inwardness of man or an inwardness of nature. The requisite method must accordingly be one that turns its face inward as well as outward. It will not for example be one which hopes to discover the nature of mind by experimenting with the brain or with animals. It will be based on recognition that the source of what *comes* from within can only be found by *looking* within.

The first thing we notice is that a method of this kind is by no means an unheard-of thing. Objections of the kind I have been raising were felt, and strongly felt, up to two centuries ago by the *Naturphilosophen* of the late eighteenth and early nineteenth centuries, some of whom turned their attention to this very problem of method, though very little attention has been paid to *them*. In England for instance Coleridge wrote eight essays on method, in which he sought to resolve the ruthless Cartesian dichotomy between mind and matter, between inward and outward, and at the same time to grant, as it were, the anthropocentricity of what we call "nature" by equating the laws of nature with "ideas" as he defined them. In one place he formulates it like this:

> That which contemplated objectively (that is, as existing externally to the mind), we call a law; the same contemplated subjectively (that is, as existing in a subject or mind), is an Idea.

And of course, while Coleridge was pioneering a fresh *theory* of method, Goethe was systematically pursuing that very method in his botanical and other studies and investigations. The "*Urphänomen,*" on the apprehension of which his method is based, like Coleridge's "idea" (from which it is perhaps hardly distinguishable), is at the same time both mind and nature; it is neither subjective nor objective; or it is both at the same time.

Does not this, incidentally, apply also to the ordinary, recognized "laws of nature"—if they really *are* laws of nature; if, that is, we are not now to begin treating even *them* as "occult qualities" about which the less said the better? I do not wish to enter into a philosophical disquisition, but when the nature of objectivity itself becomes (as for instance in modern physics) part of the problem of method, science is in a measure *pitchforked* into philosophy. I shall therefore allow myself a brief word on the difference between "ideas," as Coleridge for one conceived them, and those transcendent and superhuman ideas which are associated with Platonism. For

Coleridge, and I think also for Goethe, an idea is on the one hand a constitutive antecedent unity in some natural process; but on the other hand,
howsoever objective it is, howsoever *super*individual, it is also the act of an
individual thinker. Only, in thinking—in pure thinking as distinct from an
abstract chain of thoughts based on remembered sense-impressions—the
individual human being functions, not as a skin-confined personality, but
as anthropos. That is really the heart of the matter: that the less personal a
man is—the less merely and egotistically personal—the *more* truly individual he is. And the more individual he is, the more universal he is. That
is of course a difficult thought; but if, as I am convinced, it is also the
mystery at the heart of creation, it would be rather naive to expect it to
be anything less. It is also the reason why the method for investigating
qualities, unlike the method of traditional science, must have a moral as
well as an intellectual coefficient.

I said that for both Coleridge and Goethe the idea (in the sense in
which Coleridge used the word) is, notwithstanding its objective status or
reality, an act of the individual mind. I should now like to stress the grammatical tense of that word "is." It is *now*. It was not always so. That is because, if we look back far enough into the past, there *were* as yet no
individual minds; and what is not there cannot act. Emergence into our
contemporary psychology of subject and object was gradual. Thus, if you
go back a rather shorter distance, only to the age of Plato for example,
you find that minds were even then somewhat *less* individualized, and thus
less capable of self-originated activity, than they are today. This is something that cannot be proved by the traditional scientific method. There are
ways of discovering it for oneself, into which I have no time to enter; but
it is a discovery which, in one way or another, an increasing number of
people show signs of making in our time. It is important, because it is just
this principle of an *evolution* of individualized mind or spirit, as the occult
or unconscious basis of personal human consciousness, which is the first
thing that distinguishes the methodology and the cosmology—or, as I prefer to say, the findings—of Steiner's spiritual science from the work of the
Naturphilosophen, of whom I have spoken, and of which it can from one
point of view be seen as a development. (I dare say it is known to most of
those present that Steiner first came conspicuously before the public as
the definitive editor of Goethe's scientific writings.) One way of characterizing anthroposophy would be to call it a systematic treatment of the
evolution of consciousness. But of course it follows from all I have been
saying that that will have been at the same time the evolution of the
macroscopic world. It follows, that is, if we accept (as I have suggested we

must) that macroscopic nature is anthropocentric. If we do accept it, then I think we must concede that the evolution of nature and the evolution of consciousness cannot be separated, but have amounted together to what I will venture to call "the evolution of anthropocentricity." And that is of course very different from the evolution that was assumed by the Darwinians and is taught to our children. For we have to assume, if we adopt it, not that man, after having been for a long time nonexistent, eventually emerged as one of the higher animals, but rather that anthropos was present from the beginning, though without the "centric" consciousness which we experience today focused clearly and sharply into body and brain.

Here let me revert for a moment to the pre-Scientific Revolution ("Aristotelian") world-picture. It assumed as a matter of course that mind or intelligence is operative in nature as a whole and not exclusively in the human brain. This assumption was vociferously abandoned. Indeed rather more than abandoned. I believe almost any biology student will tell you that it is absolutely taboo with the scientific establishment, so that it is as much as your academic life is worth even to hint at such a possibility. It is true that rumblings of discontent with the official doctrine of a totally mindless nature are now making themselves felt here and there in both physics and biology. One thinks in that connection of such names as A. N. Whitehead or of Michael Polanyi and his disciple Marjorie Grene. But by and large what I have said is no exaggeration. How is it then that there is not only intellectual conviction but also this emotional defense-reaction, or taboo? I believe the principal reason is the historical one. It is because any suggestion of anything like intelligence in nature (no matter *whose* intelligence) smacks too strongly of those repudiated "occult qualities" to which I began by referring. You will recall that it was on the exclusion of these that the Scientific Revolution actually rested. It is felt that to re-admit them, or anything remotely like them, would be to shake the very foundations of science.

But there is also another way of looking at it. We may choose *not* to forget that it is just this exclusion of occult qualities, and eventually of all quality, from nature which has brought about what I have called our anthropocentricity. Rudolf Steiner was, as far as I know, the first to point out that the Scientific Revolution betokened the culminating point in that long drama of individuation which is the evolution of consciousness, and further to maintain that this will be seen in future to have been its most important feature—far more important than any of the technological discoveries that have resulted from it, though he did not underrate the importance of these.

Ousted from nature, the qualities, whether occult or manifest, had to go somewhere and they have reappeared in the human psyche. It is significant that in their new home not even the occult ones are altogether taboo. Apart from a certain number of hard-boiled empiricists and behaviorists, most people today concede to the psyche that "inwardness" which they deny to nature, and they call it the unconscious mind — or the unconscious. In other words there is mind of which we are unconscious as well as mind of which we are conscious. And, since we do not consciously *devise* qualities, it must be the former which is responsible for those qualities which we classify as subjective, but which look so very much as if they actually belong to nature. Nevertheless we must not speak of any mind or intelligence *in* nature — because it is taboo. Might it not make things less complicated if we were now to infringe the taboo and concede that what we call unconscious, or unself-conscious, mind is in fact the inwardness of nature as well as of ourselves? Coleridge, who was also a kind of pioneer in the true psychology of the unconscious, put it succinctly when he propounded that:

> ... the productive power, or *vis naturans*, which in the sensible world, or *natura naturata,* is what we mean by the word, nature, when we speak of the same as an agent, is essentially one (that is, of one kind) with the intelligence, which is in the human mind above nature.

"The intelligence, which is in the human mind above nature," is of course the conscious mind, and the unconscious mind, which is also "the productive power in nature," is of one kind with it.

Steiner had no notion of reverting to medieval Aristotelianism. Anthropocentricity has advanced too far for that. It is true, the *Naturphilosophen* made good use of the abandoned world-picture and its terminology; for example the concept of a *natura naturans* as well as a *natura naturata.* But Steiner really began from where they left off. And in doing so he introduced quite a different terminology; a terminology which he made his own by careful definitions, though he usually refrained from inventing actual new words, employing instead those already in existence whether in occidental or oriental usage. Moreover he went into details where the *Naturphilosophen* reached only to generalities. Thus, where they spoke of such things as the productive power in nature, or *natura naturans,* and of its essential oneness with what we call intelligence, his spiritual science is developed in terms of the "etheric," of a human etheric body imbedded, so to speak, in an etheric Earth and indeed an etheric cosmos, and linked to it by immaterial, interpenetrating forces, which make the relation between the two very different from that which obtains between the physical body and the physical Earth. It is there, and in what lies still further behind it, that we must look, if we are really setting out to investigate the qualitative as well as the quantitative universe. I feel justified in throwing out such observations, without any attempt to develop them, because I conceive it is matter of this sort which will be engaging some of your attention in the conference before us.

Steiner did not want, as a good many people have now begun to want, to undo, as it were, the Scientific Revolution. He wanted to use it in a new way. But in order to do that we must understand its total significance. And its true significance includes the anthropocentricity which it has made possible, or at all events hastened, as well as the physical accuracies it has enabled and the *habit* of accuracy it has fostered. He would have us *begin* from the acknowledgment that, if qualities are "occult," or apparently unknowable, that is precisely because they are one with ourselves, or better say our Self. And that (he held) is the really vital contribution of science to humanity, not (up to the present) its knowledge-content — although we are so often and so confidently assured that the "frontiers of knowledge" are still receding. No doubt they are, but only in one strictly limited direction. For the knowledge-content to be won from traditional scientific method alone is valid only to the extent that both nature and man are treated as mechanisms. That has been its strength because, if our principal aim is to be technologically effective, we *have* to think in terms of mechanism. Traditional scientific method has done so; and it has been effective. Hence also its other strength: the firm hold of its consequential world-picture on the mind of Everyman in our time. The philosophy of Everyman could perhaps be summed up in the simple proposition: Science must be true, because it works.

It is becoming its weakness, because traditional scientific method is coming more and more up against the fact, the really fairly obvious fact, that neither man nor nature *is* only mechanism. Please do not forget the word "only." It often is forgotten by enthusiastic protesters against the evil aspects of our technological civilization. As you know, the general principle of mechanism is usually, and rightly, contrasted with the principle of organism, or organicism. Mechanism treats every whole as resulting, by aggregation, from its parts; organicism treats the parts as resulting, by progressive development and individuation, from an antecedent whole; mechanism relies exclusively on differential causality, organicism looks also to formal causality. The principle of mechanism is the accepted basis of traditional scientific method; the principle of organism is virtually taboo because formal causality, and indeed form itself, is not quantitative and is therefore in the category of the occult. But it is also a feature of our time that an increasing, though still small, number of those concerned with the life sciences are emphasizing the sheer impossibility of apprehending, of *cognizing,* any living organism, if the principle of formal causality is excluded. Nor is this movement of the contemporary mind, if I may so call it, limited to the realm of science. Awareness of a polar opposition between mechanism and organism, as universal principles, is, if anything, more widespread in the humanities. Anyone at all familiar with the revival of interest in the literature and philosophy of the Romantic Movement, which has characterized the last thrity years or so, will know how popular the term "organicism" has become in the vocabulary of literary criticism.

Of course it is assumed in such circles that organicism is only valid for art and poetry and has nothing to do with knowledge. Did not Immanuel Kant himself say so in his *Critique of Judgment*? Nevertheless there is some danger here, if we link this trend with certain incipient signs of a popular reaction against technology and even against modern science itself. Nonscientific enthusiasts for "organicism" are apt to see the contrast between mechanism and organism as one of pure black and white. Mechanism is the villain, organism the hero of the play. Mechanism is the root of all our woe, organism the spring of all our hopes. It will not be well if this naive reaction should spill over into science itself. We do well not to forget that both nature and physical man *are* also mechanisms. What is important is to distinguish the two *principles,* not to condemn one and exalt the other. What *is* important is to distinguish two active principles—of free *life* and confining *form*—while perceiving their interpenetration at all points. And if we do so, we find, once more, that the ultimate distinction lies between "inward" and "outward." Coleridge, as usual, formulated acutely when he defined as follows: "Whatever is organised from without, is a product of mechanism; whatever is mechanised from within, is a product of organization." It would be along these lines, I think, that one would reply to those who mistakenly identify organicism, or holism, with the so-called argument from design and reject it for that reason; since "design" is essentially a pattern imposed from without rather than emerging from within. And as such it is applicable to products of mechanism rather than to products of organization.

It is commonly emphasized, especially in artistic circles, that what is mechanical is *dead*, or at all events lifeless, whereas what is living is always organic. It is possible to accept this truth without rejecting the principle of mechanism as irrelevant even to the life sciences. Neither osteopathy nor surgery, let alone dentistry, would have got very far by ignoring it. For spiritual science, mechanism does indeed reflect the death-principle in the universe, but the death-principle is itself indispensable to life, and particularly to human life. It is to the death-principle that we owe the existence of a *conscious* mind in addition to that unconscious mind which is hardly distinguishable from life itself and is one in us with the life and instinctive intelligence present in nature. It is at this point that a research worker in spiritual science has to take into consideration, and to investigate with exactness, not only an etheric world and etheric body (which I have already mentioned) but also a form-giving "astral" world and "astral" body.

I want to conclude with a further consideration which arises from the polar opposition between mechanism and organism. The cognitive approach through the principle of mechanism *alone* involves that we perceive and think about the world and man *as* mechanisms alone. I have been reminding you that, so far at all events as the macroscopic universe is concerned, the world itself on the one hand and the way we perceive and think it on the other hand are inseparable. It must follow from that that, if enough people go on long enough perceiving and thinking about the world as mechanism only, the macroscopic world will eventually *become* mechanism only.

But I dare say the objection has all the time been at the back of some of your minds that I began by distinguishing sharply between the macroscopic world, which we actually perceive with our normal senses and our minds, and that microscopic and submicroscopic one which is only accessible to instruments and inference, and which is the special domain of physical science. Further, that all I have been saying applies only to the former, the macroscopic world. How can this be justified, seeing that practically everyone—science, the humanities, and the man in the street—concurs in assuming that it is precisely the other, the submicroscopic world, which is objective, independent of man, *not* anthropocentric . . . which is the only *real* world?

Well, I have done it on purpose—as I also did some years ago in a modest little book called *Saving the Appearances.* I have done it partly because I was particularly anxious to keep this lecture as far as possible within the perimeter of science, without encroaching much on philosophy; but also because, as I have tried to show, as far as the *life* sciences are concerned, the macroscopic world is *in any case* more than enough to be going on with. But I may as well add now, in parenthesis, that in my own view the submicroscopic, or inferred, world is no less anthropocentric than the macroscopic one. It is still the world we perceive and think about, only in this case there is a very much larger ingredient of thinking and a very much smaller one of perceiving. Certainly, as far as the problem of *method* is concerned, the approach to biology through physics is a way of thinking, another way from the macroscopic approach. Moreover it is the way of mechanism without organism. It is the way which treats any whole as constructed from its parts by aggregation; which assumes organization from without and not from within. That is no doubt why the method which springs from it is the familiar one of concentrating attention on ever smaller and smaller units—atoms and particles in physics, molecules and atoms in chemistry, chromosomes and genes in biology. Whether or no we add a hypothetical assumption—to my mind an entirely unwarrantable one—that as a matter of world history the macroscopic world was actually built up from these units, the fact remains that pursuing them further and further towards the infinitesimal is not the only possible method of discovery. In human history many of the most crucial discoveries were made quite otherwise—the discovery of wheat, for instance, and of the way to cultivate it and turn it into bread.

If mankind as a whole follows only the current trend of identifying biology more and more with physics, of learning how to *manipulate* life by treating it as the product of mechanism, no doubt many results will be achieved. But the achievements will all be technological; because the method itself entails treating nature as lifeless mechanism and treating man as a natural object, instead of what he is, a human subject; which means a human spirit. You may not be with me in everything I have said, but if I have rightly divined the impulse behind this conference, you are with me in this conviction and you share the determination not to leave other methods unexplored simply because they are unconventional.

The Coming Trauma of Materialism

Theodore Roszak's *Where the Wasteland Ends* (1972) is a book which seems to me to deserve a somewhat extensive consideration, not only on its proper merits as a literary and intellectual product, which are high, but also in the whole context of its appearance and reception. His earlier *The Making of a Counter Culture* was, I suppose, "radical" in most senses of the word, but it was radical in a mode that is already becoming fairly familiar, as indeed its title suggests. Essentially it was yet another attack on the establishment. In the second book his own "countering" passes from strident protest into quiet, if emphatic, argument. It goes much deeper, inasmuch as its blows are aimed, not primarily at our "power structures," etc., and our ruthlessly technological civilization themselves, but through them at the historical and metaphysical roots from which they spring. His quarry now is not modern life, whether plutocratic, bourgeois, or proletarian, but the "mindscape" it expresses.

Nevertheless — and this is the surprising thing — it seems to have been fairly well-received. It is in paperback in America; its publication in England last year was greeted by substantial, and by no means contemptuous, reviews in many English journals; the *New Scientist* observes that it "goes to the heart of the issues so clearly disguised from view by those who maintain that all is well, or will soon be well, with the world"; and so on. This in spite of the fact that what the book explicitly and repeatedly, one must even say repetitively, seeks to undermine is something which everyone, whether establishment or revolutionary, really takes for granted — namely, the whole scientific and commonsense concept of "objectivity." "The act of knowledge," he quotes a historian of science as observing, "is

187

an act of alienation." And for Roszak the "alienation" of which we hear so much nowadays is merely a synonym, an emotive synonym but still a synonym, for the very principle of objectivity, on which all science is and has been based since the Scientific Revolution.

The vaunted progress of "knowledge," which has been going on since the seventeenth century, has been progress in alienation. The alienation of nature from humanity, which the exclusive pursuit of objectivity in science entails, was the first stage; and was followed, with the acceptance of man himself as part of a nature so alienated, by the alienation of man from himself. This final and fatal step in reductionism occurred in two stages: first his body and then his mind. Newton's approach to nature was already, by contrast with older scientific traditions, a form of behaviorism; and what has since followed has been its extension from astronomy and physics into physiology and ultimately psychology.

Technology, he argues, is inhuman, and is proving baneful, because it is based on reductionism, and reductionism is the product of alienation. Therefore he makes it his principal business to contrast the principle of reductionism, explicit and implicit, with the opposite one of "transcendence," which has characterized the thought and feeling of all civilizations prior to our own. His case is that our behavioral interpretation of nature is not, as has been generally assumed, a reflection of fact but an arbitrary mental construct. It is a convenient and necessary one for the purposes of manipulation (technology), but insofar as it is assumed to reflect the whole truth, or the most important part of it, it is an illusion. Moreover it is *the* illusion, the one from which the whole of our cultural alienation springs, and we cannot find our way out of the one without finding our way out of the other. He sees the way out of the great illusion as proceeding, naturally, in the reverse order from the way in: first psychology and then the natural sciences. It will perhaps not be so difficult to cease taking behavioral psychology very seriously; we really *know* that another person is something more than his observed behavior, because we know that *we* are. "But now," he continues in a passage which I will quote nearly in full,

> Suppose this ability we have to find something of ourselves in people should be expanded, so that the same personal transaction occurred with animal and plant. . . .
>
> Suppose that ability began to reach out further still, discovering a reality of inventive pattern and communicative vitality even in what we once regarded as the dense, dead stuff of the world. . . .
>
> Suppose the whole of creation began to speak to us in the silent language of a deeply submerged kinship. . . .

Suppose . . . we even felt urged to reply courteously to this address of the environment and to join in open conversation. . . .

Roszak attempts no prophecy; he leaves it at that; perhaps because he does not underrate the shocking nature of what he is supposing. It would involve no less than the removal of all those metaphysical and psychological premises which have become "the subliminal boundaries of the contemporary mindscape," since we absorb them "as if by osmosis from the artificial environment that envelops us and which has become the *only* environment we know." Nevertheless it is possible to take his advice and go ahead from supposing it; and that is in effect what I propose to do on this occasion. The reasons why I do not feel the supposition too fantastic to be worth making will I hope appear as I proceed.

Our contemporary "mindscape" dates back roughly to the Scientific Revolution. It has developed and strengthened since then, but it was then that it began. It was preceded by a very different mindscape, which had endured from some time in the first millennium B.C. to about the seventeenth century A.D.; and which I will, for convenience, call "Aristotelianism," not because it originated with Aristotle, but because he was the thinker who formulated most competently the presuppositions on which it was based. This earlier mindscape was one which assumed an intercommunion between man (the microcosm) and nature (the macrocosm) not limited to the mode of passive sensation and active manipulation. Assumed, not merely "believed in." Either men actually experienced it so, or they were subliminally assured that it was so, or both. One way or another it was, as Roszak effectively points out (borrowing the term from Freud), their Reality Principle, just as precisely the absence of any such participation is ours. We may perhaps designate our own Reality Principle, and the mindscape that goes with it, "Cartesianism" on the same principle as above; not because it was invented by Descartes, but because he was the thinker, fairly near its beginning, who most competently formulated the felt alienation of matter from mind, and thus of nature from humanity, of which it consists.

For Cartesianism, as for Aristotelianism, its own Reality Principle is and always has been the truth, not for itself alone but for all men at all times. Any other Reality Principle by which some men may appear to live, or to have been living, is subjective illusion. Thus, for Cartesianism which came later, Aristotelianism itself had been such an illusion. This is where Roszak takes his departure. He accepts that the alienation of matter from mind, and of nature from humanity, *is* the subliminal Reality Principle of Western humanity and increasingly of humanity as a whole. He denies that

Aristotelianism and still earlier "mindscapes" were, by contrast, illusionary. By and large they were a good deal *less* illusionary than Cartesianism. What he asks us to suppose therefore, in the passage quoted, is an abandonment by the Western mind as a whole of Cartesianism, which should be no less total and effective than was its earlier abandonment of Aristotelianism.

It might be thought that (outside of strictly scientific circles, of which more later) such a change could take place without any very great upheaval. After all even in our Cartesian world quite a number of people seem to hold theories about the relation between man and nature which are incompatible with an absolute gulf between mind and matter. Quite a number of people for example take a respectful interest in astrology, not only on the puerile level of popular-press horoscopes, but also, as was the case with C. G. Jung, on a highly intellectual one; and astrology is based on an extrasensory relation between macrocosm and microcosm. Others bridge the gulf with an idealist philosophy or a religious faith; and so on. But any forecast based on such considerations overlooks Roszak's point about the Reality Principle; it overlooks the extent to which Cartesianism has progressed from conscious to unconscious or "subliminal" conviction. "Materialism" in my title means, not any materialist philosophy, *à la* Haeckel or Lenin, but the mental habit of taking for granted, *for all practical purposes and most theoretical ones,* that the human psyche *is* intrinsically "alienated" from nature in the manner indicated, a habit so inveterate as to have entered into the meanings of a great many common words and thus to have become accepted as common sense itself. Materialism in this sense is not, for instance, incompatible with deep religious conviction.

The habit is one which owes a good deal to a certain secondary consequence of Cartesianism that is not often recalled or alluded to. Roszak himself has less to say about it. He emphasizes that the alienation of man from nature brought about "alienation from himself," but not that the transition from the first to the second came *via* his alienation from his own origin and *history* as man. It was this that was effected by the secondary consequence I am referring to. "Uniformitarianism," as it was called a hundred and fifty years ago when it was first postulated, is the maxim "that no causes whatever have, from the earliest time to which we can look back to the present, ever acted, but those now acting, and that they never acted with different degrees of energy from which they now act." So it was formulated by the geologist Lyell, as an obviously unprovable but very convenient postulate, at about the time when Western man was first becoming deeply interested in his own and nature's "evolution." Adopted as a habit, and eventually by force of that habit accepted as a fact, it has determined the whole development of evolutionary theory. Causality not only is now, but always has been purely physical, untouched by "transcendence." Nature, alienated now from man, must always have been so alienated (so runs the tacit argument) and must therefore have evolved by its own objective and unchanging laws. Thus, other concepts of evolution, such as Goethe's, to whom Roszak devotes some attention, were quickly lost from view and the Darwinian theory triumphed. Fortunately the whole catenation is succinctly traced in the historical section of the article on "Evolution" in the 13th edition of the *Encylopaedia Britannica:* uniformitarianism depends on Cartesianism and Darwinism depends on uniformitarianism. This is of course not realized by more than a tiny minority, and Darwinism, inculcated from childhood as fact, intertwines with, deepens, and spreads the subliminal roots of Cartesianism. It is the combination of the two which has been decisive for the Western mindscape and is now almost synonymous with it.

Intensive reflection on these lines is really indispensable if we are to take seriously the kind of change Roszak tentatively envisages, since to reject the permanent alienation of nature from mind is to reject also the concept of an exclusively biological evolution, that is, of Darwinism; and it is just a fact that Darwinism is immanent in our mindscape at all points. In order to convince oneself of that, it is only necessary to adopt for a few weeks the habit of reading or listening to contemporary literature and journalism in a rather special way. Pause every now and then and ask yourself: is one or other aspect of Darwinism (whether struggle for existence, sexual selection, or the simple animality of man) implicit in that last observation or in the terminology it employs? You will not need to continue the experiment very long. Begin with Women's Liberation if you like. You will find three-quarters or more of the arguments both for and against unquestioningly based on it. Or begin wherever else you choose – child care, educational theory, environmentalism, ecology – and when you have done with sociology in all its branches, spread your net wider. You are likely to get a still bigger haul from psychology; and the result will not be so very different with paleontology, anthropology, archaeology, aesthetic theory, linguistics, and even philosophy as now generally taught. I have left out biology itself, with genetics, physiology, medicine, etc., because in those cases the special attention I am suggesting is hardly necessary, the conclusion being obvious even without it. Indeed the whole point is that it is *not* only biologists who (to borrow a phrase from George Steiner) "biologize the data," but that, either discursively or semantically or both, we are all doing it all the time.

Thus, if Roszak is right, as I personally think he is, and all this is not twentieth-century enlightenment about objective fact, but simply an ingrained mental habit, it still looks to be a pretty ineradicable one. Nevertheless I believe it is worthwhile taking a look at the possibility of its *being* eradicated in the foreseeable future and trying to foresee some necessary consequences.

At this point I think it will help if we vary his metaphor of a "mindscape" by substituting that of a frozen liquid mass; a frozen mass *on* which the psychological and physical structure of our technological civilization is erected, and *into* which are imbedded deep-down foundations determining even the minor details of the edifice they support. The mass, to repeat myself a little, consists of a collective conviction, mainly subliminal and by now amounting to certainty, (a) that nature is an objective system which man can only affect by manipulation from without and (b) that each individual man is a separate part of that kind of nature. Less important, but as following from the above, one might add (c) that one mind can only communicate with another through the medium of physical processes.

That is the mass, and its surface looks at first sight firm enough. Yet for those with eyes to see there are a good many indications that it is not nearly as firm as it looks; and further that the likelihood of the mass as a whole continuing solid is being seriously threatened from both above and below. Cracks are appearing in the surface, where the foundations first become visible to the naked eye, as the result of impacts from above, while from the opposite direction the frozen mass itself appears to be growing thinner, becoming more like a crust than a mass, as it is thawed by a gradual increase of warmth uprising from the depths below. The impacts from above represent instinctive human reactions against the *results* of the uncritical objectivity that has dominated intellectual life for the last two or three centuries; the warmth from below represents the beginnings of criticism.

As to the cracks, they seem to be of two kinds, the first originating more in the will and the second more in the intellect. As evidence of the first I would instance the truly remarkable, though scattered, proliferation of small journals and pamphlets, often the product of some voluntary association of human beings, widely diverse from each other in many respects, but having one thing in common, namely, violent reaction against technological civilization and its consequences. They are of course insignificant in terms of publicity, but anyone who goes a little out of his way to look for them is almost bewildered by the cataract of names: Alternative Society, Responsible Society, Confrontation, Dwarfs, Friends of the Earth, Resurgence, etc., etc. It would be unwise to ignore the presence among us of all those communes of mostly young people who are, with varying degrees of firmness, seeking to opt right out of technological society. Such at all events is the situation in England and I imagine it is the same or more so in America. The particular names I have cited may well not be the most important ones, and the reader may prefer to compile his own list of overt manifestations of what Roszak calls the Human Potentials Movement.

How widespread is the movement and what prospects are there of its becoming effective? It is difficult to say. The media, which constitute the mouthpiece of a democracy's mindscape, handle any widespread but new and radical movement of opinion in three stages: (1) silence, except for an occasional facetious and probably misleading reference; (2) if the movement does not fade away, but begins to organize within the silence (for instance, by attempting to influence legislation), it is disparaged, in the name of democracy, as a "pressure group" or "lobby"; (3) since it cannot be disparaged without being mentioned, this may bring about the third stage, at which it is at last openly discussed and thus begins to emerge from a collectively subliminal to a collectively conscious level. Roszak's Human Potentials Movement is clearly for the most part at Stage 1; the groups are small and widely scattered and presumably know little of each other; but straws in the wind such as a recent "Communities" issue of the Boston *East West Journal* and in England the *existence*, at least, of a "Directory of Communes" seem to suggest an incipient resolve to federate and thus to move towards Stage 2. Or perhaps some of them may be said to have already reached Stage 2; I am thinking of those groups and movements which derive their energy from what may be called the impulse of "practical ecology"—abhorrence of treating animate nature as an object, opposition to factory-farming, to wholesale experiments on animals, to test-tube babies, and of course to pollution in all its aspects. Roszak himself fills an Appendix with horrific instances of the things ecologists are objecting to.

There is another kind of external impact from another source, namely, an increasing awareness of phenomena that simply do not fit in to the mindscape. It must be fifty years or more since Charles Fort filled one or two books with a huge collection of these *inexplicabilia*—"the data that Science has excluded," as he called them—culled from an astonishing variety of sources. Arthur Koestler's *The Roots of Coincidence* has recently mounted a more systematic attack on a similar footing. Less anecdotal and probably more persuasive is the continued incidence of things like second sight, or telepathy, the sort of thing in which the older institutions for psychic research, and more recently the followers of J. B. Rhine, are specially interested. These however are still outsiders, if rather insistent ones. What is more striking is the growing number of *systematic* ideas and practices, sufficiently established to form a positive part of the structure of society but occupying a sort of scientifically *demimondaine* existence because they are counter-Cartesian. A good deal of psychoanalysis comes within this category. Hypnotism was the name given to the discredited "Mesmerism" that fascinated the early nineteenth century when it was found it could not be dismissed. The label was considered more scientific but in fact did nothing to render the phenomenon more explicable in purely physical terms. Yet it is actual and empirical enough to have called forth protective legislation to prevent its abuse. The "high-potency" remedies in use in homeopathy are prepared by carrying dilution to an extreme which excludes the possibility of physical causation, and for that reason are rejected as a flight of fancy by a large part of the medical profession. Yet they are in regular and organized use all over the place by fully qualified doctors. Acupuncture, which contradicts all established medical theory, is in use for anesthetic purposes in the Royal Victoria Hospital, associated with McGill Medical School, in Montreal. If I am reluctant to add the Anthroposophical Movement and the many practical activities which have been inconspicuously pursued for half a century by the followers of Rudolf Steiner, it is only because they call for so much more than the passing mention that alone is in place here. Familiarity with the incredible breeds, not contempt but respect, and it is no wonder if there is less readiness than there was to dismiss out of hand even such seeming *grotesqueries* as Michel Gauquelin's "cosmic clocks" or the claims of the Findhorn Group in Scotland to be fostering the growth of plants with the help of friendly nature spirits.

But once again the reader will be able to compile his own list. Some will no doubt recall the astronomical paperback sales achieved by the publishers of Edgar Cayce or Carlos Castaneda. As I write, the British *Daily Telegraph* is running in its weekly Supplement a series of articles covering the "paranormal" in general, including such diverse instances as extrasensory perception, psychokinesis (with special reference to Uri Geller), faith or psychic healing, astrology, acupuncture, and others. The writer reminds us that, until James Reston proved it on his pulses during a visit to China, acupuncture was "dismissed as a load of old Chinese rubbish"; he speaks of "trends emerging which are pointers to the future" and he wisely forecasts "a long hard struggle ahead," during which, whatever has been going on outside the medical schools, medical students "may expect to be taught from the same old biology and physiology textbooks."

Fixation by textbook, to which T. S. Kuhn also pointed in his *The Structure of Scientific Revolutions* (1962), plays and will play of course a major part in maintaining the compactness of the crust; and this really brings me to the underside of it and the opposite of surface cracks, namely thermal dissolution from below. But before going on to it, I ought to mention a contemporary manifestation, which may be thought to work from both directions at once. I referred in passing to Castaneda but without pausing to point out that the widespread use, and the literature, of psychedelic drugs has fairly obviously been loosening for a vast number of minds the reassuring opacity of the five senses and therewith of the Reality Principle which science has chosen as its base and on which technology rests. The increasing vogue for literature from the East, itself largely untouched by Cartesianism, is no accident.

When however I speak of dissolution from below, I am thinking more of those places—intellectual, academic, and occasionally scientific—where the basic presuppositions are less buried and more explicit, a little less subliminal and a little more conscious; the kind of thought-process that is observable in Koestler's *Beyond Reductionism,* logical appraisal of the presuppositions of materialism and no longer from a standpoint fixated within them—objectivity in fact about objectivity. There is some danger here of my metaphor leading to confusion, since we are accustomed to think of unconscious in terms of depth and conscious in terms of surface. The movement I am now considering is still "underground," but only in the sense that it is largely unknown to the general public. Nevertheless I have the impression that it cannot remain so very much longer. I can only mention one or two out of the many indications on which that impression is based. The metaphysical implications of advanced physical research are perhaps the most obvious, where quantum theory and its consequences are already leading here and there to point-blank questioning of Cartesianism itself and thus of the possibility of continued scientific dependence on "objectivity" as it has hitherto been understood.

Less noticed as yet, but more ominous, is the condition of the crust in its other aspect of congealed Darwinism. (I use this term to cover *any* exclusively and mechanically biological theory of evolution, so that from this point of view later developments such as the substitution of "mutation" for chance variation, of "genotypes" for species, or of "adaptation" for survival of the fittest make no difference.) I have a strong impression that here too the crust is thinning from the bottom upwards. It is true the surface looks firm enough. For the British *Guardian*, commenting on legislation in Dayton, Ohio, to insist that the Darwinian theory should be taught as theory rather than fact is indistinguishable from insisting on Fundamentalism, and requires the like facetious treatment. For the media, today no less than yesterday, to doubt the Darwinian theory is to be a flat-Earther. Evolution means Huxley, Monod, and Bronowski. But underneath, and not now so very far underneath, it is a rather different story. Thus, the *Everyman Library's* (1967) edition of the *Origin of Species* includes an analytical Introduction, which remarks on "the hymn to Darwin and Darwinism that introduces so many text-books on biology and evolution," reveals the existence of "a great divergence of opinion among biologists, not only about the causes of evolution but even about the actual process," and records the writer's own conclusion "that Darwin in the *Origin* was not only not able to produce palaeontological evidence to prove his views but that the evidence he did produce was adverse to them."

There is nothing specially new in such ideas. There have always been pockets of open-mindedness here and there kept hidden for fear of common sense. There have always been crypto-skeptics, such as the Cambridge Professor of Zoology, Adam Sedgwick, mentioned by E. L. Grant Watson in his *The Mystery of Physical Life*, who used to teach his pupils orthodox Darwinism in the early part of the century—and then privately assure them that, if they took the trouble to look at the *facts*, they would find whole groups of them which contradicted any theory of evolution so far advanced; adding that he himself believed archetypal forms of plants and animals to have been "precipitated."

But it is a long step from an eccentric professor's study with the doors shut to *the* popular cheap edition of the *Origin of Species.* Is the surface quite so solid as it looks through the media? According to the *Los Angeles Times* in October last, an Indiana professor of anthropology criticized his colleagues *sharply* for declaring "as a fact" that man descended from ape-like creatures and suggested that they did so "for fear of not being declared serious scholars or of being rejected from serious academic circles." George Macbeth's *Darwin Re-tried* (1971), which is not the only radical critique in the English language published in the last two or three years, consists almost entirely of the quoted utterances of contemporary biologists ranging from Sir Julian Huxley (on television): "The first point to make about Darwin's theory is that it is no longer a theory but a fact" to Professor Ernest Mayr of Harvard: "The basic theory is in many instances hardly more than a postulate." Divergence of opinion on subsidiary details is not less striking; and the book leaves one with a startling impression of head-on conflicts of opinion and a state of general disarray in the citadel, which do not suggest that the garrison is particularly well-equipped to withstand a daylight assault from pure reason.

Suppose such an attack should be mounted, and that it should be successful: the question I am asking myself is what will happen, in the first place to the general public? What will the effects be, as the crust grows too thin to go on bearing even the media, and the mental and verbal clichés they stand on begin collapsing under their feet? Roszak paints his roseate picture of a new and quite other mindscape. I do not think, as he appears to do, that it must involve the virtual abolition of technology; but leaving that aside, let us hope it might come true, at least in some measure. Well, but what of the "long hard struggle ahead" that comes first? I doubt if he has given much attention to this. I am certain his *New Scientist* reviewer has not. In Stevenson's story the transformation of Mr. Hyde into Dr. Jekyll was accompanied by convulsions. It seems clear that, as far as the elites are concerned whether of the sciences or the humanities, the first phase of the struggle must be one of powerful and even reckless resistance. Is there a hint of this already when a scientist of repute is heard committing himself to such a wildly unscientific statement as Sir Julian Huxley's on television? Does not that sort of thing sound by now rather less like common sense and more like mulishness? But there are other and more aggressive forms resistance can take. Twenty-four years ago, when Dr. Immanuel Velikovsky propounded certain astronomical and geophysical theories which, if accepted, would oust the uniformitarian hypothesis, Albert Einstein expressed the opinion that he had nevertheless made out a prima facie case on the evidence, which ought to be carefully investigated. The point here is, not the theories themselves but what happened to them. The trouble was that, if established, they *would* oust the uniformitarian hypothesis; and *The Velikovsky Affair* (1966) sets out in documented detail various measures, including the threatened blacklisting of a publisher, which were taken to ensure that they should remain not only uninvestigated but also as far as possible unheard of.

I fear the long hard struggle will involve repressive and other measures compared with which the Velikovsky affair will look like bow-and-arrow warfare.[1] How could it be otherwise when one thinks of what will be at stake for the defense? One has to imagine a twentieth-century biologist being asked to accept that the whole library of textbooks from which a man learned at school and university, from which he has himself been teaching all his life, and to which he has perhaps added an original contribution of his own, is in fact largely irrelevant. By way of comparison suppose a consulting engineer in high repute with his clientele who, as he

1. Perhaps, who knows, they will begin with the scientific *demimonde* referred to above. In some European countries active steps are already being taken to outlaw the use of "high-potency" homeopathic remedies.

believes, has spent his life examining and improving a vast central heating system, and who is now asked to accept that what he was working on was really only the thermostat! Why was Velikovsky ostracized? With the collapse of uniformitarianism the *actually* would again become the *obviously* unverifiable; and this must apply to all calculations of past time based solely on physical data—for example the age of the Earth itself. With that of Cartesianism similar extrapolations of the geometrically measurable into "outer space" (the sidereal macrocosm) must evaporate into adroit brain-spinning.

Let us nevertheless suppose that the resistances are eventually overcome and try to imagine a second stage of transition. This must surely be a climate of extreme depression amounting in many quarters to despair. Certainly if I myself, forsaking generalities, endeavor to focus on particular goings-on at the point of time where it shall at last have become incontestable that the age of postmaterialism has dawned, I am simply forced to envisage an epidemic of something like nervous breakdowns, with probably some suicides, within such solid fortresses of conformity as M.I.T. or the London School of Economics and among their alumni.

There will be problems for the many as well as for the elites. And here I seem to see not so much depression or despair as a period of total confusion. For example, what exactly will happen to popular sexology, as the cracks start and widen between habits of behavior and habit of mind? If it becomes as much a matter of common sense as the converse is now that an individual human being is a unit of dignity transcending birth and death and not a lump of galvanized meat? Darwinism, directly and through Freudianism, has been responsible for the artificial abstraction of "sex" from gender or humanized sex. One's imagination boggles at the convulsions that must accompany any struggle of anal and oral eroticism to turn into something like romance or the marriage of true minds or even something altogether new; at the incertitudes, the qualms, the misgivings, the deflated egos, the sagging self-assurance of a permissive society, as its whole vast monkey ethic of solemnly inculcated sensuality, masturbation, perversion, abortion, hitherto fed to it from school, university, parliament, press, and sometimes pulpit, begins to subside beneath its feet.

One way and another there is an opportunity here for a good book in the genre of science fiction by a really imaginative writer, who should fill out in terms of concrete events and experiences the issues I have merely glanced at, and no doubt introduce others. It need not for instance be assumed, as I have implicitly done, that the whole of society would resist, weaken, and capitulate at the same pace. It might become sharply divided against itself along the lines I hinted at in an article in this quarterly in the winter of 1972, with a consequent development of widespread domestic and civil strife. In any case the *order* in which various sections of society may adjust to the new mindscape would be an interesting feature to work out. The humanities should in theory lead the way; but it is by no means a certainty. Possibly, if I were capable of writing such a book myself, I might be tempted to depict the avant-garde movements in art and literature as the last of all to toe the line. Because, ever since Marinetti's hymns to mechanism at the turn of the century, their whole *raison d'être* has been self-appointed leadership of a culture advancing towards more and more materialism and more and more technology; and because, when a marching column turns about, the vanguard automatically becomes the rear guard.

But I hope this flight into fiction will not lead the reader to treat all my speculations as an idle exercise in crystal-gazing. They are intended more seriously. If a society is really faced with startling changes and fairly imminent ones (and there is a good deal of evidence that ours is) it cannot be amiss for a few people here and there to be peering ahead, however inadequately, by way of preparation for them. I must add in conclusion that I regard the speculations as applicable only to an open society. I have no space, nor am I sufficiently well-informed, to consider what is likely to happen in Czechoslovakia or elsewhere behind the iron curtain. But it looks as though, both above and below the surface of the crust, it could be very different from anything I have envisaged here. Above it, they have their own way of dealing with dissentient voices and dissident groups. Below, the difference is perhaps even greater. It is the weakness of most of our own counterculture groups that they evidently think it possible to abolish or tame technology and its *sequelae* while still retaining materialism (in the sense of course in which I have been using the term). It is the strength of Roszak's book that it does not balk this issue, though in sum he handles it rhetorically rather than acutely. But if the information available from Ostrander and Schroeder's deplorably journalistic *Psychic Discoveries behind the Iron Curtain* (1970) is reliable — and it seems to be well-documented with references unverified by me — the course they have set themselves there is exactly the opposite. Their back-room boys are quite ready to abandon materialism, provided they can maintain and even enhance technology by doing so. Research into *psi* phenomena of all kinds, but particularly psychokinesis, far from being discredited as reactionary mysticism, is now being enthusiastically financed by the state. But the research is strictly technological and the aim is operational not cognitive. What matters is, not the nature and highest function of mental energy but the problem of quantifying it as manipulable "psychotrons." In this way it is incidentally disinfected of all philosophical and moral implications and the trauma of thermal dissolution may well be averted. If so, we should do well to reflect that the presence among us of a powerful impulse no longer to deny the spirit but to impound it, or rather no longer to doubt it but to deny it—to materialize as it were the immaterial itself, or in other words to turn from theoretical to practical reductionism, may be pregnant with the gravest possible consequences for humanity as a whole.

Participation and Isolation:
A Fresh Light on Present Discontents

I suppose everyone would agree that one of the particular things we observe when we try to take a general look at the world as it is today is a growing demand on all sides and by every kind of human being for a greater share in the control of his own life and destiny. This ideal used to be called "democracy," and still sometimes is, but it seems to be becoming apparent to more and more people that, although there is a great deal of what is called democracy about, there is little if any of that distributed control. One manifestation of this, often noted, is the fact that on a particular occasion where people do have the opportunity to exercise their democratic rights, that is, at an election, either municipal or parliamentary, it is extraordinary how very few people take the trouble to go and do it. "Electoral apathy" it has sometimes been called. Arising out of this feeling of dissatisfaction there is a tendency nowadays to speak less of "democracy" and more of "participation," as a better name for the thing that we ought to have but haven't got. Demands for participation are heard everywhere, as loudly on the other side of the Atlantic as on this, and indeed throughout the world, and they grow louder and louder. Some years ago I suppose we rather thought we had done something towards participation when we converted an empire into a commonwealth; but I doubt whether very many simple citizens of the Commonwealth countries feel themselves participating much more in the control of their own lives than they did under the Empire. Meanwhile, in almost any direction we turn we get the same demand. The manual and other workers in industry demand participation in the management: students call for participation in the policy decisions of their university: women want to participate in the structures

201

of a man-made society: and we even hear it solemnly argued that school-children are being oppressed unless they are allowed to run their own schools!

There is another widely prevalent frame of mind that looks at first sight rather like the opposite to the demand for participation, although from another point of view it is perhaps the obverse or back side of the same thing, and that is the feeling that is sometimes called "alienation": the impulse not only not to assume responsibility for the conduct of society but, as far as possible, to keep out of the whole rumpus. Some time ago I happened to read in the newspaper that Timothy Leary arrived in Algeria wearing a button inscribed with the motto, "Turn on, tune in, drop out." I suppose that puts it not only on a button, but in a nutshell. Of course it *is* an attitude that is often associated with drug-taking, but not always; and I, for one, feel considerable sympathy with it as one possible conclusion to be drawn from the experience of today: when we look round us and see everywhere social organizations based on oppression, violence, and war; human life and intercourse dehumanized; and nature either denatured or polluted or both, by the monster of technological progress—now, it may be felt, too powerful ever to be controlled. I am not asking whether the impulse is justified, I'm merely pointing out that it is there. It is there and it is fairly obviously a root cause, not only of dropping out, at one extreme, but also of things like motiveless violence, vandalism as we call it in England, at the other. Now very likely in this second case, overt manifestations of the feeling I'm talking about are less widespread than the mainly sensational media we've come to rely on for our news would lead us to suppose, but I have the impression that the feeling itself is very much there, both consciously and subconsciously, in the minds even of the majority who do not go to the length of acting it out in melodramatic behavior. Altogether there is a great deal of bewilderment about, and a great deal of that paralysis of the will which bewilderment engenders.

The circumstance that led to my being honored to come over here[1] and address you is the fact that in the course of my life I have written a few books which have attracted some attention amongst scattered groups of people here and there—in Continental terms, rather more here than there—and if in the course of the evening you find me referring rather frequently to one or more of these books and hardly at all to any others, you will understand that it is not because of a secret conviction that they are the only books worth reading—a conviction which has been known before

1. This paper is a slightly revised version of a talk given at Dalhousie University.

now to accompany the onset of senility—but simply because that is what, as I have understood it, I am expected to do. There is one additional reason. When I began thinking of what I would say, I found myself in something of a dilemma. It seemed to me that the alternatives before me were either to use the time in a rather hopeless attempt to do all over again, in a single hour, what the books have already done, whether successfully or unsuccessfully, in a great number of pages, or else to try and add something new. In the end I chose the latter alternative as the more likely to be what was expected of me. But then the trouble arose that, if one speaks of "adding," it presumes some previous acquaintance with what is being added to, in this case of course the content of the books. But I think it unlikely that more than a small number of my hearers already possess such an acquaintance. The only apparent way to meet this difficulty is to begin by giving a sort of outline sketch of what that content is, and I decided to use about the first quarter of my time in attempting to do so.

I have been told that the books themselves are already rather highly condensed. If anyone feels that he is losing touch in the course of my preliminary attempt to condense the condensed a further thousand per cent or so, I can only hope that he will not give up in despair or disgust, but will hang on in the hope that the argument will become clearer when I go on afterwards to apply it to the symptoms I began by describing. It can happen you know. If you've tried to master a game, a new game you haven't played before, by reading the little booklet found inside the box, it is almost impossible to understand what it is talking about: but when you actually start to play the game, it often turns out to be fairly plain sailing. Well, one book in particular, called *Saving the Appearances,* is expressly on the subject of participation, and its opposite: only in a very different context, and also in a rather different sense of the word from the sense I was using it in in my opening remarks; at all events, it looks at first sight very different.

Very, very briefly, absurdly briefly, the argument of *Saving the Appearances* is, first, that the human mind is not an onlooker on, but a participant in the so-called outside world. Secondly, that this fact—namely that in perceiving the world we do not passively observe what is already there, but participate actively in its process—is today accepted in theory by most educated people who think about it at all, but is nevertheless ignored in practice. Thirdly, that this includes the practice of science, except for the case of a few philosophical physicists. We all know that physicists and, to some extent, chemists, no longer deal with the world we actually perceive, but with a world whose existence they *infer* from what they perceive. As far as the world which we do actually perceive is concerned, the ordinary macroscopic world, the *Lebenswelt* or *monde vécu* as I think the phenomenologists call it, or "familiar nature," as I call it in another book, *Worlds Apart*, where this point is argued in more detail, as far as all that is concerned, what the mind perceives is mainly itself; some would say wholly, not mainly; but on the factual issue of participation, it doesn't matter a great deal which of the two you say. What does matter is to grasp the fullness of what it signifies, to grasp it and not to substitute a caricature of it. Why do I say caricature? Because participation does not signify that by virtue of some kind of aggregated or collective consciousness, some "coenesthesis," or "intersubjectivity," or whatever new word may be found for it, a number of separated minds join in projecting into a world already there, a kind of cinematic picture which each isolated mind then separately experiences as the objective world common to all of them; that is the caricature, the caricature with which C. G. Jung, for example, tried to live. It is the attempt to concede participation and handle it philosophically, but without abandoning idolatry: I shall be explaining this use of the word "idolatry" in a moment or two. Whereas, if the concept of participation is thought faithfully through to the end and not hurriedly dropped at the point where it begins to look too uncomfortable, it entails that the world itself, the objective world that most of the scientists deal with, is not outside of man in the sense of being independent of him, but is *his* outside in the sense that every inside has a correlative outside; that it is the obverse of his self-consciousness: his self-consciousness displayed before him, so to speak, as his perceptions.

Of course, to use the term "man" in this way already implies that man, or mankind, is a real totality, as well as an abstract class of quantitative units. So that one may legitimately speak, as Rousseau did, and as Coleridge and others have done, of *l'homme général* as something no less real than *l'homme particulier*; and this I'm afraid at the moment, I must ask you simply to accept, simply to let me assume it, though many, indeed most people today, would sharply contest it. To the skeptical or the irritated among my hearers, I would say that I am very thoroughly aware of the objections that can be raised to any such assumption — I simply have no time to argue them — the arguing part of the business has been done already in the books to which I am referring. Another thing which these books of mine have in common is that their standpoint is always historical: the history of participation is perhaps most fully stated in *Saving the Appearances,* but they all, in one way or another, seem to draw attention to the fact that there was awareness of participation between man and nature, down to about the sixteenth or seventeenth century—or let us say, to the Scientific Revolution—since when it has been more and more rapidly disappearing; that is to say, the *awareness* of it has been disappearing, not the participation itself, which is built into the structure of the universe. The "Scientific Revolution" did not, because it could not, destroy participation; it did evidence a change in the center of gravity, or in the predominant *direction,* of participation between man and nature. And since then it has been increasingly the case that, although participation is still a fact, we are no longer aware of it; not only so, but this nonawareness culminated in a positive, but quite erroneous, denial of the very fact of participation itself. That denial was expressly formulated by the philosopher Descartes in his partition of the universe into "extended substance," or matter, on the one side, and "thinking substance," or mind, on the other. And it is on that denial of participation that the whole methodology of natural science is based. That is why the denial of participation has become implicit in the whole elaborate structure of hypotheses which constitutes the current world-picture, including, of course, our mental image of our own past. The denial was not only positive but also very sweeping, inasmuch as it affirmed, not only that there is no participation *now*, but also that there never was, or could have been any such thing. The fact remains that the denial is an illusion, and I should mention that in the book I have been mainly speaking from, that illusion is called "idolatry," the full title of the book being *Saving the Appearances—A Study in Idolatry.*

It is an illusion, but the fact also remains that on that illusion, or idolatry, the whole form and pressure of our age and its culture—the textbooks available to our students, the way we educate our children, what we tell them, for example, about evolution, almost our definitions of truth and untruth—have become inveterately and fixedly based. To question it therefore is subversive in the most literal sense, and for that reason it has become more than an illusion, it has become a taboo. That is a point I tried to make with rather more emphasis, both in *Worlds Apart*, and a year or two later, in a little book called *Speakers Meaning.* It is a taboo because, although you may refer to it in a proper and reasonably learned context (for instance, psychology of perception, cerebral neurology, idealist philosophy, atomic theory), you must never on any account bring it into connection with anything outside itself. You will never, for instance, unless you are prepared to face something like ostracism, point out that it is irreconcilable with the received theory of evolution, according to which inanimate matter preceded any form of life, and the Earth, very much as we perceive it today, was in existence millions of years before there was ever any kind of consciousness; still less will you go on to point out that, if it's taken seriously, it hopelessly upsets as much of psychological theory, and of behaviorist psychology as depends on the presupposition that all soul qualities originate from physical events. The trouble in fact is, that although it can be admitted in theory and even, as I have said, very commonly is admitted, to take it seriously would mean turning the world as we see it upside down.

And yet, you know, the world as men were seeing it has been turned upside down before now. Marx himself did something of the sort, though to a much less radical extent, less radical because the prejudice of which I am speaking is so much more widespread and more deeply ingrained than the prejudices he attacked. For this one is clamped as ferociously on the minds of revolutionaries as it is on those of conservatives; it shapes their protests and ideals no less tyrannically than it shaped the structures of the establishment they seek to overthrow. Or rather, to me, it *is* the establishment *par excellence* if we define establishment as "an obsolete structure which ought to be overthrown."

This brings me at last to the question I want to open up, which is, whether there is a vital connection between the aesthetic participation I have written about, and the sociological participation to which I referred at the outset of my lecture. I use "aesthetic" of course in its widest sense of having to do with perception in general, and not having to do with the fine arts only. I shall try to show that there is such a connection, and I will begin by making a very general observation without pausing to develop it. We have just been looking at the curious phenomenon of an aesthetic fact which almost everyone admits while his attention is being exclusively directed to it, but which is nevertheless forgotten or ignored by almost everybody in the theoretical and practical conduct of affairs, because of the startling consequences it entails. The question may be asked, Is there a similar sociological fact? Is there anything analogous to this in the sociological realm? Well I think there is, and it's this. There is the fact that modern industrial society is based through and through on the principle of altruism. It doesn't feel much like it, you say—well I couldn't agree more, but I am talking about altruism, not as a feeling or even as an awareness, but as a fact. Here too, the fact is nonetheless a fact because it is forgotten or ignored. However much we choose to ignore it, it remains a fact that in modern society, structured as it is upon a more-or-less universal division of labor, everyone works, not for himself, but for everyone else, and conversely each relies upon everyone else for what he consumes. I need not labor the enormous contrast between our own time and earlier agricultural communities. A single worker may spend most of his day, say, producing half a hole in a line of steel plates passing before him on a conveyer belt. Conversely the mind reels before the task of computing the number of human beings who must have been concerned, in one way or another, in the production and marketing of a single package of cereals: design and manufacture of the agricultural machinery; design and manufacture of the jigs and tools for producing that machinery; large-scale farming; and then the same all over again for the manufacture of the packages, the packaging itself, transport and manufacture of vehicles for it; wholesale and retail marketing, and finally the erection and maintenance of the large supermarket where our steelworker's wife eventually picks up her package of cereals. Those are still only a selection. What is unquestionable is that the principle on which it is based is that of all for each and each for all, of each individual human unit participating in a vast whole, which we call industrial society.

I ask you to keep that in mind while I now go on to consider a third contemporary ideal, or demand, or complaint, or slogan, or warcry (they are becoming very much the same thing) in addition to the two I've already mentioned. If *participation* and *alienation* are being very much insisted on, so, in the same breath, is *equality*; or rather, the ideal of social equality is not so much insisted on as it is presupposed, taken for granted. It is presupposed for instance, every time the suffix "ism" is added to the word "elite," to produce the vogue word "elitism." Whatever his income, his class, his nationality, his race, his color, political and social equality is assumed to be the inalienable right of every human being, as much, or even more so, as hot and cold water and a refrigerator. Now I'm very far from thinking that it is not an inalienable right: what I do think we might do with advantage is to take a rather closer look than usual at the *idea* of equality, before we start embodying the *ideal* of equality in elaborate schemes of social engineering; an analytical look at it in fact. That is what I now propose to do. It will mean limiting myself rather severely to a single aspect of a subject which has many others as well, but I believe it's the best way. I believe it will be best for me to deal with one aspect in depth, rather than to skim the surface only of a good many: the more so, because if I'm right, an inveterate intellectual habit of skimming rather than digging is part of the trouble. I am here not because I have a program of social reform, but because I've been suggesting for a long time now, that we need to begin thinking about things in general in a rather different way. At worst then, what follows may serve as an illustration of the sort of ideas which may come to the fore if we start thinking about sociology in that different way.

So let me begin by asking, what do we mean by equality (equality, in

the most general sense, not simply between human beings, but equality between any two or more units)? Consider an example: a student has lost his
textbook, he asks another student in the same course if he has seen it lying
about anywhere. "Yes," says the other, "I saw one lying on the floor in
the Students Union; here it is. Had yours got your name in it?" "No."
"Well *this* one has no name in it." "It must be mine then." "Wait a minute," says the second student. "How do you know? Everyone in the course
has got one." And, of course, the question that has to be settled is not just
whether the book that has been found is "the same" as the one that was
lost: all the copies of that book are "the same" as each other, they're equal
in every respect, they're identical with each other. But how do we distinguish *this* kind of identity from the kind of identity between the lost book
and the found book, which the first student must establish before he can
claim it as his property? Well we generally call the latter kind "numerical"
identity, if we're philosophers, and if we're not philosophers we don't
bother to have any name for it at all. Because one can only use such a notion for the purpose of avoiding confusion, or clearing it up when it has
occurred. That's for the very simple reason that we're talking about identity as though it were a *relation*, and "numerical identity" is no relation at
all. To say that a thing is identical with itself is to say nothing about the
relation because, for the purpose of a relation, you've got to have two or
more things. Moving backwards then from numerical identity (which is no
relation at all) the first thing you come to is this—what shall I call it?—
"replica" identity. Replica identity, or uniformity, is the relation that
comes as near as possible to being no relation at all. When we say of two or
more things, copies of the same book for example, that they're identical
with each other, we are saying that the only relation between them is that
they are *not* "numerically" identical, that they are two and not one. The
only relation between them is their separateness, their side-by-sideness in
space, their isolation. Now we do not always use the semilearned word
"identical," we sometimes use the commoner word "equal," as though it
meant identical, equal in all respects. The one book is exactly equal with
the other. What I'm trying to bring out with all this is that the closer any
two or more units come to being equal with each other in all respects, the
truer it is to say that the only relation between them is their separateness.

Reflections of this kind on the abstract notion of equality may sound
at first like a rather trivial academic exercise, but I believe they are not so.
I believe they are not so because if you take them in conjunction with
what I've said earlier about, for instance, the economic structure of modern society, you are digging down to the roots of the characteristic malaise

of modern society; and I cannot put that better than was done in a book that appeared last year, called *The Passing of the Modern Age*, where the author describes this malaise as "integration contradicted by disintegration."

Now there is one thing to be noticed about the notion of absolute equality, or identity. It is also the foundation of all merely *abstract* thinking. Abstract thought looks at a number of diverse and separate units — individual trees, or chairs, or human beings — and concentrates exclusively on the respects in which they appear identical with each other. That apparent identity is indeed precisely what it "abstracts" and gives a name to. And yet it is quite unreal. The diversity, the disintegration, is real; the integration is only a convenient fiction.

The opposite of abstract thought is imagination, which deals not with identities, but with resemblances; not with side-by-sideness, but with *interpenetration*; and if we want to see the whole system of abstract thought, in which we're so deeply immersed, from outside of itself, so to speak, we must begin by seeing it in the light of imagination, which is what I have been trying to get you to do. By the way, if anyone is in doubt about our immersion in abstraction and equality as abstraction, he need only to take a look at the educational policy of the British Labour Party. It calls for equal opportunity for all. Yes, but that's not enough; there must also be equality in the final results. As long as the schools continue to turn out a few who are better educated than the rest, the hated "class consciousness," it is insisted, will continue to survive. Political equality is not enough, the real aim is personal and social uniformity. Well, of course, there is a reason for it. There is a reason for everything, including fatal road accidents. You haven't got in Canada quite the same nagging echo of defunct social status, with its roots going back to the feudal system and beyond, back to the hierarchical social structure that was based not on merit, nor even on wealth, but simply on the bloodstream. So you're not in as good a position as the British Labour Party is to appreciate the disadvantages of classconsciousness. But I only took the demand for uniformity in education — ending in the belief that uniformity is the *object* of education — as an example. How many well-intentioned programs of integration seem to suffer from the same disability, so that they turn out in the end to have been programs of disintegration!

In the case of aesthetic participation, I spoke of an historical development, and I emphasized that that development can be seen as a diminishing awareness of participation, culminating in total *un*awareness, which is what we have today. This is what, in fact, I have mainly written about, especially from the point of view of the history of language, and of myth, as the earliest form of human consciousness to which we can look back with any confidence. Others who are better known have also treated myth from this point of view; a few, like Cassirer, have interpreted the history of language in a somewhat similar light. It is above all when we observe the historical process at work in the development of language that we see how this diminution of participation has accompanied the increasing prevalence of abstract thought. Indeed, they are virtually one and the same thing. It's the increasing power and the predominant use of abstract thinking reflected in the altered meanings of his words which have brought about man's isolation from nature; an isolation which is both a curse and a blessing, or perhaps it would be better to say, a potential blessing. It is a curse because it involves his apprehending nature, not as a nursing mother, or as a fecund and benevolent companion, but as an inhuman and meaningless mechanism. It is a blessing inasmuch as our very existence, as fully individual beings, depends on it.

Sociologically speaking I believe the principle of equality to be both a curse and a blessing in very much the same way, and for very much the same reasons. It is a blessing, and an indispensable one, where it belongs, particularly for instance, in the rule of law: it is a curse when it takes the bit between its teeth, or goes to and fro like a roaring lion, seeking what it may devour, because then it involves the reduction of human relations to side-by-sideness, as I've called it, and so it eliminates mutual participation. So you see, if you look at the evolution of consciousness in the light of that principle or process of participation-versus-isolation, as I do, you inevitably see it not only as applying to the relation between man and nature, but also to the relation between human beings themselves. There is the same transition from unindividualized to individual consciousness, and that also is borne out by the historical study of language. But it is not borne out only by the historical study of language, nor need you go anything like as far back as that will take you, in order to observe the process at work; I'm often amazed when I read a novel written as recently as one hundred fifty years ago at the totally different experience on which personal relations were obviously based; family bonds, common ancestry, position in the social hierarchy—these were still matters of immediate inner experience and therefore matters of course for everyone, in a way that has altogether faded from us. For instance, we laugh at Lady Catherine de Burgh in *Pride and Prejudice,* and so did Elizabeth Bennet, but Jane Austen accepts her *fundamental* assumptions as a matter of course. The idea, for instance, of there being any social equality between Lady Catherine and Elizabeth, or between Elizabeth herself and her coachman, except perhaps at the moment of death, would have been as preposterous to Jane Austen as Lady Catherine's ideas are to us. In other words we assume the contrary as a matter of course: *they* could not do so, because in their whole way of thinking and feeling, you could not possibly be a gentleman or a lady unless you were born one; everything depended, not on yourself, but on the blood in your veins and arteries. Go back a little further still and you come to that concretely participating bond that united the members of the clan or the tribe. There's a note in one of Scott's novels, I think in *Waverley,* giving an account of a conversation with a Scottish clansman who was asked how he felt about the head of the clan, "I'd cut my bones for him," the man replied. It just makes no sense to interpret this sort of relation simply in terms of exploiter and exploited. We're dealing with a different kind of human being from ourselves. We think only with our brains, but *they* were still thinking partly with their blood as well; and thinking with your blood is the real meaning of what is loosely referred to as "instinct."

Another thing you'll notice in the older books is that the negative emotions like envy, resentment, hatred of superiority, whether real or assumed, petty tyranny, snobbery, all come into play between individuals occupying *the same* rank in the social hierarchy, practically never between one rank and another. They are symptoms of a demand, not for political equality (which is already enjoyed by members of the same class), but for social uniformity. And this, or course, is one of the disadvantages of the supersession of the principle of hierarchy by the principle of equality. However idle and foolish he might be, the airs and affluence of the eighteenth-century fop, the Victorian dandy, and, even later, almost within my own memory, the Edwardian toff, were taken for granted, and often much admired by the Cockney in the gutter. There was mostly very little resentment against what was called "the quality." But once the principle of equality has been extended to cover everyone, there is nothing to restrain everyone from having those negative feelings about everyone else. At least there is nothing given in the nature of things, and requiring no effort on the part of the individuals concerned.

Let me just epitomize the point I've been trying to emphasize with the help of that little digression. Firstly, confused as they now are in most people's minds, equality and uniformity are two entirely different principles, and the demands for them are differently motivated. It will be found that, whereas the idea of equality is rooted in the strength of the superpersonal idea of justice, the demand for uniformity is rooted in the meanness of the personal sting of envy. Secondly, if we contemplate human society historically, we find ourselves looking back into a state of affairs where a saving *instinctive* awareness of mutual participation underpins the social structure. We find, as a matter of history, that the social structure itself was not the product of a social contract made between individuals constituted like ourselves, but that it arose out of the bloodstream, out of the *life* of human beings, of human beings very unlike ourselves; just as man's existence as an individual being has arisen out of the organic and hierarchically structured unity of the life of nature. But we also see this participation inextricably associated with political and social inequality. We find a continuing awareness of participation going on just about as long as we find an *inner* experience of inequality going on, or one could say, an experience of inequality as hierarchy.

So now if we turn and look again at our own time, we find that inexorable, almost universal, demand for equality: a demand which (confused as it may be) I am convinced arises out of the deepest nature of human beings as they are *now* constituted. The practical question is then, Is it possible to retain the kind of participation that makes human society possible without abandoning the relatively new principle of equality, of social equality? There are few more important questions, because the plain truth is that if it is *not* possible, democracy as an experiment has failed.

That was why I thought it worthwhile to try and analyze the notion of equality with some care and precision: because it seems to me that the future of democracy will depend on whether or not there are soon to be enough people about with sufficient understanding to grasp the respects in which all human beings are equal, and enough imagination to apprehend the respects in which they're not. It needs to be grasped that they are equal precisely in the regard that they are independent or, if you prefer, alienated and isolated from one another. Every single one of them is entitled to have assured to him his separate existence as an independent being, free of any such paternalist or authoritarian control of his choices, as was inseparable from the hierarchical construction of society, and free also from such other interferences as mass-disseminated propaganda disguised as news. And this equality, this political liberty he is entitled to, just because he is *now* capable not only of participating with his fellow men, but also of *not* participating. Participation is no longer instinctive; it comes only as a result of conscious effort. But insofar as they genuinely participate with one another, human beings are *not* equal, because they are not merely side by side but are interpenetrating. We had a glance at one domain in which they're willy-nilly interpenetrating to a degree that has not previously been approached in the history of mankind; that was the economic domain, where everyone produces for everyone else and consumes the product of everyone else. But there can be no equality in economic cooperation *as such*; it depends on a combination of different skills, of skilled and unskilled labor, managers making decisions and issuing orders which are obeyed, and so forth; otherwise it just won't work.

The same is true at the other end of the scale, in the life of the mind; there is no equality here, and it is on the *in*equalities that participation in a large measure depends. This man's capacity for growing wiser participates in that man's acquired wisdom: an ability to learn dovetails in with an ability to teach; the creation of works of art with their appreciation, and so forth. And the survival of democracy depends not on abolishing or castrating these activities because they entail or disclose inequalities, but on devising a social structure nervous and flexible enough to accommodate them within the overall guarantee of political equality to which I have referred. And that, in its turn, will, I am convinced, be achieved (if it is achieved) only out of a much deeper understanding of what human beings are in their fullness than is to be found anywhere today in the proliferating departments of sociology.

Perhaps I've been unfortunate in the bits of sociology that I've come across, but a sociology that is based on behaviorist psychology, and very probably on experiments with rats, whatever benefits it may confer, is almost by definition totally abstract, since it has preselected for study precisely the areas over which men are uniform, the respect in which they are identical. At best therefore, all the hurrahs, both of the researcher and of the sociologist who applies his findings, will be for discoveries within that area. At worst, this willed abstraction of psychological identity will be carried to its logical conclusion in the extremer sort of philosophical Marxism, where words like "bourgeois" are applied pejoratively, not only to capitalism, but also to any kind of individuality, and ultimately to the very fact of self-consciousness.

I spoke of the survival of democracy and suggested the need for a social structure nervous and flexible enough to reconcile the principle of political equality with economic and spiritual diversity. I cannot, of course, tell you how to build such a structure: I can only tell you, in my opinion, the best place to go for advice on it, and that is to the threefold sociology of Rudolf Steiner. The habit of pointing to Steiner, by the way, is another feature which has been observed on by a good many reviewers of those books of mine, as well as by one or two who have written on them at greater length. If you want my justification for doing so, you will find it in a book called *Romanticism Comes of Age*, where I endeavor to show that we had in this man a portent, I don't think that's too strong a word, of an incredibly learned and well-informed mind, which did not simply confront abstract thinking with its opposite, imagination (as many poets have done both in the Old World and in the New, as all the alienated do subconsciously, and a few of them explicitly), but whose genius succeeded in combining the two in an altogether new and intimate way.

A little earlier in this lecture I myself was looking at the concept of equality in a decidedly analytical and abstract way, but that kind of analysis was only rendered possible by the historical imagination that had interpenetrated it. And that is where the importance of history comes in; I mean of history, not just as an abstract study, but as what the Dutch historian Johann Huizinga called an "existential encounter." We study, or we ought to study, history not simply for the purpose of producing more and more specialized books, or dissertations, but because the only possible way of grasping in any depth both what as individuals we are, and where we are, is by grasping with imagination, where we came from and how we got here. We must realize that our important abstract thought arose out of the imaginal, instinctive awareness of participation that preceded it; and we must realize that our important ideals of liberty and equality, however vigorously they function in revolts against the establishment, were themselves originally nurtured and grew out of a different kind of establishment, which itself had grown out of the whole nature of the human being. It was a nature, it was an establishment involving paternalism and hierarchy. We no longer want the paternalism or the hierarchy, but we still want the roots from which they sprang and from which we spring. Cut flowers fade, and we shan't have many flowers in the garden if we work on the principle that there are no such things as roots.

I might add that this has an important bearing on education, on theories of education, because in the development of the individual from childhood to maturity, the phylogenetic development of the whole race is reflected and, in a manner, repeated. It is the child who has been educated in a climate of respect and reverence for authority who will have some chance of growing up into a really free human being, capable of criticizing that authority with judgment, as well as with passion and prejudice, not the deprived adolescent who has never heard that it is possible not to sneer.

I'm getting very near my conclusion and I'm wondering whether you will find anything I've said worth your consideration when you go away and reflect on it, should you pay me that compliment, or rather I should say that further compliment, since you've already paid me the big one of asking me all this way to address you. I know there is one very grave objection to it. If the history, whether of mankind as a whole or of the individual human being, is an evolutionary process of participation followed by isolation, if it marks a slow growth from the dependence of original participation, through isolation, which is a kind of adolescence, to the spiritual adulthood of what I call in *Saving the Appearances* "final participation," then unfortunately it is meaningful. And to see the world as a whole as having any meaning is enough in itself to infringe the taboo of which I spoke earlier, the embargo on admitting that the so-called inner world of human consciousness is as real and as old as the so-called outer world of nature. Until that embargo has been lifted, it will not be possible for many people to appreciate that imagination is the opposite, but not the enemy, of abstract thought, and that true knowledge depends on each of them penetrating the other. The idea therefore, of participation, vital though I believe it to be, will have little chance of taking hold. Participation is graspable not in terms of abstract thought alone, but only by the use of imagination in conjunction with it. Until, therefore, the taboo is discredited or, as I put it in *Saving the Appearances,* until "the idols are smashed," we shall go on with the cosy old twentieth-century image of history as the meaningless and absurd, and therefore of life itself as meaningless and absurd. How tired I am of it: how I should like to see it beginning to be replaced by the image of history as a process of transition from original to final participation; from the individual being shaped by the community, to the community being shaped by the individual, just as evolution for me is a process of transition from man being shaped by nature to nature being shaped by man. I should like to see, before I go the way of all flesh, the beginnings of both an ecology and a sociology based, not on ingenious abstraction, but on the concrete realities of nature and human nature.

If I am right, the possibility of its coming depends on the smashing of those Cartesian idols and they, in turn are protected by the taboo, or in other words, by the establishment. Infringing a taboo is not much fun for the infringer, that is, not until it has already largely ceased to *be* a taboo, then indeed, as in the case of sex, it's great fun. The infringer of *today's* taboos, on the other hand, will be lucky if nothing worse happens to him than being thought a crank or a maverick.

I expect there are a good many here who are likely to follow the teaching profession. Let me conclude by quoting a paragraph from the book I have referred to, *The Passing of the Modern Age* by John Lukacs, which, incidentally, I recommend strongly to anyone who feels at all sympathetically inclined towards the general tenor of the rather wide-ranging observations I have been trying to put before you. It comes from the end of a chapter bearing the ominous title "The Dissolution of Learning," and it runs as follows:

> The sometimes hopeless slowness in the movement of ideas makes life difficult for the young who, even more than adults, are very much dependent upon the ideas of others. This is why the dissolution of learning will not at all eliminate their dependence on teachers, rather the contrary. And the great teachers of the future will be those who, through a kind of wisdom, will direct their attention to all kinds of public untruths, very much including those propagated by the established public intellectuals.

Form in Art and in Society

A work of art is generally distinguished from other products of human labor by the fact that we recognize an intrinsic value in its *shape* or *form*. Most works of art have other values too, and many objects and parts of objects, which we do not think of as works of art at all, have this value in some degree. A thing is a work of art, however, only insofar as it has this value.

Can anything useful be said about the nature of "form"? In appreciating, let us say, a great picture, the consciousness oscillates between, on the one hand, a delighted observation of—and a *dwelling* on—detail, and, on the other, apprehension of the whole as such. One may forget about the whole in concentrating for a space on the perfection—yes, and even self-sufficiency—of the part; and then one returns to the contemplation of the whole, and the part is seen to possess an even greater perfection because of the way in which it is articulated into, and somehow reexpresses, that whole. Indeed, this peculiar relation to the whole is an essential element in the perfection of the part.

It is possible to forget this—there is even a necessary tendency for the artist himself to do so, a tendency inherent in the very nature of his activity; for the richer and more powerful the art, that is, the more perfect its form, the more independent life of their own will these parts or details try to possess. Anyone who has dabbled in lyric poetry knows how easy it is to become engrossed in the improvement of, say, a single line, forgetting all else. At last it seems perfect—and then he looks again at the rest of the poem and he sees that it is not perfect at all; because it has ceased to be a true part of its whole. In another poem it *might* be perfect, but, alas, not

217

in that one, and it must accordingly be scrapped — not without heart-burnings.

The "part" of Barnardine in *Measure for Measure* is an example, I think, of a part which has life of its own but has it at the expense of its "partness" and therefore at the expense of the whole, rather than as a contribution to it. Perhaps the last two acts of that play are in the same category. *Hamlet*, on the other hand, or *Bleak House*, or — to skip rather nimbly sideways — Chartres Cathedral, all are composed of a variety of entities, each with an independent value and even life of its own, yet each stamped with the peculiar quality that renders it indisputably a part of that particular whole and no other. In the case of *Hamlet* not only the characters, but many much smaller units of expression — the metaphors for example — bear the same unmistakable stamp. The play is hallmarked *Hamlet* in every link.

But, just as a distinct part may have a life of its own without fitting in to the whole, so another may fit in without having any life of its own. When this happens (as in a picture which is well-designed and no more, or a plot that is cleverly constructed but is operated by mere lay-figures), there is adequate structure and unity, but inadequate form. Artistic form, then, may be resolved into a peculiar relation of part to whole, and of whole to part.

The next question is, whether it be possible to expound still further the nature of this relation. I have spoken of the part being "articulated into" the whole, but of what kind is the articulation? Clearly, much more is required than articulation in a serial or spatial sense, and I was prompted to attempt this essay by the curious experience of finding in a book not concerned with art at all one of the best expositions of just this ideally "formal" relation of part to whole which I have ever come across. I refer to *The Meaning of Love*,[1] by Vladimir Soloviev, and, in particular, to the author's conception of "organic solidarity." This principle, he says, is to be found first in the world of nature, which it builds up by stages leading from gravitation to the animal organism, and subsequently in human consciousness. Gravity is "the general power of attraction, by which parts of the material world do not expel one another, but, on the contrary, aspire mutually to include one another, and to mingle with each other."[2] Aspire — but, as yet, without success. For Soloviev propounds, as the essential characteristics of *material* existence, what he calls "a twofold impenetrability."

Perhaps this sounds complicated, but we find that he is merely referring

1. Translated from the Russian by Jane Marshall, London, Geoffrey Bles, 1945.
2. *Ibid.,* p. 73.

to the commonest experience of all, namely, the limitations imposed by time and space on ordinary human consciousness, and a moment's reflection convinces us that he is obviously right. Let us have this "twofold impenetrability" in his own words:

1. Impenetrability in *Time,* in virtue of which every successive moment of existence does not preserve the preceding one within itself, but excludes it or, by itself, dislodges it from existence, so that each new thing in the sphere of matter originates at the expense of, or to the detriment of, what preceded it.

2. Impenetrability in *Space,* in virtue of which two parts of matter (two bodies) cannot at the same time occupy one and the same place, *i.e.* one and the same part of space, but of necessity dislodge one another.

In this way that which lies at the basis of our world is Being in a state of disintegration. Being dismembered into parts and moments which exclude one another. . . . To overcome this two-fold impenetrability of bodies and phenomena, to make the actual external medium conformable to the inward all-one idea—there is the problem of the process of the world. . . .[3]

This "inward all-one idea," which finds active and more outward expression as "organic solidarity," seems to me to throw light on the true nature of artistic form. Soloviev begins by pointing out how the overcoming of impenetrability is accomplished, and the "all-one idea" gradually realized, in the world of nature. In the first place, he says, the unity of the world of matter is itself not a material unity. Or rather, there is no such thing as material unity. That is a contradiction in terms. For if nothing but matter existed, the universe would be made up of mutually impenetrable objects, doomed to perpetual isolation from one another. But in nature the all-one idea attains to a partial manifestation, "in a spiritual-corporeal fashion," by means of the worldwide force of gravity, and by means of light and other kindred phenomena, which serve to knit material objects together and to establish some sort of communication between them. *Yet, the fullness of the idea demands that the greatest possible unity of the whole should be realized in the greatest possible independence and freedom of the particular and single elements.* And it is in pursuance of this tendency that the cosmic process, as it reaches the organic, attains to

3. *Ibid.,* p. 72.

the creation of animal life—to that unity of the living body, wherein is realized "a complete solidarity and reciprocity of all the particular organs and elements."

Now the imagination or *mens creatrix*, the faculty to which we impute the provenance of art, has also frequently been spoken of as "organic," and indeed this quality is in some degree implied by the very use of such an adjective as "creative." But if "organic" in this connection is to signify anything more than a loose analogy with the mysterious ways of "nature," we need to have a clearer idea of the general principle underlying "organic" processes. In short, we must know what "organic" means.

And it is here that Soloviev comes to our aid, building up, through his concept of "organic solidarity," the image of a special relation between part and whole, which is neither serial nor spatial nor—as we shall see— hierarchical; the kind of relation, in fact, which the imagination, and only the imagination, detects between the parts and whole of a living organism, and both creates and detects between the parts and whole of a work of art. For imagination is, precisely, that which experiences form.

Thus the body of a single animal—when regarded as a whole—manifests the principle of organic solidarity. But nature goes further than this. Though each body is in itself a whole, yet each animal, regarded as a unit of consciousness, is only a part. As such, it is a part of the *race*; and it experiences, says Soloviev, the unity of the race in its full force at the moment of sexual impulse, when the inward unity or community with the "other," with the "all," receives its concrete embodiment in the relation to a single being of the other sex, which represents this complementary "all" in one.

But since the process of individualization is carried furthest of all in the human being, it follows that it is in human society that the all-one idea can be most fully realized. For man, too, that inward unity or community receives its concrete embodiment in the relation to a single person of the other sex; but the unity which he thus experiences, or ought to experience, is the unity, not merely of the physical race, but of the social organism. The social organism "is produced by that same creative life-force of love, which gives birth also to physical organisms." The love between two human beings (and this strangely packed little book is primarily a disquisition on human love) is true to its own essence only if it functions as a sort of biological cell, with the potentiality of expanding to the entire social organism. We may suppose that Soloviev would have approved the words of Thomas Traherne:

That violence whereby sometimes a man doteth upon one creature is but a little spark of that love, even towards all, which lurketh in his nature. When we dote upon the perfections and beauties of some one creature, we do not love that too much, but other things too little. Never was anything in this world loved too much, but many things have been loved in a false way, and all in too short a measure.

Of course it is, in a way, characteristic of human experience that it can *not* be divided up into parts at all, and this is the discovery of the "association-stream" school of writers and painters, who strive to represent the flux, and call it art. Nevertheless, experience is imaginal (a better word, I think, than "imaginative" for this purpose) precisely to the extent that it *is* organic in the sense already given. Certainly its parts are virtually inseparable in space and time—everything slides into everything else. But it is characteristic of imaginal, or aesthetic, experience (they are the same thing), as distinct from reverie or doodling, that its parts are *spiritually* separable in a way in which the parts of nonaesthetic experience are not. And it is just this separableness which constitutes their "organic" quality. It is this which draws them from the living but unorganized stream of consciousness, as it is this which draws the vegetable or animal "organism" from the primeval ocean. Admittedly the parts of an organism are also *in*-separable, but it is precisely this paradox, or tension between two opposite states, which makes a thing an "organism." Its parts are inseparable, inasmuch as it is not dead; they are (at least, notionally) separable, inasmuch as it is not *merely* living, but something more.

A work of art, then, is characterized, not by the absence of distinct parts but, on the contrary, by the greatest possible distinctness and self-sufficiency of its parts—provided only that we do not think of them as mutually impenetrable. It is equally clear that interpenetration is a quality which the parts possess, not as mere objects, but precisely as being (a) wholes in themselves and (b) "parts" of the same whole. They interpenetrate and are *pro tanto* inseparable, not because the whole is a formless waste, but because the whole has form, and that form enters into each of them. Can we therefore go further and affirm that the ideal organic relation of part to whole is a sort of *identity* of the one with the other? That, in musical terms, ideal counterpoint is fugue—where the whole melody is found again in each part?[4] Now, according to Soloviev, this is or ought to

4. This is intended as an illustration of my meaning, not as a musical judgment, for which I am not competent. It may be that there is a *mechanical* element of identity in the fugal form, which mars its perfection as an "organism." I do not know. There has at all events been a persistent notion to the effect I have indicated; and for my own ear the fugure possesses a spiritual quality, like that of light itself.

be true of human society—that whole of which individual men are the "parts." Not only man in general, but each individual man "may *become* all" (he says), as he lives and learns to do away with that inward boundary which severs him from the rest.

And again: the ideal "person, or embodiment of the idea, is only an individualization of the all-oneness, which is indivisibly present in each of its individualizations."[5] Thus, in the "all-one idea" realized, the part *is* the whole, not by merger, but on the contrary by intensive development of its true individuality or part-ness. Or rather the whole is the part; for, whereas when we think abstractly *about* being, as in the processes of logic and classification, the whole is predicated of the part, so that we say "A horse *is* a quadruped," in the actual *process* of being, the order is reversed, and the race or archetype *is* the species or individual—because it gives it being.

If it is important to know as much as possible of what we mean when we call art "organic," there are other common epithets which would repay as close an inspection. It has, for instance, long been the fashion to speak of art as "creative." Anyone who follows that fashion would do well to ask himself which of three things he means. He may use the term, meaning simply that an artist makes something, without implying anything at all about the manner in which he does so. If so, "creative" is not much more than a complimentary endearment. Or, secondly, he may mean that the maker of a work of art works in the same *way* as does the process of natural creation. One might hold this view and still conceive of art as being primarily mimetic. Or thirdly—and this is the notion to which Romantic theory of art has always tended—one may mean that the *same* process (denoting thereby not similarity but identity) is at work in the artist as in nature. It was in the development of this theory that the word "creative" first came to be applied to human, as distinct from divine, activity, and, unless this theory is accepted, it is really a solecism. The name by which English writers have usually designated such a supposed "creative" faculty is imagination.

Now the most distinctive feature of Soloviev's book is that it propounds an adequate conception of Christian love, without at the same time setting this over against nature and the natural. On the contrary, by applying his concept of "organic solidarity," he reveals the same spiritual principle at work, on the one hand in nature and on the other in man and society. The aim and object of this principle is everywhere the same—the establishment of an "organic" relation between part and whole—and, when the "whole"

5. Soloviev, p. 61.

in question is human society, the principle is usually called love. Such a conception of love, not exclusively as the fruit of "grace" supervening on "nature" from a contrasted source, but rather as a normal extension of the natural process itself, carries far-reaching implications; and it is my whole contention that these implications may be profitably considered and better understood in connection with a similar theory of imagination.

At the present juncture of affairs the establishment of a true relation (by which I mean one that will satisfy the deepest needs of human beings) between part and whole in society is a problem of great practical urgency. Indeed it is a truism that civilization is threatening to break down because of man's failure to solve it.

In the period that ended, we will say, with the French Revolution, this problem was solved for Europeans by a wide acceptance of the spiritual principle of hierarchy, and its social expression, feudalism. The feudal structure endured and withstood shocks, because hierarchy is also "organic" in another—perhaps commoner—sense of the word; though it is not organic in the sense intended by Soloviev in his phrase "organic solidarity." Now if that principle of hierarchy is a permanently valid one, it follows that the abandonment of feudalism in society has been an aberration and the way back to health and sanity lies through its restoration, however difficult that may be.

For my own part I would not too lightly dismiss such a view: too many people have rendered themselves incapable of discerning the healthy principle of hierarchy at all, by keeping their eyes narrowly glued on its disease, exploitation. An excellent and very sympathetic account of the true principle and of its value not only for society but also for the individual human soul may be found in C. S. Lewis's *Preface to Paradise Lost*.[6] In a community based on that principle, where "degree" (as Ulysses calls it in the well-known speech in *Troilus and Cressida*) is accepted as of course and felt as divinely ordained, no individual human "part" would dream of thinking himself from any point of view commensurate with the whole or the equal of every other "part." But neither, on the other hand, would he feel isolated or insultingly inferior.

Yet, when all this has been well considered, the question still remains, whether the principle of hierarchy *is* in fact paramount; beyond the reach of historical development; a permanent and necessary element in human consciousness and therefore in the form of human society; or not. We must not turn a blind eye upon a truth, merely because it happens to lie in

6. Oxford University Press, 1942.

a direction in which many shallow-minded, many shortsighted, and many ignorant people are pointing; and I cannot avoid a conviction in my bones that the fall of the Bastille did betoken much more than the bursting of a temporary imposthume of exploitation on the healthy body of feudalism. I believe it did mark the fact, though not necessarily the moment, of transition to a period in which the old principle would no longer serve.

Either there has been such a real change or there has not. We must make up our minds which we believe. I think that the change (place it in the "unconscious," if you prefer) was greater, not less, than is supposed by the philosophy of the Left. Moreover, the eradication of feudalism and, indeed, of all notion of "degree" from the structure of society is accelerating as it approaches completion. Is the present chaos partly due to the fact that our thinking has not kept pace with it? Is our thinking—not merely its product (notions) but its very form and structure—still too hierarchic in a world whose underlying spiritual form demands an egalitarian social structure?

The structure of feudal Europe was based on two parallel hierarchical systems, the secular and the spiritual. And in feudal Europe the form of thought which was pursued by the learned with enthusiasm, worked out, developed, and all its possibilities investigated, was logic. Now hierarchy in society is logical classification realized—allegiance being substituted for predication. Thus, hierarchy in the social structure was not a thing to argue about. Classes were the structure of society as self-evidently as classification was the structure of thought. May it not be that a valid and enduring new form of society will take shape only as and when the principle of its structure is generally felt to be self-evident in the same way?

If this be so, and if the new principle is to be something like Soloviev's "organic solidarity," we may see a new significance in the fact that the form of thought which began to be pursued with enthusiasm, worked out, developed, and its possibilities investigated in the present period (which I have for convenience taken as beginning with the French Revolution) was imagination. Should *imagination*, as the Romantics tried to expound it, take as firm a hold of the minds of the intelligentsia (or clerisy, as I prefer to call them) as *judgment* did in feudal Europe, it would furnish the necessary mental foundation for a viable democracy. Necessary, because the existing foundation of Newtonian, atomic thought, can only be realized either in *laissez faire* or in the totalitarian reaction from it.

We need not trouble ourselves here with supposing the various channels by which such a prevalent thought-form could overflow from the clerisy into the minds of the masses; as, in the Middle Ages, the forms of hierarchy and judgment were soon there for all in pageants, mystery plays, in ubiquitous frescoes of the Last Judgment, and otherwise. This part of the process can be left to take care of itself, once the thought is made clear, established, and accepted.

The demand for social "solidarity" and the conviction of its necessity are today realities; they cannot be denied. If the attempt is made to deny them, they revenge themselves by attacking the denier — man or nation — in the rear; confusing his mind, weakening his will, and reducing him to a condition of impotent *malaise*. But the demand for individual liberty, spiritual as well as political, is no less real. Unfortunately it appears all too evident to most people that individualism is incompatible with collectivism and "fellowship," and that to propound as a good the unlimited expansion of individualism in any sphere would be to preach moral egoism and social anarchy.

Herein lies both the moral and the sociological importance of Soloviev's doctrine of organic solidarity. If this doctrine be true, it is not for the individualist to go cap in hand, apologetically, to the collectivist, saying: After all, you must leave something to the individual! Life will not be worth living if you don't! Nor should he merely argue: Society is only the means; the individual is the end for which it exists! Rather he should proclaim with all his might: You cannot *have* an enduring society *at all,* unless you provide for the free spiritual expansion of the individual. So far from individualism leading to social anarchy, the solidarity of your society will vary directly with the extent to which the individuals composing it become and remain individuals. If you are aiming at collective unity, you *must* also be aiming at individual liberty!

This is exactly what Rudolf Steiner sought to drive home from so many different points of view in his book, *The Threefold Commonwealth*; and I am sure that this book has met with so little understanding principally because the ideas it expounds need, in order to grasp them, the kind of thinking and perception which is normally reserved today for the appreciation of works of art. Yet if — as I believe to be the case — a modern social structure must, if it is to be healthy and durable, be somehow *artistically* right, this is exactly what we should expect. For such a structure will have to transcend the impenetrabilities of which Soloviev wrote.

If our thinking accepts the impenetrabilities, we shall conceive of the state as something put together by aggregating units — pyramidally or otherwise. Or we may arrive at it by adding together the three estates, each estate being composed of a separate collection of human beings. Perhaps, allowing imagination to creep in at one point, we may allow one man at the head to feel and to say: *L'état c'est moi*. But in Steiner's democracy each man is at the same time a member of all three estates; since his deeply threefold nature, as it becomes increasingly self-conscious, will be satisfied with no less.

It follows that men dare not destroy, but should rather amplify, the touch of imagination with which they have hitherto clothed the institution of monarchy. The characteristic of a true democracy will be, not the absence of one king, but the presence of many, the fact that every member of it will feel, howsoever dimly, *l'état c'est moi*. Politically and economically, at all events, each, in Soloviev's phrase, will have "become all"; although—or rather *because*—the foundation of the whole structure is the liberty of the individual human spirit. For Soloviev the Christian concept of a Mystical Body implied that the spirit of man is in fact "organic," after the same principle as the world of nature, from which he derives his physical body. Steiner pointed out that in future, even for practical purposes, no social structure stands a chance of surviving unless it takes full account of this fact.

What I am particularly suggesting here is, that the establishment of such a society seems rather to presuppose a mental climate, wherein the function of imagination in thought will be as self-evident to the effective mass of minds as the function of judgment has been since the epoch of Scholasticism. It is inherent in the nature of judgment that the judge is separate from and set over against the judged. It is characteristic of judgmental thought that the thinking subject is set over against the object of thought. Over here the thinking mind, over there the laws of nature. This is the form of thought which was sown, perhaps, when the Jews were forbidden to make graven images, and which culminated in the theological doctrine of nature and grace and in the mechanistic view of nature achieved by Western science at about the close of the eighteenth century. Since then, however, something has been strongly pulling the Western mind towards a view of man, not as contrasted with nature but as part and parcel with her. It is at this point that judgmental thought broke down. In biology it could produce nothing better than the Darwinian theory—which is nonsense (as an exclusive explanation) to anyone who looks, with an imagination that has not been atrophied, at such a phenomenon as a colony of bees. In philosophy and psychology the breakdown was a far more pitiful affair, as may be seen from the strange contortions of the behaviorists or the verbal morass of Korzybski's "non-Aristotelian" system of science.

Both Soloviev's "all-one idea," and the principle underlying Steiner's Threefold Commonwealth, require for their comprehension a kind of thinking in which imagination – the image-making faculty (which is hardly distinguishable from the image-apprehending faculty) – plays as great a part as judgment. That is why it is easier to detect in its aesthetic than in its ethical or sociological manifestation. For in appreciating works of art we are still obliged to think imaginally, even if we do so nowhere else. We have seen how, for Soloviev, it involved also a conception of the organic in *nature*, based on the same principles of mutual penetrability, of a dependence which is at the same time independence, and a separableness that is inseparable – tensions or polarities which are head-splitting paradoxes to judgmental thought, but child's play to the imagination. Provided, of course, that it is an imagination which is accustomed to sharing, at least in contemplation, the life of art or nature.

Kant defined judgment as "the faculty of thinking the particular as contained under the universal." Imaginal thought substitutes those same tensions or polarities for the "universals" of judgmental thought. In the judgment we affirm our own existence as a subject separate and distinct from the object thought about (and therein lies its true function), but in the same moment we exclude from our consciousness the life of the object. We "murder to dissect," as Wordsworth observed. Both ways of thinking are apprehensions of unity in multiplicity, but whereas, in the mind, a universal is a static abstraction from the object apprehended – a fish which died in the moment of entering the net of our subjectivity – a polarity is (like Goethe's *Urphänomen*) a dynamic participation in the process of actual life as it manifests itself in the production of nature's ordered multiplicity.

It is beyond the scope of this essay to speculate on the probable effect of the development of imaginal thinking on the natural sciences, or to consider the effect which it has actually had in the small area over which it has already begun to take effect. My object has been to stress the relation between form in art and form in human society; I could not achieve that object without seeking to penetrate to the underlying unity from which that relation springs; and, at that level, as Soloviev's little book suggests and I have tried to show, the true principle of form in nature is also relevant.

Note: For the final form of this article I am deeply indebted to the judicious criticism and wise suggestions of Mr. Charles Waterman.

Philology and the Incarnation

Sir Thomas Browne, that mystical, or quasi-mystical, author of the seventeenth century, wrote a book which he called *Religio Medici*, "The Religion of a Doctor, A Medical Man." Many, many years later—in my own youth, in fact—Professor Gilbert Murray, who is well-known in England and is probably known over here as a Greek scholar and humanist, wrote a little book (or it may have been no more than a single lecture reprinted) called *Religio Grammatici*, "The Religion of a Scholar, or Man of Letters." It occurred to me after I had given the title of this lecture, that if I had been a little more pretentious or a little more brash, perhaps I might have ventured to call it *Religio Philologi*, which I suppose would mean "The Religion of a Student of Language," perhaps especially a student of the historical aspect of language.

It is impossible to give much attention to words and their meanings, and more especially the history of words and the history of the changes which those meanings have undergone, without making a number of interesting discoveries. Moreover, in my experience the discoveries one then makes are of a kind which it is impossible to make without being forced by them to reflect rather intensively on the whole nature of man and of the world in which he lives.

Let me give you a very simple example. Has it ever occurred to you, I wonder, that the epithet "charming" as people use the word today, has certain very odd features about it? In the first place, it is the present participle of a verb active, namely the verb "to charm." Grammatically, therefore, when we speak of an object, a garden, for instance, or a landscape, or perhaps a person, as "charming," we make that object or person the sub-

228

ject of a verb which denotes an activity of some sort. That is what we do grammatically, but it is not at all, or it is only very rarely, what we mean semantically. When we speak, for instance, of a child as charming, we do not mean that the child himself is actually doing something. On the contrary, as soon as we notice that anyone, a child or a woman, is "charming" us in the verbal sense (in which case we rarely use the simple verb by itself, but we find some other expression such as "putting on charm" or "exerting charm" so as to bring out the notion of a willed activity), when that happens, the charmer who is charming in the verbal sense generally ceases to be charming in the adjectival sense!

Well, you could say the same thing about the word "enchanting." I mention these two words because they're good examples of a whole class, quite a noticeable group of words in our language which possess the same peculiarity. One has only to think of such words as *depressing, interesting, amusing, entertaining, entrancing, fascinating,* and so on to realize that we tend to allude to qualitative manifestations in the world outside ourselves by describing the effect they have on us, rather than by attempting to denote the qualities themselves.

The next thing that you find about this little group of words, if you go into the matter historically, is that these words, when used with these meanings, are all comparatively recent arrivals. Most of them first came into use in the eighteenth century—none of them is earlier than the seventeenth, I think. The kind of question one is led to ask is: Is this just an accident, or has it any wider significance? That is just the kind of question which the philologist, the student of language in its historical aspect, is led on to ask himself. Is the appearance of these words at this comparatively late stage just something that happened to happen, or is it a surface manifestation of deeper currents of some sort? So you have a linguistic habit, one must say, arising in the West in the course of the last few centuries, of describing or defining or denoting the outer world in terms, as it were, of the inner world of human feeling.

Now, let us take a look at another group of words, a very much larger group this time, indeed an almost unlimited one. I am referring to all those words which go to make up what the nineteenth century utilitarian philosopher Jeremy Bentham called the "immaterial language." In other words, I mean all those innumerable words in any modern language which do not refer to anything in the outside world at all, but only to the inner world of human feeling, of human thought—only to states of mind or mental events—*hope, fear, enthusiasm, conscious, embarrass, humility, ambition, concept*—you can go on reeling them off, any number of them, of course.

If you take the trouble to look up the etymologies of these words, you will find that in every case either they or their predecessors in older languages from which we have taken them, at one time referred not only to states of mind or mental events but also to some thing or some event in the outer world; that is of course what one might call elementary etymology. Only this time it is not usually a matter of looking back just a few hundred years into the past. We have to take a much longer survey if we wish to observe the historical process to which I am now seeking to draw your attention.

First, let me make this point—everyone is agreed, and I repeat, *everyone,* that there *was* such a historical process. Now you may ask, How do I establish that rather bold proposition? And the answer is: I establish it because I am in a position to call two witnesses to it from the very opposite ends of the earth. In saying "the opposite ends of the earth," I am not only alluding to the fact that one of them is American and the other is English, though that happens to be the case, but I am thinking much rather of the fact that they represent diametrically opposite philosophies, diametrically opposite points of view and beliefs about the whole nature of man and his relation to the divine disposition in the world. The two witnesses I'm thinking of are the transcendentalist, Emerson, and the positivist philosopher to whom I've already referred, Jeremy Bentham. You'll find in the section on language in the longer of Emerson's two essays which are entitled "Nature" the following passage: "Every word used to express a moral or intellectual fact, if traced to its root, is found to be borrowed from material appearance. *Right* means *straight; wrong* means *twisted. Spirit* primarily means *wind; transgression,* the *crossing of a line; supercilious,* the *raising of the eyebrows.* We say *heart* to express emotion, the *head* to denote thought, and *thought* and *emotion* are words borrowed from sensible things, and now appropriated to spiritual nature. Most of the process by which this transformation is made is hidden from us in the remote time when language was formed." Well, that is Emerson.

Then you find Jeremy Bentham, hard-headed positivist Jeremy Bentham, in an essay of his entitled "Language," (it comes in section four of the essay), writing as follows: "Throughout the whole field of language, parallel to the line of what may be termed the material language, and expressed by the same words, runs a line of what may be termed the immaterial language. Not that to every word that has a material import there belongs also an immaterial one; but that to every word that has an immaterial import there belongs, or at least did belong, a material one." When, therefore, we approach this immaterial language, these words which refer to the inner world only, we know that we have to do with words that at one time were words of the material language. We know that there has been a transition from the material language into an immaterial one.

Can we go still further and, at least in some cases, observe the transition taking place? The answer is that in some cases we can. You see, if in the case of any word of the immaterial language, we can lay our finger on a period in its history when the older material meaning had not yet evaporated, if I may put it that way, while the later immaterial meaning had already appeared, then we shall have located the transition itself.

Now let me take one of the examples Emerson himself gives, where he writes: "*Spirit* primarily means *wind*." I imagine that is as good an example as any you could choose of an immaterial meaning which was originally a material one. In this instance we have the best possible evidence that there *was* a particular time when the material meaning and the immaterial meaning still operated side by side in the same word. Not only so, but we know that that time was the time, about the beginning of our era, in which the New Testament was being written. Because in the third chapter of John's gospel you read in the account of our Lord's encounter with Nicodemus, first the words, "That which is born of the flesh is flesh and that which is born of the spirit is spirit." And then, in the next verse, "The wind bloweth where it listeth, and thou hearest the sound thereof, but canst not tell whence it cometh, and whither it goeth." And then again, "So is every one that is born of the Spirit." But in the Greek it is the same word "*pneuma*" that is used, whether it is wind or spirit that is being referred to. In rendering the two phrases, which occur in one and the same verse, "the wind bloweth where it listeth," and "every one that is born of the Spirit," the translator has to use two different words for what in the original text is one and the same word. The two meanings, the material and the immaterial, were present side by side, or mingled, in the *one* Greek word.

Now I want to suggest that if we set side by side the two linguistic phenomena which we have been looking at, we see on the one side the thing I spoke of first, the relatively recent tendency to refer to the qualities in the outside world (call it the world of nature, if you like) in terms of their effect upon ourselves. Then you see on the other side a much older habit (I call it a habit, because this time it is too widespread to refer to it as a mere "tendency"), that much older universal habit of referring to ourselves and our thoughts and affections in terms of the world of nature, the outside world. So we see, reflected in language, a curiously equivocal relation between this outside world and the inner man, the self or ego of the human being which experiences it. But we see something more than that. If you survey that equivocal relation, as I've called it, historically, you can't fail to be struck by the fact that there has occurred in the course of ages a change of emphasis. One could really say a change in the center of gravity, a change of direction in the way in which this equivocal relation operates. Looking back into the past, we observe an external, an outer language, a material language referring to the outer world of nature, which becomes more and more used in such a way that it becomes an inner language or an immaterial language, as Bentham called it. And this is clearly a very important process, for it is only to the extent that we have a language in which to express a thing that we can really be said to be properly conscious of the thing at all. That may sound a controversial proposition, but I think it's an experience which we all have as children, when our learning to speak on the one hand, and on the other our whole awareness of our environment as a coherent and articulated world, increase side by side as correlatives to one another.

What then was the thing of which this gradual historical development of an inner or immaterial language out of an outer or material language enabled mankind as a whole to become aware? The answer is clear, I think. It was none other than the existence, hitherto unsuspected, of an inner world in contradistinction to the outer one. In other words it was the existence of a man's self as a conscious individual being. Clearly, it was with the help of language — it was through the instrumentality of language — that individual men first began discovering themselves.

But now, what do we imply when we say that something has been "discovered"? If it was discovered at a certain point or during a certain period of time, as it must have been, we imply that there was a previous period during which it was not yet discovered. But please note carefully that, although this must always be the case, it may have been the case for either of two reasons. The thing may have been undiscovered because, although it was already in existence, although it was always there, no one had so far happened to notice it. That's the one reason. Should I be in order, I wonder, here in placing the discovery of America as an example of that category? I don't know. But anyhow, there are plenty of other examples. Take the planet Neptune, for example. That's the first kind of discovery: not discovered because it didn't happen to be noticed although it was already there. But the thing might also have been undiscovered, for a different reason. The reason might be simply that it wasn't yet there. It you discover a new, wild flower in your garden, next spring, let's say it's an annual, the reason you didn't discover it last spring may be that the bird or the wind which carries the seed didn't happen to have passed that way, whereas this year it did. That is the second kind of discovery. We cannot always be certain which of the two causes any particular discovery belongs to. It is conceivable, for instance, that even the planet Neptune *might* not have been in existence until about the time it was discovered, though I expect we are right in classifying that as a discovery of the first kind.

But there is one case where we *can* be absolutely certain that the discovery was *not* of the first kind, and therefore *was* of the second kind (the discovery of something which did not exist until it was discovered); and that is the discovery by man of his own existence as a self-conscious being. The reason is plain enough. It simply does not make sense to say that at one time self-consciousness was an existing fact which had not yet been discovered. You can be unaware of many things, but you cannot be unaware of being aware. In this case, therefore, the discovery and the birth of the thing discovered are one and the same event.

We see, then, looking back into the past, a condition of affairs in which it was not yet possible to speak of an inner world or an individual self in contradistinction to an outer world. And when this did begin to become possible, the inner world at first could only be suggested by the way in which one employed the language of the outer world. We see this particular way of using words, the (if you like) "symbolical" way, or the way of imagery, gradually growing in strength and variety until there comes into being a whole rich, immaterial language, a rich treasury of words, which had at one time, indeed, an external reference, but from which, in common usage, all external reference has long since passed away. That is what we see when we look back into the past. And then we see looking at the present a state of affairs in which the tables have been turned. The tables have been turned in the linguistic relation between man and nature, or between the individual self and its environment. Because, as I pointed out at the beginning, if a man now wants to say anything about his natural environment, anything rich or qualitative, as distinct from the purely quantitative measurements of natural science, he has to do it by employing a language whose literal reference is to something that is going on within himself, but employing it in such a way that he somehow *suggests* that those qualities exist not in himself, but in the world outside himself.

I have, it is true, given only a single indication of this last, namely, a particular small group of words. There are, in fact, plenty of other indications of what I am saying, but it would take too long to go into them. I'm not, and I should like to make this very clear, attempting to argue a case. I can go no further than stating it.

Now, a change of direction is, by its very nature, a change which must have taken place at a definite point in time. The moment of change may be easily observable, may be easy to determine or locate, or it may not. In the case of a billiard ball hitting the cushion and rebounding, it is easy enough. In the case of a more complex phenomenon, it may be very much harder. The waves, for instance, keep on coming in even after the tide has turned. And an extra large wave may make us doubt whether it has turned yet after all. In the case of an infinitely more complex phenomenon, such as the evolution of human consciousness, it is even less likely that the actual moment of change will be easily observable. But that there *was* such a moment, even though we are unable to locate it exactly, is a conclusion to which reason itself compels us; for otherwise, there could not have been a change of direction at all. Moreover, if the moment of change or reversal cannot be exactly pinpointed, that does not mean that it cannot be placed at all. I don't know the exact moment at which the incoming tide changed to an outflowing one, but I do know that it is an outflowing one now, and that five minutes ago, let's say, it was still coming in.

And now, if I may leave my analogy of the turning of the tide, and return to this change I have been speaking of, this reversal in the direction of man's relation to his environment, this change from a period, in which, with the help of language, man is drawing his self-consciousness, as it were, out of the world around him, to a period in which he is, again, with the help of language, in a position to give back to nature something of the treasure he once took from her, then a student of the history of word-meanings can certainly be as definite as this: he can say with confidence that the great change of direction took place between, well, let's say between the death of Alexander the Great and the birth of St. Augustine. Indeed, there are indications which would tempt him to be much more precise.

Again, I'll only give one such indication. If one contrasts the meaning of the Greek word for *word* or *reason* or *discourse* (for it could mean all three: I'm referring to the word "*logos*"), if one contrasts the meaning of that word, as it stood in the time of Plato and Aristotle, with its later meaning; or to put it another way, if one contrasts the meaning of the old word "*logos*," with the meanings of the words which we have to use to translate it; and if one then moves the microscope a little nearer, so to speak, so as to determine, if possible, the moment, or at least the single century, of transition from the old to the new, then one is struck immediately by the way in which this word "*logos*" was being used, in Alexandria, for instance, used by Greeks and used also by Jews, in the first century B.C. One may even be a little more pedantically precise, and remark that

that particular word was in especial use in the Stoic philosophy, and that it was in expounding the Stoic philosophy that the concepts *objective* and *subjective* first make their appearance in a clearly recognizable form. In other words, it was then that the fundamental duality with which we are now so familiar was first clearly formulated, was first sharply focused, a duality no longer merely between *mind* on one side and *senses* on the other (which had been long familiar to the Greeks), but a duality between a *self* on the one side and its *environment* on another.

And so, if it were possible (and of course it is not) that a man should have pursued the kind of studies I have been speaking of, without ever having read the Gospels, or the Epistles of St. Paul, without ever having heard of Christianity, he would nevertheless be impelled by his reason to the conclusion that a crucial moment in the evolution of humanity must have occurred certainly during the seven or eight centuries on either side of the reign of Augustus and probably somewhere near the middle of that period. This, he would feel, from the whole course of his studies, was the moment at which the flow of the spiritual tide into the individual self was exhausted and the possibility of an outward flow began. This was the moment at which there was consummated that age-long process of contraction of the immaterial qualities of the cosmos into a human center, into an inner world, which had made possible the development of an immaterial language. This, therefore, was the moment in which his true selfhood, his spiritual selfhood, entered into the body of man. Casting about for a word to denote that moment, what one would he be likely to choose? I think he would be almost obliged to choose the word "incarnation," the entering into the body, the entering into the flesh.

And now let us further suppose that our imaginary student of the history of language, having had up to now that conspicuous gap in his general historical knowledge, was suddenly confronted for the first time with the Christian record; that he now learned for the first time, that at about the middle of the period which his investigation had marked off, a man was born who claimed to be the son of God, and to have come down from Heaven, that he spoke to his followers of the "the Father in me and I in you," that he told all those who stood around him that "the kingdom of God is within you," and startled them, and strove to reverse the direction of their thought—for the word "*metanoia*," which is translated "repentance," also means a reversal of the direction of the mind—he startled them and strove to reverse the direction of their thought by assuring them that "it is not that which cometh into a man which defileth him, but that which goeth out of him."

Lastly, let me further suppose that, excited by what he had just heard, our student made further inquiries and learned that this man, so far from being a charlatan or lunatic, had long been acknowledged, even by those who regarded his claim to have come down from Heaven as a delusion, as the nearest anyone had ever come to being a perfect man. What conclusion do you think our student would be likely to draw?

Well, as I say, the supposition is an impossible one, but it *is* possible – I know because it happened in my own case – for a man to have been brought up in the belief, and to have taken it for granted, that the account given in the Gospels of the birth and the resurrection of Christ is a noble fairy story with no more claim to historical accuracy than any other myth; and it is possible for such a man, after studying in depth the history of the growth of language, to look again at the New Testament and the literature and tradition that has grown up around it, and to accept (if you like, to be *obliged* to accept) the record as a historical fact, not because of the authority of the Church nor by any process of ratiocination such as C. S. Lewis has recorded in his own case, but rather because it fitted so inevitably with the other facts as he had already found them. Rather because he felt, in the utmost humility, that if he had never heard of it through the Scriptures, he would have been obliged to try his best to invent something like it as a hypothesis to save the appearances.

The Psalms of David

In common with many of my generation, I grew up with an aversion from the Old Testament. Later on, I came to envy, for literary and historical reasons, that close acquaintance with the Bible which was forced on our fathers in *their* youth and which remained with them as a cultural endowment long after so many of them had felt the emotional reaction which I had inherited or acquired. But I still disliked the people portrayed in the Old Testament, their whole attitude to life, their everlasting preoccupation with sin, their perpetual backslidings and the abject, cringing way in which they confessed them. Sometimes, it seemed, they had a very low opinion of themselves (an opinion in which I fully concurred):

> *But as for me, I am a worm, and no man: a very scorn of men and the outcast of the people . . .*
> *For I will confess my wickedness: and be sorry for my sin.*

At other times they evinced a revolting self-righteousness:

> *I have hated the congregation of the wicked: and will not sit among the ungodly*
> *I will wash my hands in innocency, O Lord: and so will I go to thine altar.*

Their religion seemed to me a loveless and a joyless affair or, when any joy did break in, it was of a kind which I could not easily approve, much less share:

237

Behold, how good and joyful a thing it is: brethren, to dwell in unity!

It is like the precious ointment upon the head, that ran down unto the beard: even unto Aaron's beard, and went down to the skirts of his clothing.

This is not my idea of a good and joyful thing at all. But, worse than this, through it all ran the central theme of obedience and disobedience, rewards and punishments. Cruel and violent, alike to their enemies and to the offenders in their own ranks, and that not only by nature but by the express commands of their Deity, the only sin of which they seemed to be really ashamed was disobedience, the only virtue they recognized (and even this they spoiled by claiming rewards for it) obedience; obedience, not to the dictates of conscience, mark you, not to the words of a beloved Lord, but to their stern and even vengeful Jehovah. And this is not my idea of religion at all.

With all this I contrasted the frank and free atmosphere in which, for example, the Greeks lived their lives and out of which they created their art and their literature with its calm dignity and its saving grace of humor. They well understood the distinction between modesty and self-abasement. *They* were not mawkishly preoccupied with sin like the Jews, but knew how to clothe the theme of human guilt in the dignified vestments of tragedy.

One day however (I can still recall the time and place) a friend pointed out to me that the Jews were historically remarkable precisely because they were the *only* people in whose consciousness the naked sense of right and wrong was so powerful a reality that it took precedence of all else. I began very slowly and painfully to readjust my ideas. I began, in fact, to try and give to the Jews of the Old Testament the benefit of that historical imagination which I had applied so liberally elsewhere but for some reason had withheld from them. By historical imagination I mean the habit of mind which endeavors to approach a past epoch by seeing the world through its eyes instead of by seeing *it* through the eyes of the twentieth century and which, in assessing the contribution of that epoch to the history of human consciousness, carefully refrains from judging it by later standards—especially if the creation of those standards is part of the very contribution to be assessed.

Nowadays, we approach the Old Testament, if at all, through the New Testament. Our mental picture of a pious Jew is that of the lowest type of Pharisee as Jesus found him, our emotional reaction to the Law itself is colored through and through by the reaction of St. Paul after his vision on the way to Damascus. The first task of historical imagination is to peel all this away. I at any rate had criticized the religion of the Old Testament as something too external, not truly of the heart, but enforced from without. Now I endeavored to appreciate that it was largely because the Jewish nation had lived and struggled that I or anyone else was in a position to make such a criticism at all. Moral choice, responsibility, freedom—whence do we get our absolute conviction of these things? Not from Nature:

> Ah, child, she cries, that strife divine,
> Whence was it? for it is not mine!

Not from any of the heathen nations. In a pagan world of myth and imagery and idolatry, where in the sentient body and sentient soul Nature in living pictures was herself active as human impulse, the Jews alone were forbidden to make graven images. It was their whole historical task to introduce into human consciousness the very inwardness which I had pertly accused them of lacking! I had, as it happens, already accepted this from the writings of Rudolf Steiner as a fact, but it had remained for me what I will call a historical cliché, a proposition which I could support with a few isolated quotations and which I believed because it fitted into the general scheme of things. I had never *experienced* it outside idea, as one experiences Shakespeare or springtime or breakfast. I now wished to do so and among other lines of approach I read and reread the Psalms.

The Psalms are the Old Testament in epitome. Of three or four of them (the 78th for instance) this is true in the most literal sense, inasmuch as they consist of brief *résumés* of the history of the Israelites; but it is true in a much deeper sense of the whole body; for the Psalms express in spirit both the Law and the Prophets. Contrast with the well-known 23rd Psalm ("The Lord is my Shepherd"), or the magnificent hymn of praise and ode to Nature, which is Psalm 104, the 119th Psalm (really a group of Psalms, one for each letter of the Hebrew alphabet). For instance:

> *I hate them that imagine evil things: but thy law do I love.*
> *Thou art my defence and shield: and my trust is in thy word.*
> *Away from me, ye wicked: I will keep the commandments of my God.*
> *O stablish me according to thy word, that I may live: and let me not be disappointed of my hope.*

Hold thou me up, and I shall be safe: yea, my delight shall be ever in thy statutes.

Thou hast trodden down all them that depart from thy statutes: for they imagine but deceit.

Thou puttest away all the ungodly of the earth like dross: therefore I love thy testimonies.

My flesh trembleth for fear of thee: and I am afraid of thy judgments.

I think that most of us feel that, while we can admire and love the "prophetic" element in the Psalms, the Law is a very different matter. Why such enthusiasm about it? The prophetic is, for us, the poetic:

Thou deckest thyself with light as it were with a garment: and spreadest out the heavens like a curtain . . .

Whither shall I go then from thy Spirit; or whither shall I go then from thy presence?

If I climb up into heaven, thou art there: if I go down to hell, thou art there also.

If I take the wings of the morning: and remain in the uttermost parts of the sea;

Even there also shall thy hand lead me . . .

or

By the waters of Babylon we sat down and wept: when we remembered thee, O Sion . . . .

But we feel the Psalmist committed an error of taste when he attempted to speak in the same exalted style, and with his singing robes about him, of anything so dry and authoritarian as the Law.

But this, if we are seeking to use the Psalms as a pathway to sympathetic understanding of the Jewish consciousness, is exactly what we must try *not* to feel. The contrast between the Law and the Prophets was no contrast between prose and poetry. The Law, with all its severity, was not Katisha to the righteous Jew; it was Yum-yum herself:

O how sweet are thy words unto my throat: yea, sweeter than honey unto my mouth.

It was written in their hearts:

In the volume of the book it is written of me, that I should fulfil thy will, O my God: I am content to do it; yea, thy law is within my heart.

They loved it because in their eyes it was lovely. It moved them at times, as music and memories and children move *us* at times. You never knew when it was going to give that little tug at your heartstrings or bring that lump into your throat.

A modern Jew has tried to convey this by means of a comparison. Suppose a well-regulated and affectionate family, living in a district inhabited else by gangsters and hooligans, a family where law and order and routine mean much and are sedulously enforced; where at mealtimes, for instance, not only every person, but every saltcellar and flower-vase have their exactly appointed places; where all must be done "duly" and ceremonially, one day following another in smooth succession; where none must be late or come with unwashed hands; but where all who belong are welcome and glad. The very table-talk has gradually developed into a private language, intimate, allusive, and half-secret. The ritual of bowing to the head of the table on entrance, of holding the knife correctly, chewing properly, passing the dishes to and fro, and all the *minutiae* of decent manners, is all-important. Then think yourself a child, a member of this family, coming in out of the street or from a day of harsh contacts with the hooligans outside, who would neither understand nor value these family customs, whose language is crass and vulgar and their conversation larded with jeers and catcalls, who do not bother overmuch with trifles like soap and water. It is not a perfect analogy, but it may help you to feel how it was possible for the Jews, not merely to praise obedience as a duty, but to delight in it as an end in itself, not merely to revere their Law, but to love it:

With my whole heart have I sought thee; O let me not go wrong out of thy commandments.

Thy words have I hid within my heart: that I should not sin against thee.

Blessed art thou, O Lord: O teach me thy statutes . . .

I have had as great delight in the way of thy testimonies: as in all manner of riches.

I will talk of thy commandments: and have respect unto thy ways.

My delight shall be in thy statutes: and I will not forget thy word.

Human nature does not remain the same. It has developed, and in the

course of history quite new potentialities have been added to it. It is indeed often possible to trace how these have been unfolded especially in
one place by one people and later spread over a large part of mankind; and
the meanings of many common words are living relics of this process. One
may trace, for example, how meanings, quite foreign to the original speakers, distinctively *Christian* meanings, were brought into the Greek language, when this was used for writing the literature from which the New
Testament canon has been selected, and in that way dispersed, either directly or through the Latin tongue, over a large part of Europe and Asia.

But that is not my purpose here. These Christian meanings had first
themselves to be created. How? Not out of nothing. By the Christ himself
then? But even he needed something that would come part of the way to
meet him; some soil prepared and thirsty for the seed he came to sow;
some souls for whom his Gospel, though new and startling, would yet,
owing to their predisposition, not be so new as to seem wholly meaningless. Such souls he found in Palestine, either Jews themselves or living in
intimate communion with Jewish society. There he found what he could
have found nowhere else in the world, namely a peculiar quality of love, a
tender personal affection, which embraced as its object not persons only
but the fountain of righteousness itself. The Greeks, and no doubt other
nations also, knew something of this tenderness ($\sigma\tau\acute{o}\varrho\gamma\eta$), but only in the
family circle as between parent and child or brother and sister. The Jews,
as has been already indicated, had come to feel the same *sort* of tenderness
for the *Torah*. There is much else besides feeling to be taken into consideration, but it is feeling which I am considering here and it was just *this* feeling which Jesus was able to win for himself and, by so doing, to transmute
it into Christian love and charity.

So much I think any man of reasonably sensitive perception would have
to concede, whatever his beliefs about the underlying causes. Is it such a
very big step further to perceive that a metamorphosis so pregnant with
meaning for the human race could hardly have taken place by accident, or
that it was possible only because the two beloved objects were in substance
the same? In loving Christ the first Christians were loving him whose pre-
venient shadow the *Torah* (that is, the Law) had always been. Read in the
Gospels the remarkably inconsistent references made by Jesus himself to
the Law, which at one moment he ratified to the last jot and tittle and in
the next proclaimed to be superseded by himself.[1] There may well be
verbal confusion and paradox, and abrupt changes of heart, where a sharp

1. The dominical utterances on the Law will be found admirably assembled,
analyzed, and considered in Hort's *Judaic Christianity*.

contrast apparent on the surface springs from identity in the depths. The
sudden electrifying perception that this Christ whom, out of his deep reverence for the Law, he had been persecuting so actively in his followers,
was not only no enemy, but actually *was* the Beloved, the Law itself—was
the very center and source of its reflected radiance—this surely is the bare
concept of St. Paul's experience on the road to Damascus:

> *I will preach the Law, whereof the Lord hath said unto me: Thou*
> *art my Son, this day have I begotten thee.*

St. Paul must have known this verse from the Psalms well enough (he was
to allude to it later in one of his Epistles); but hitherto, we may suppose,
he had only taken the one half of it really seriously. Now he realized that
both parts must be given equal weight, if the truth was not to slip through
his fingers. And at once the old thought became so new that he was temporarily blinded by the revelation. There is no question here of devising a
"rational explanation" for a miracle. Whatever physical disturbance accompanied the *volte face* of consciousness is, for me, of relatively slight
importance.

At this point it will probably make my meaning clearer if I say that I
personally have long accepted Steiner's account of the Incarnation, according to which it was (*inter alia*) the event which made possible the complete "descent" of any and every human ego into a physical body; it is
thus at the root of the increasing self-consciousness which, for good and
ill, has marked the subsequent psychological history of mankind. The
Deity portrayed in the Old Testament, he affirmed (for reasons and with a
background into which I need not enter), was related to the Christ as light
reflected is to radiant light. For the point which I am seeking to make in
this paragraph, however, it is sufficient to suppose that the Old Testament
includes a partial or imperfect revelation of certain facts of the spirit
which were later to be much more fully expressed in the New—a supposition which, although not now widely accepted, is neither particularly new
nor particularly startling. The point is that this fact, if fact it be, is also
one of which it is possible to hear both halves, but to grasp and live with
one only.

That the Law, and indeed all that is contained in the Old Testament,
was *sub specie alternitatis* "only" a reflection of what is contained in the
New—this in this postrevolutionary era is a truth which can be quickly and
gratefully grasped by most of those who attach a more than anthropological significance to both documents. It is the other half which costs some

trouble in the uptake; I mean the at least equally weighty half of the truth, that it *was* a reflection—not, that is, something contrasted and repugnant, but a reflection, with all the faithful likeness of a reflection. Our difficulty, though its solution is less important, is the exact opposite of St. Paul's.

But it is time to return to the Psalms. Keep in mind the special love and tenderness for the Law which I have tried to indicate and suppose a soul imbued and saturated through and through with this tenderness. The Psalms express nothing less than the intimate and personal conversation of such a soul with God. Intimate, because a sense of the actual and immediate presence of God breathes so strongly through them; personal, because the God who is so present is nevertheless so *other*, and therefore so distant. He is addressed indeed as if he were actually another person. He can be argued with:

> *What profit is there in my blood: when I go down to the pit?*
> *Shall the dust give thanks unto thee: or shall it declare thy truth?*

admonished and exhorted:

> *Up, Lord, why sleepest thou: awake, and be not absent from us for ever.*

held to a bargain:

> *O Lord in thee have I trusted: let me never be confounded.*

The trouble here is that, through all the splendor of the diction, we can hardly help feeling faintly uneasy, as we do with the Oxford groups and those evangelical pastors who inform us readily, and sometimes perhaps a little glibly, that God likes this and does not like that, that he wants us to do so and so and will be disappointed if we do the other; referring to him rather too much as though he were the Headmistress or Mr. Churchill. In other words, it is above all this imputed personal otherness which constitutes a stumbling-block when, throwing historical imagination to the winds, we turn to the Psalms as we should to a book written yesterday and strive to let them speak afresh to our hearts, and *for* our hearts, as they have done to so many generations of our fathers. I think it is for that reason that for many souls today they seem most answerable to its despondent moods. This is certainly the case with those who (like myself) talk, or think much, and also perhaps sometimes a little glibly, of the Ego, thereby identifying ourselves with the spiritual world or at all events affirming ourselves as already its inhabitants. But there may be times when we feel reason to doubt whether, in doing so, we have been speaking with quite the precision which such a subject demands. And then the spiritual world, and the Ego, too, may look quite as overshadowing and remote and "other" as did the God of the Old Testament to the Psalmist, when he cried:

> *Take me out of the mire, that I sink not: O let me be delivered from them that hate me, and out of the deep waters.*
> *Let not the waterflood drown me, neither let the deep swallow me up: and let not the pit shut her mouth upon me.*
> *Hear me, O Lord, for thy loving-kindness is comfortable: turn thee unto me according to the multitude of thy mercies.*
> *And hide not thy face from thy servant, for I am in trouble: O haste thee, and hear me.*

Most of those to whom the presence of the spiritual world is a stark fact and not merely a habit of speech and a voluble assumption, know what it is to feel something of what these words express, that is, to feel how precious little all their talk of the Ego and its divine origin and prospects seems to amount to in practice:

> *By the waters of Babylon we sat down and wept: when we remembered thee, O Sion.*

It will be some time yet before there is no longer any place in humanity for writings which affirm in the same moment, and with the beauty and intensity of the Psalms, alike the nearness and the otherness of the Divine Spirit.

How comes it, then, that the Psalms express these two contrasted attributes with such special intensity? Without trying to answer this, let us ask another related question: How comes it that they *lack* something else, something all-important, if we are endeavoring to assess their contemporary value as, let us say, a book of devotion? I mean the sense of the *indwelling* Spirit, of all that is implied in the word "sacramental." The second question is really the obverse of the first, for it is implied in that "otherness," the consideration of which led up to it.

Once again we are brought face to face with the peculiar destiny of the Jewish nation. The gods were immanent in pagan and gentile souls, in the Midianites, the Hittites, the Perizzites, and the Jebusites, in a way they

could never be, *must* never be allowed to be, in the Jewish. The old sacra-
mentalism represented a direct inflow of the astral and spiritual world into
the human astral body and sentient soul. The new sacrament, that is the
new *union*, the new transcending of that "otherness" of which we have
spoken, can only take place in and through the ego itself; and it presupposes the full incarnation of the ego in the physical body—an event which
had not yet taken place when the Jews were making history. But an ego is
not merely, like the astral part of man, a "soul," it is also a "self." Hence,
almost by definition, it is "other" than all that surrounds it, including the
Spirit from which it derives its being. The Jews made possible the physical
incarnation of the ego, prepared the physical body in which it first took
place. But this was not all. It was they, also, who bore the brunt of the
ego's tragic, almost self-contradictory, task of affirming its separateness
from, while maintaining its identity with, the Divine Spirit. I think we are
allowed to overhear something of that brunt in the Psalms.

Nor in the Psalms only, but also in the whole of the Old Testament. For
the whole history of Israel before the Incarnation is a panorama of the
progressive incarnation of the ego, experienced as a moral problem. They,
for the whole human race, were custodians and stewards of that process;
tender nurses protecting the nascent ego and guarding it in their midst.
Egypt, Jerusalem or *Sion, Babylon, Jordan,* why are they now such colos-
sal and abiding symbols for the experiences of each individual soul on its
way? Is it because someone has drawn adroit poetical parallels? Not for a
moment. It is because, in the Jews, a whole nation was engaged *as* a nation
in solving a moral problem and achieving a moral task, which have since
become *the* problem and *the* task facing every individual soul.

I began by endeavoring to approach the Psalms through historical imagination and then I made some attempt to appraise, purposely excluding
historical imagination, their value as a book of devotion or vehicle of expression for contemporary religious experience. I am now trying to suggest
a sort of *via media* between these two avenues of approach, which if we
follow, we may be able to share the poetic and spiritual treasures in the
Psalms without being chilled and repelled by that lack, of which I have just
spoken. The Psalms lack the peculiar sacramental grace. Inevitably so, because the individual Jew was not able to say, "Now is the Prince of this
world cast out," or, "Our lives are hid with Christ in God," or "No longer
I live, but Christ liveth in me." He could not feel the unfathomed inwardness in himself, because it was not there. But the Jew could and did say to
himself: In the world is Judea, in Judea is Jerusalem, in Jerusalem is the
Temple, in the Temple's inmost holy of holies is the Ark, and in the Ark

is—nothing—everything—the invisible beating of the wings of the cherubim—a voiceless Breath forever uttering the unutterable Name, I AM—the two stone tables with the Ten Commandments of the Law engraved upon them! Here was *his* mystery of inwardness, not his own, but his nation's; and when he reflected on it, the low mood of despondency beneath the remote and frowning majesty of Jehovah vanished away like smoke, and instead it was:

Sing we merrily unto God our strength: make a cheerful noise unto the God of Jacob.

Take the psalm, bring hither the tabret; the merry harp with the lute.

Blow up the trumpet in the new-moon; even in the time appointed, and upon our solemn feast-day.

Having, then, learned something with the help of historical imagination—that "peeling away" of the intermediate past of which I spoke earlier—we should abandon the special effort this required but retain in the background of our minds the fruits of meditation on the peculiar destiny of the Jewish people, so that there hovers in our apprehension the picture of the Israelites, wandering long years in the desert, homesick, restless, and unhappy, but caring the more tenderly because of that very unhappiness for the Ark and its mystery, which they carried with them in their midst; until they could bring it safe to rest on the holy hill at last and build the Temple to surround it. Then we shall find that the sacramental element, the unfathomed inwardness, is not so entirely lacking as we at first felt. We shall feel its breath stirring over and over again, when the spatial focus of the *nation's* inwardness is alluded to, that is to say, when Jerusalem or the hills on which it stands are mentioned or poetically invoked:

They that put their trust in the Lord shall be even as the mount Sion: which may not be removed, but standeth fast for ever.

The hills stand about Jerusalem: even so standeth the Lord round about his people, from this time forth for evermore . . .

Our feet shall stand in thy gates: O Jerusalem.

Jerusalem is built as a city: that is at unity in itself . . .

As the hill of Basan, so is God's hill: even an high hill, as the hill of Basan.

> *Why hop ye so, ye high hills? This is God's hill, in the which it pleaseth him to dwell: yea, the Lord will abide in it for ever . . . Out of Sion hath God appeared: in perfect beauty.*

There are many similar passages, but I must forbear further quotation. The Psalms are not there for any one nation alone; but for the English-speaking peoples they possess this added significance, that there is probably no piece of literature, not even excepting Shakespeare's plays, which has exerted so deep and abiding an influence on their history. Hundreds of those who have played leading parts in that history must have known the Psalms practically by heart. Dig down and you would find their sentiments and cadences intertwined with the roots of the national consciousness. Accordingly, in this time, when there is a strong and growing impulse at work in many quarters to sharply cut off the present and future from their roots in the past, to sabotage all feeling and tradition and to start building the world afresh on a foundation of naked will guided by shallow doctrine, it is well that there should be no unnecessary hindrances in the way of anyone's approach to a document of such ancient and majestic import as the Psalms of David.

The "Son of God" and
the "Son of Man"

If you were approached by someone who had never heard of Christianity and were asked for a definition of it, not a description but a definition for the purpose of distinguishing it from other religions such as Parseeism or Mohammedanism, I suppose the correct reply would be: Christianity is the belief that Jesus Christ was the Son of God. It is an error, though a common one, to suppose that the justness of such a definition depends somehow on the justness of the belief. It is a correct definition, not because it covers everything (in which case it would be a description), but because it cannot be applied to any other religion. Nevertheless, if your questioner were then to turn to the Gospels, he would be surprised, as a great many people have been surprised in the past, to find that in the Gospels Jesus is in fact scarcely ever referred to as the Son of God. The title by which he almost invariably referred to himself was the "Son of Man."

A great deal has of course been written on both these titles, and in particular the "Son of Man" is never explained anywhere in the New Testament. It may of course be said: After all it is not so very surprising, in view of the fact that it is also the central teaching in Christianity that Christ was both God and man. But I feel myself that the difficulty is not so easily disposed of, for it is noteworthy that Christ uses the title "Son of Man" of himself, not exclusively in those contexts where one might expect it, where for example he is emphasizing his humility and his identity with the tribulations and sufferings of humanity; but he also uses it just where one would expect the other title, the "Son of God," to be used. In what are sometimes called the apocalyptic passages, for instance, he speaks of the Son of Man coming in "clouds of glory." There, if anywhere—surely one would expect the "Son of God" instead. There are several pages of comment in I suppose most theological works—there certainly are in Hastings's *Dictionary of the Bible*—on the meaning of the term "Son of Man"; and Hastings, having quoted them at length and in number, sums them up by saying that they express two different conclusions, one of which is that Jesus used it in order to emphasize the fact of his Messiah-ship and the other is that he used it in order to *conceal* the fact of his Messiah-ship! I think, where one finds experts differing as widely as that, one is entitled to try to form ideas of one's own for what they may be worth.

It is obvious that both expressions are "metaphorical," if we take the literal meaning of the word "Son" as connoting a physical begetting, with obstetric accompaniments; and that is certainly its literal meaning today. But it is also obvious that the tenor or hidden meaning of the metaphor is very different in the one case from the other.

The first metaphor emphasizes that Christ was a man having a relation to God that is somehow different from all others. The second seems to call attention to a something, whatever it is, that Christ has *in common* with all men. Moreover this cannot be the bare fact that he was physically begotten (even if such were the case); or why should he have chosen precisely this name as the "tag," as it were, by which to identify himself? That is why I say this term must be no less metaphorical than the other.

It is of course the teaching of the Church that Jesus is a man having a relation to God that is somehow different from that of all other men. That is the belief of (I suppose) nearly all Christian sects. But that conviction is in no way essential in order to understand what I shall be trying to say. What to my mind is *essential* is to understand, as far as one can, the real meaning that lies behind such momentous appellations.

If we now go a little further and ask ourselves how we are to describe the difference between the special relation of Jesus to God and that of all other men to God, then of course the difficulties begin. They certainly began very soon as a matter of history. Thus, in the Nicene Creed, it is emphasized that Christ was "begotten, not made"—which is usually taken to imply that ordinary men were "created," and are creatures therefore, but that Christ was not. He was the Son of God. He was "begotten of His Father before all worlds." But even this does not dispose of the difficulty for me; for there seems to be an admitted sense in which man (ordinary, natural, unredeemed man) is also a "son," or "child," or "descendant" of God. I cannot believe myself (however much the "creatureliness" of man ought to be emphasized) that it entails thinking of man in any sense as a manufactured article. In some sense he, too, is much more like a son or

descendant of God. And this view seems to be confirmed by the Bible itself in many places. Jesus himself, though he refers often to "My Father in
Heaven," also refers, when speaking to others, to "Your Father in Heaven."
Again, there is the genealogy near the beginning of St. Luke's Gospel,
where his descent is traced back to Adam, "who was the son of God." In
what sense then was *Adam* presumed by the writer to be the son of God?
In the Book of Genesis we read how "The Lord God formed man of the
dust of the ground, and breathed into his nostrils the breath of life." Certainly this, as described, is not a physical "begetting" in any ordinary
sense. But equally certainly it is much more like a begetting than it is like a
manufacturing or a creating-out-of-nothing. For the Breath of God is after
all not nothing!

It seems to me then that we must say that man had his origin in the Divine Being. He is a son, or descendant, of God. You will observe that I have
used for the third time the word "descendant." Why? The sonship which
Luke attributes to him in his genealogy was not an immediate one. It was
traced through a long descent. And that reminds us that here we are confronted with the difference between the word "man" and the words
"men" or "*a* man." We sometimes speak of "Man" as a unity, leaving the
relation between this "man" and "men" unclear. If we say that "Man" as a
whole is a descendant from God, it certainly does not follow that any particular man, considered as a personality, can claim to be the Son of God.

Rather he is a "descendant" by virtue of his descent, of his blood, of his
history, of all that he carries in his organism of the past, not of himself
alone but of mankind as a whole, in a word because of his *heredity*. A fallen, a prodigal son, no doubt, but still a son. And this part of him is just
the part of which he is *normally unconscious*. It is the part of him *which is
as much there when he is asleep as when he is awake*, unlike his personality. I think it is because a very young baby is so largely unconscious—so
that he has as yet *no* personality—that we feel so strongly the presence of
the Divine when we look at him. Wordsworth knew something about that.
But beyond that, if we look at a full-grown man (even a wicked man)
sound asleep and we think of the marvels of his organism, of the heart that
began to beat as soon as he was born and will continue to do so (in spite of
all the strains he places on it) until the day of his death; if we think of the
lungs, miraculously performing their priestlike task of transforming the
outer air into the redness of his arterial blood, and all the marvels of the
circulation, combustion, and rhythmic reoxygenation of the blood; if we
have all this before our minds, we have to say, no matter how wicked the
man is: "He came down from Heaven." We can do no other. We say it, as

we would say it of nature, perhaps, of a beautiful landscape, or a spring flower.

It seems to me this is where the psychology of the unconscious, which has made such a noise during the last fifty or sixty years, is up to now so inadequate. I think for instance of Freud's equation of the unconscious with the bodily functions, with all that is there and beats in the blood as instinctive drives. And then of course there has been its much wider extension, as it left the psychiatrist's couch and expanded on the wings of literature and art. One thinks first, I suppose, of D. H. Lawrence; but he is only one of a phalanx, whose name is legion. I am thinking of the whole amorphous impulse among writers, painters, and others to contrast this unconscious element in themselves with the arid intellectualism, or moralism, of their conscious life and to try to bring it up to the conscious level, *so as to fertilize the conscious personality with the unconscious man.* As the one penetrates, or at least impinges on, the other, they feel (or hope) that the conscious personality may somehow acquire something of the primordial life, the archetypal majesty, the invincible strength, of nature herself. But by "nature" they generally mean physical nature, as we know it today. They tacitly assume that the unconscious is rooted, not in mental or spiritual but in bodily energies. They forget, or up to now they have mostly forgotten, the descent, the heredity, the divine origins of the body itself. They forget that man is, precisely in his physical organism, already a "son of God." One must always oversimplify in an hour's lecture, and I am well aware that what I am saying is subject to significant exceptions. It is certainly no longer true of all psychologists. It has perhaps always been less true of Jung and his followers than of Freud and his followers. But it is something which characterizes the psychology of the unconscious, as it has up to now developed, whether as clinical procedure or as the blithely assumed cosmology that underlies our literature, art, and philosophy.

When we look for origins, we invoke, not Heaven but an essentially mindless Darwinian animal. But what if that should prove to have been an aberration on our part? One way of testing whether it is so or not is to try approaching a number of different problems *without* assuming it, and see what we make of them. And it is so that I approach this problem of what is meant in the New Testament by the terms "Son of God" and "Son of Man."

We must remember that all I was saying about man asleep applies not only to man asleep, but also to that part of him which *remains* asleep even in his waking life; which remains unconscious even during his waking hours. And from this we know that we must distinguish the individual, waking personality. It is the personality of the ordinary wide-awake man that we mean normally when we use a proper name, Alfred Smith. Alfred Smith is indeed the son of John Smith. He is a son of man in the ordinary sense of the words. But this little waking personality, so empty as it is, so aridly intellectualized in the nineteenth and twentieth centuries, by contrast with the sleeping depths of the unconscious, has one thing, which the unconscious (its Big Brother, the Unconscious) altogether lacks, and that is freedom—or potential freedom. It is just to the extent that man is *not* determined by his past—his heredity, his blood—all that comes from the past—it is to the extent that he is *not* the son of God *in the sense that I have tried to use the phrase* that he can say he is free, that he can choose one thing or another, a better or a worse. Now in the old times, in the pre-Christian era and to some extent afterwards, religion as a whole, or let us say the pagan religions and cults, were always aiming at the *reawakening* of the unconscious son of God. That was, above all, their characteristic. But it was not so in the case of Christ. By contrast, it was always just that little mite or morsel of nascent freedom in human beings to which he addressed himself, and which he sought to draw after him. And that to me is at all events one reason why he preferred to refer to himself as the Son of Man rather than as the Son of God.

If I am right, it was the most important reason. He also was a son of God in the sense that I have been using the term, as a matter of course, as all men were. But that was not the element in all men he was to appeal to. There is another element in all men, which is not—or which is no longer—the son of God; but which, in the course of the generations, man himself has been progressively developing for good or ill, and that is his weak, but waking, personality. The Christ, it seems, was there to call on these weak personalities, and not only to call, to *energize* them—to do what? To resume in themselves, as personalities, the sonship already given to them as organisms, and thus to become sons of God in another sense as well. It was because he himself, unlike any other man, was *already* a Son of God in this *other* sense also, and not only organismically, that he was able to do this.

I at least feel that all this is made very clear in the opening verses of St. John's Gospel, where the Evangelist writes, speaking of the coming down of the Word: "As many as received Him, to them gave He power to become the sons of God." What does this mean? We have seen that, as I have been using the term, there is no need for men to *become* the sons of God. On the contrary, there should be nothing easier for man than to resume the divine sonship. All he has to do is to fall asleep or, without actually falling asleep, to relapse into the semiconscious, instinctual life, to be the mere product of his heredity, to sink back into the dim, strong life of the blood (as many have sought to do in our time). It should be as easy as slipping on a well-worn shoe. But St. John makes it clear that it is not *this* kind of "resumption," not this kind of "sonship," to which he was referring. For he goes on to distinguish the two kinds of sonship. In the next verse he defines the words: *"Tekna Theou,"* which he has just used: "the children, or sons of God." There is, as we have seen, the normal, and if I may so call it, the "given" kind of sonship, which is derived through the blood, or through heredity, and which (*pace* Darwin) implies a man's original descent from creative spirit, but St. John makes it clear that it is not this kind he means. For he goes on, speaking of these children of God (which it had now become possible for man to *become*): "which were born, *not* of blood, nor of the will of the flesh, nor of the will of man, but of God."

There seem then to be two kinds of divine sonship: a direct one, if I may use the expression, which is the one I mentioned last, and to which it is possible for man to attain, but which he has not yet attained. *This* kind of divine sonship is reached, if at all, in freedom, through the Word, and this is an aspect on which theology as a whole has had plenty to say, emphasizing either moral obedience or "conversion" and salvation. Much has been written, much has been preached, much has been worked over in thought. Secondly, there is the other kind of sonship, which perhaps I may call, in a kind of shorthand, the "Adam," or Adamic," one, the one from which history really began, and which is by its nature powerful, and also by its nature unfree. This other kind is divine in a quite different way. I suggest it is divine almost *because* it is unfree. The sonship of man, as descended and derived from God, could be perhaps called an "archetypal" sonship. Of this the churches and those who have been most outwardly active in the development of Christian tradition have had very much *less* to say. There have, of course, been, and there are, references to "the old Adam" and "the new," but in general this has not been worked over and preached about in anything like the same depth as the other, direct, kind of sonship. This kind is something which, as I have already suggested, the pagans really knew far more about than the Christians do today. It is something which was at the heart of the pagan cults and of the mystery religions in general.

I have suggested that in the West a certain stirring or awakening of our consciousness has recently become apparent; and that it is evidenced by an increasing awareness of precisely that *un*conscious or subconscious sleeping element in the being of man, *by virtue of which he is already a son of God.*

It is true that this new awareness does not often extend to its having any-thing to do with divine sonship; but it is also true that, in the last fifty years or so, a great deal of interest has been displayed not only in individ-ual consciousness, in the individual status of man as a spirit, but also in what we may call his "collective" spirituality. It was there that C. G. Jung, for instance, placed the archetypal shapes he detected in the subconscious dreaming experience of present-day humanity. Philosophically it may be seen as the single root in which consciousness and conscience are still one. There is however yet another of those movements of thought and feeling that appear to have been going on in my time, to which I want to draw at-tention; and that is a new concept of *history* in the air, a new feeling for its true significance. It is beginning to be realized that history is not simply a chronicle of events, which is to be enjoyed as a story, or from which a moral is to be drawn. We have witnessed the dim dawning of a sense that history is to be grasped as something substantial, as something essential to the being of man, as an "existential encounter." The phenomenon has been called "historicism"; and it has been called "historicity"; the Germans call it "Historismus." It was R. G. Collingwood who remarked that this historicism can almost be regarded as a revolution. He compared it to the sudden awakening of interest in natural phenomena which occurred at the time of the Scientific Revolution in the seventeenth century.

Now all this, in my feeling, helps to suggest that man is in process of discovering, or rediscovering, the first kind of divine sonship, the kind which in a way is "given" independently of his efforts. And it is important precisely because it is *not* specifically Christian. In my feeling, it is a some-thing which, as it comes to be more and more realized, will be seen to be *that which Christianity possesses in common with the old pagan religions,* and not less so with the extant and very widespread religions of the East. For that reason I wonder if we may hope that its further realization may help towards a reconciliation or a reunion of the religions of the world. It is something which I should like to see the World Council of Churches pay more attention to. Schweitzer has pointed out somewhere that religion, in the West, has narrowed or atrophied in this respect; it has become more and more exclusively equated with ethics. Thus, it has become supposed that religion is *solely* a matter of personal relations and individual and moral development. This, he feels to be a constricting atrophy and one rea-son for its pathetic weakness. It is perhaps the main reason.

So I ask myself: Is man becoming aware that he cannot become a son of God in the *second* sense, in the sense St. John was drawing attention to in the opening verses of the fourth Gospel, without reawakening to, and entering into, his "inheritance" as the son of God in the first sense? (You will remember that, in that sense, it is literally an "inheritance," it is in fact "heredity.") Conversely, is he becoming aware that an awakening to, an increasing realization of, this inheritance may be a necessary step towards the attainment of divine sonship in the *second* sense? How can that be so? It seems from what little we can imagine of those who have become sons of God in the second sense (the sense to which St. John is pointing), that they must have reached a state where they inevitably do the will of God rather than their own personal wills, or where their own personal wills have become identical with the will of God. They must not merely have acquired a new relation, a relation as it were of "dragged obedience," to the divine will, like the rest of us, who do our duty often with great reluctance. No. They will have resumed or become aware of, or resumed by becoming aware of, an *existing* relation. They will find themselves doing the will of God, as the lungs find themselves breathing and the heart finds itself beating, simply because the whole world of nature (I would even say the whole universe) is breathing and beating *in* them.

This, in my understanding, is the secret of that *energeia* of which St. Paul often speaks. English has the equivalent word "energy." It is a sad thing that it is not actually used in the translation of the Epistles. "Energy" can be used both for physical force and also for positive impulse, for *power*, in the human being, in the human spirit. It was a word St. Paul was so fond of that he more than once uses it twice in the same sentence. It was the experience, I believe, which the early Christians had, when the world was still nearer to paganism. They felt the *strength* in them. And they were strong because, through their uniting themselves with Christ, the universe was strong in them. They knew that it is not only present nature, the animal in nature, which can become invincible in man, when he resumes the divine sonship: it is the divine *source* of nature . . . it is God the Father. It is there that we too must look for God the Father, within the son of man. It is there we must look, under the deepening troubles that afflict and threaten us. Not, I believe, to any outside intervention or any *deus ex machina*. But we must first have realized that God is there.

Here I feel I must revert for a moment to the familiar phenomenon of sleep. It is commonly forgotten by those who deal with the nature of man, whether they are scientists or theologians, that they are dealing with a being who spends approximately one-third of his time asleep. What is sleep? No one really knows. But I do not see how such a being can ever be understood without taking into account this mysterious, regular swing between the two poles of conscious and unconscious being, one could say between the son of man and the son of God. And the new stirring and awareness of which I have spoken will come to nothing, I believe, unless such things are taken really seriously, with all their consequences—in a way which has not yet been done—unless they are investigated in detail, and indeed in a scientific spirit, as was done, for instance, by Rudolf Steiner, to whom I point so often.

The new approach to history, of which I have spoken, could perhaps be summarized as an endeavor to look back *into* the past, as well as merely *at* it. By looking still further back into their past than recorded history will take them, men may come to see themselves as sons of God in the original way in which I have tried to present it. By looking forward to the future with the same new impulse they may come to see themselves as sons of God in the other way, the way that is only open to the sons of man through the Son of Man. But then how are they to see themselves in the present? First of all, what do we mean by "the present" in such a context? To my mind we mean all history! There was a time before "history" and there will be a time after. Meanwhile, history is the story of the Son of Man. It might be called the biography of the Son of Man. In the present, then, man seems to live precisely *in this rhythm* between the opposite poles—between his conscious and his unconscious being. His progress, if that is the right word, through history is not to be conceived as a steady march onward, a linear motion. Rather the waves from his past—with, as it were, an ebb and flow of the tide—inch their way into the future. I have hitherto referred only to sleeping and waking. But the essential rhythm is repeated on other scales, with other tempi. We shall find a hint of the same rhythm in our breathing. Our in-breathing turns us towards our waking life, and our out-breathing more to the sleeping part of our being. And even the seasons, and other experiences related to nature, which we all go through as human beings, disclose a similar directional alternation. But I am convinced it goes further than this. I believe the same swing between the poles of consciousness and unconsciousness (or relative unconsciousness) holds true of life and death. Only words like "life" and "death" can easily mislead. On Earth we can only equate the *un*conscious with the "life" element in our being. We reach it by a kind of death of our conscious personality, our waking part. Physical death is *also* the death of this limited personality, so far as it has remained limited to its private interests as such a personality. But physical death is *life* for a son of God in the second sense and thus for a son of man himself in the true sense—in his *entelechy*. To look however at life and death as a rhythm, as the longest so to speak of a series of rhythms passing to and fro between the poles of the conscious and the unconscious, implies more than one life. I have become convinced that some awareness of reincarnation as a fact will be found a necessary corollary of "historicity." A gradual, rhythmically developed and guided progress from a "collective" spirituality of the past to the fullness of the individual spirit—that, it seems to me, is how we must understand the present. A process in which the individual man is in course of becoming whole and, in a measure, becoming *the* Whole, precisely because he becomes the true Representative of Humanity; precisely because he begins to overcome in some measure that unclear distinction between "man" and "men," of which I spoke at the beginning. I do not think myself that the mysterious and unclear relation between man and men will ever be understood without some understanding of the working of repeated Earth lives. For me it is also the only way out in the long run from the misery of the social problem—the clash between developed and undeveloped individuals, the clash between the developed and the undeveloped races, black and white, man and woman, the clash between East and West.

In this connection I would like to stress again the importance of such a threefold view of man's being as I have tried to put before you. Collingwood, to whom I have just referred, defined the historical process as "a process in which man creates for himself this or that kind of human nature *by re-creating in his own thought the past to which he is heir.*" What do we mean when we speak of Christ as "Logos"—the "Word"? We mean that the Son of God and of Man is so constituted that he cannot help creating. And I believe that our increasing miseries result from the fact that, ever since we began to create in a feeble way in literature, in art, in science, we have been trying to do so in forgetfulness of our heredity as the sons of God. It is there, I think, we must look for the cause of that emptiness, that hollowness, that loss of meaning from the interior man of which he is becoming more and more aware in our time. That is why we look like becoming, not the sons of God, but the husks of man. Man is a being with a past relation and a future relation to God, as I said, but he also has a present relation, which rhythmically links the other two—which indeed *is* precisely that link. And this threefold relation to God is reflected everywhere in his being, in his psyche; as for instance, in his *thinking* and *willing*—with *feeling* between; in his physical structure; in his *head* and his *limbs and lower organism*—with, between them, the *rhythms of his breathing and the circulation of his blood,* which link and harmonize them.

It may be felt in some quarters and I have altogether overstressed the importance of the historical process, indeed of history in general. Such a point of view is almost inseparable from the "techniques," as they are sometimes called, which have come to us from oriental religious traditions, and in which so many Western circles are now interesting themselves. They seem to speak of a relation between the individual soul and the Divine, to which history is completely irrelevant. Such an ahistorical conception is indeed possible; but it is one which I have never been able to accept, because, when I look round at the firmament or at the majesty of the Earth, of the universe, and at all the vast long tragedy of history, I find it impossible to conceive that all this is simply put there as a stage on which a play should be enacted, in which out of every million there are about 999,999 participants who are completely ignorant and have no idea of what they are there for and of what they are doing; and here and there, now in one age and now in another, among those millions there happened to be a mystic of one kind or another who knew what he was expected to do.

This indifference to history, and ultimately to time itself, seems to me to be a fundamentally Eastern approach. But the barriers between East and West are rapidly melting away. Is that perhaps why the misunderstandings between them, just in our time, are so sharp? I would suggest that the East will only understand its own "path" in the terms demanded by our own time, if it learns to link to its own tradition all that the West has been developing as history; and conversely I hold it equally true that the West will only understand its own history—its own child, as it were—by learning to interpret it in terms of a "progress," somewhat resembling that Eastern "path" of the individual soul from terrestrial to divine. I believe we are approaching a time when no individual path to salvation, or what you will, will be valid for men, which does not also take consciously up into itself the longer and greater path of the progress of man, through the long agony of history, from the son of God in the *Garden* of Paradise to all that is represented and implied in that great picture of the son of man in the abiding *City*, which we find in the Apocalypse of St. John. If we do take up that picture into ourselves, if on that foundation we can become creative and re-create in our own thought the meaning of the past to which we are heirs, then we shall in the world of action not simply re-create the past, but create the future in its light. Can we unite the *weakness* of our freedom with the *strength* implicit in our *un*freedom? That is the question. What in the last resort is the meaning (in the perspective which I have been trying to put before you) of the past? Is it not really the throne of God the Father? If we realize the past in the sense in which I have spoken of it, then and only then can there be a descending of that throne into the free will of each one of us.

Then and only then can there be a development of true power on Earth.

Meanwhile there are many different kinds of power. There is the physical kind, which the physicists and all those concerned with the development of our technological civilization are concerned with, which they are continually (because it is their business) tampering with, interfering with, investigating with a kind of curiosity—and of which they have no real control; which is indeed in danger of getting *out* of control, as we know all too well! There is secondly, psychic power, which arises (as the psychologists have been discovering) from the unconscious depths of our being, whether these are understood in and for themselves or as animal instinct; and thirdly, there is the spiritual power, which comes only of a direct "contact," of a direct identifying of the being of the individual with the will of the Father; only from the setting up of the throne of the Father in that individual's free will. If we can see the troubles which are afflicting us as indicating a coming in the future of a positive reunion of these three kinds of power, which have diverged so very far from each other, then we may perhaps look out into the gathering darkness with some faint undertone of confidence. After all it is only the owl for whom sunrise is *all* disaster.

Acknowledgments

Several essays in this volume have been drawn from lectures and have not been previously published. For permission to reprint various other essays in this book and for the courtesy extended by their original publishers, the following acknowledgments are gratefully made:

"The Rediscovery of Meaning," from *The Saturday Evening Post*. Copyright © 1961 by the Curtis Publishing Company.

"Dream, Myth, and Philosophical Double Vision," from *Myths, Dreams and Religion*, edited by Joseph Campbell (E. P. Dutton & Co., 1970). Copyright © 1968 by the Society for the Arts, Religion and Contemporary Culture.

"The Meaning of Literal," from *Proceedings of the Colston Research Society*, Volume 12. Copyright © 1960 by the Colston Research Society.

"Poetic Diction and Legal Fiction," from *Essays Presented to Charles Williams*. Copyright © 1947 by Oxford University Press, Oxford.

"Where Is Fancy Bred?," from *The Golden Blade*. Copyright © 1968 by *The Golden Blade*.

"The Rediscovery of Allegory (I)," from *Medium Aevum*. Copyright © 1973 by Basil Blackwell, Oxford.

"The Rediscovery of Allegory (II)," from *The Denver Quarterly*. Copyright © 1973 by *The Denver Quarterly*.

"Imagination and Inspiration," from *Interpretation: The Poetry of Meaning*, edited by Stanley Romaine Hopper and David L. Miller. Copyright © 1967 by Drew University. Reprinted by permission of Harcourt Brace Jovanovich, Inc.

"Language and Discovery," from *The Golden Blade*. Copyright © 1973 by *The Golden Blade*.

"Matter, Imagination, and Spirit," from the *Journal of the American Academy of Religion*. Copyright © 1974 by the *Journal of the American Academy of Religion*.

"Self and Reality," from *The Denver Quarterly*. Copyright © 1971 by *The Denver Quarterly*.

262